Play

Play

The Pathway from Theory to Practice

Sandra Heidemann and Deborah Hewitt

Redleaf Press®
www.redleafpress.org
800-423-8309

Published by Redleaf Press
10 Yorkton Court
St. Paul, MN 55117
www.redleafpress.org

First edition published 1992. Second edition 2010.
Cover design by Jim Handrigan
Cover photographs by Steve Wewerka (left) and Greg Thompson (right)
Interior photographs courtesy of Steve Wewerka, Jeff A. Johnson, who took the photos on pages 113 and 127, and Jim Handrigan, who took the photo on page 182
Interior typeset in Futura, Adobe Garamond Pro, and Marker Felt Thin and designed by Michelle L. N. Cook
Printed in the United States of America
19 18 17 16 15 14 13 12   4 5 6 7 8 9 10 11

Library of Congress Cataloging-in-Publication Data
Heidemann, Sandra, 1946-
   Play : the pathway from theory to practice / Sandra Heidemann and Deborah Hewitt.—
   Rev. ed.
      p. cm.
   Rev. ed. of: Pathways to play : Redleaf Press, c1992.
   Includes bibliographical references.
   ISBN 978-1-933653-73-0
   1. Play. 2. Education, Preschool. 3. Child development.   I. Hewitt, Debbie, 1958-
II. Heidemann, Sandra, 1946- Pathways to play. III. Title.
LB1137.H38 2009
372.21—dc22   2008039424

Printed on acid-free paper

Contents

Preface

THIS BOOK BEGAN AS a simple idea. We wanted to design a play checklist that would help caregivers observe children's play skills. Little did we know that this simple idea would take so much work and time and yield such worthwhile results.

The need for a checklist was apparent to both of us as teachers and child care consultants. Often we would sit with a beleaguered caregiver and hear stories of a child who was aggressive, defiant, volatile, and anxious. Inevitably, the caregiver would also state that the child did not play with other children. We could help the caregiver reduce the aggression with a behavior plan, but this did not help the child participate more in play. We felt a checklist could help a caregiver pinpoint the play skills that needed work and plan goals for improving those play skills.

We began a long search for the right instrument to give caregivers. We adapted the components from the play inventory developed by Sara Smilansky (1968) to help caregivers understand the complex variables of sociodramatic play. However, Smilansky's components didn't give caregivers a good picture of the child's social skills. For example, the inventory didn't capture how the child entered a play group or how he handled conflict. Other play assessments were lengthy and assessed the developmental age of the child's play. We wanted an instrument that was relatively short and that caregivers could easily use in their settings. This instrument didn't need to assess the developmental level of play. It was needed more as a tool to observe play and to plan appropriate goals. This meant it had to be short, pertinent, and easy to understand.

We decided to develop a checklist that would address both socio-dramatic play (play that involves make-believe, cooperative interaction, and role-playing) skills and social skills (the ability to cooperatively interact with others, including turn taking, problem solving, and showing empathy). The process of designing the checklist proved to be longer and more laborious than originally planned. There were countless revisions as colleagues and caregivers gave us valuable feedback.

After finishing the Play Checklist, we presented it to many caregivers in workshops and individual consultations. Invariably, feedback has been positive and enthusiastic. To further help caregivers in their planning, we added suggestions and activities for children who are learning play skills. The original book based on this previous work was published in 1992. Caregivers reported that the information helped them plan for children who were having difficulty with cooperative play. It also helped them understand the complexity of play and appreciate its importance.

Since 1992, more research about play and children's development, particularly early literacy and brain development, has spurred new discussions in the field of early childhood. In that time we have observed more English-language learners, the emergence of early learning standards, discussion of authentic assessment, and the introduction of early literacy strategies in classrooms. We thought that the additions of these topics could only strengthen our book. We decided to build upon the helpful information in the last book and incorporate these new issues into this new edition. We also made changes in the Play Checklist to reflect current thinking.

We hope you will find the additions, the Play Checklist, and our suggestions for planning and activities useful and interesting. We also wish for you many playful times while you care for those who teach us the most about play: the children.

Acknowledgments

A SPECIAL THANKS TO Terry Halfin for her permission to use her case study as an example. We value the thoughtful insights offered by our readers, Diane Lerberg, Jeanne Dickhausen, Mary Hunt, and Nedra Robinson, that helped strengthen the manuscript. We appreciate the help that Marcia Zappa offered in researching topics and formatting pages. We are grateful for the trust placed in us by those at Redleaf Press as they recognize the place this book holds in early childhood literature. Our thanks to Jeanne Engelmann, Kyra Ostendorf, and Laura Maki for their careful editing and encouragement as we developed drafts.

We want to thank our families who put up with our preoccupation with the book. At times the project has been all-consuming, and our husbands, Jeff and Jim, and children, Marcia, Reid, Carrie, and Dan, have stepped in to pick up the pieces.

Finally, we want to acknowledge the many learning opportunities our work with children and early childhood educators has provided. Our work in classrooms has taught us a great deal about the importance of play and the amazing resiliency of children. Early childhood educators continually teach us about the passion they bring to their work and their desire to help children be successful.

Introduction

Nicole has seventeen students in her early childhood classroom. One of them is Manuel. Manuel is four years and nine months old. He and his family recently moved from Mexico to the United States. He knows a little English and is able to join English-speaking children as they play. He is a happy child with lots of enthusiasm and friends. Occasionally, he comes to the teacher with tears brimming in his eyes because he is unable to get the children to understand one of his play ideas. When Manuel and his parents came to fall parent night, Nicole found out that Manuel's parents speak very little English. Through another Spanish-speaking family, she learned that Manuel does much of the interpreting for his family during important communications with the apartment manager and the doctor.

Another of Nicole's students is Christopher. He is three and a half years old. He often comes to school looking dirty, wearing clothes that are either so big he could trip or so small his skin is exposed during the cold winter months. His family lives in a trailer home and is doing the best they can to make ends meet. Christopher talks about how his neighbors get into fights and then the police come. He is enamored with superhero television shows, and his backpack is full of plastic action figures. Christopher often gets into arguments with other children, and his first reaction is to raise his fist and yell. Other children are starting to avoid him.

Brooke is a four-year-old in Nicole's room. Brooke has trouble sitting for story time. She needs reminders to stay in her chair to finish snack or eat her lunch. During free play, Brooke rarely engages in lengthy play. Instead, Nicole noticed that Brooke runs her fingers over toys in an interest area and then moves on to the next. Sometimes she stops in the housekeeping area long enough to get a purse to throw over her shoulder or get a doll to carry with her as she wanders the room. One day Nicole decided to see if she was exaggerating Brooke's inability to stay with an activity. To find out, she counted the number of areas Brooke moved to during free play. She found it was no exaggeration. Her data showed that Brooke visited seven areas in ten minutes.

Early childhood educators work with children like these every day. Many have used our first book, *Pathways to Play,* to help children develop play skills. Since it was published in 1992, we have considered a revision many times. The matter took on urgency when we noticed many new challenges facing our field. We wondered what we could add to our book that would support children and their continued passionate involvement in play. What could we add to the discussion in the early childhood field that would help providers articulate the importance of play and the learning taking place? We thought about some of the recent changes in early childhood and decided to write about how these changes influence play.

What has changed in the field of early childhood? Today, new issues challenge those who work with children. One example is a greater emphasis on getting children ready for school and academics. Many interpret this as a need for drill and direct instruction, yet we know children learn best through play and by interacting with others. There is a push for testing and benchmarks, and we know that standards can help us understand widely held developmental expectations for children as well as help us plan more intentionally. Another example is that a far greater number of children come to us because their families are fleeing turmoil in their home countries. We know these children need stability and a chance to make sense of the world. Children who speak languages other than English but live in a country where English is the primary language need opportunities to develop both their home languages and their new one. Also, more children come to us from communities and families in which they witness or experience violence or are touched by violence through the media. They need the caring support of others to heal and learn that the world can offer them love and kindness. Finally, more children with learning and behavioral challenges are included in our classrooms. They need learning opportunities that encourage them to work at the height of their abilities and to develop their potential. We know that children developing typically as well as those with special needs gain from interacting with others who have differing learning styles and abilities. Special-needs children learn to play at a higher level when included with typically developing peers. Typically developing children learn to show empathy and offer assistance when needed. Whatever life challenges children experience, research tells us that play builds upon their strengths and creates a foundation for learning.

To help caregivers address these challenges, we have added a number of elements to this edition. The new elements include the following:

- A summary of several theories of play.
- A discussion of standards and how they can be addressed through play.
- Ideas about how to advocate for play with parents, administrators, and policymakers.
- A discussion of the factors that influence the typical development of play skills, including language, culture, temperament, and special needs.
- A continuous cycle of improvement that helps readers visualize the process used throughout this book.
- Information on authentic assessment, and ways to use observation and assessment in thinking about a child's play skills.
- A framework for writing goals that will help you take a child from where he is in play skill development to new, more complex skills.
- New and updated strategies for teaching play skills that correspond to the Play Checklist, including many ways to enhance literacy development.

We have outlined some new challenges, but a number of things have not changed since the first edition. Play skills remain vital to overall healthy development of all children. Play teaches children about symbols, solving conflict, and taking turns. Play is the perfect opportunity for children to address their needs and for adults to support their development. Through play, children learn the cognitive and interaction skills they need to become successful in later school settings and adulthood. Thoughtfully planned play experiences give children the opportunity to learn readiness skills. Play provides children with the opportunity to work out experiences that have confused or hurt them. Children take risks in play that allow them to learn new things. They try on a variety of roles and behaviors as they begin to learn who they are. They learn to control their emotions and behaviors as well as find out what they can't control about others. Play provides an opportunity for children to be creative, to be enthusiastic about their own ideas, and to get lost in thought. Play is fun.

About This Book

Chapter 1 introduces the most common theories of play—the place to start on the pathway to teaching play skills. This information will help you articulate why you include play in your busy schedule. A discussion of how standards can be reached through play helps you recognize the learning taking place so you can point it out to others. Ideas on how you can advocate for the importance of play are included. Chapter 2 reviews the definitions of the terms we use throughout the book. We outline how play helps a child begin to use symbols and interact with other children.

Chapter 3 gives suggestions for enhancing group play through time, materials, environment, and creating context for play. We discuss how you plan play activities to meet the needs of your group, build on their interests, and move them toward your goals. We describe how you continue to observe children's play and how to use the cycle of continuous improvement. Chapter 4 outlines factors that may influence the development of typical play skills, including culture, language, temperament, and special needs. This book suggests how to include children who are learning a second language and gives examples of how they add richness to our classrooms. A brief description of children with special needs helps you understand when to seek more information and/or the support of specialists. Knowing more about a child's abilities and possible adaptations helps you plan to meet each child's needs.

Chapter 5 looks at how to use authentic assessment to evaluate a child's play skills. An expanded version of the continuous cycle of improvement provides information about how to observe, write goals, and plan to work with a child who is having difficulty. Our Play Checklist, a tool that will help you pinpoint needed play skills, is introduced in this chapter. Chapter 6 describes a framework for writing goals that will guide your work with an individual child.

Chapter 7 shows you how to develop a lesson plan. We include questions to think about as you develop meaningful play experiences. Your role in play is an essential part of your plan. We look at when to become involved, how to become involved, and when to let the children play on their own. Chapter 8 is filled with suggestions for improving play skills. The suggestions correspond to each section of the checklist. Chapter 9 provides case studies to demonstrate how to put it all together and shows the results of putting the process into practice.

Throughout this book, a cycle of continuous improvement is presented; it includes observing and assessing, evaluating play skills, writing a goal, planning and implementing activities, and repeating the process. You will learn how to use the cycle to plan for a group of children as well as individual children.

Framework for the Book

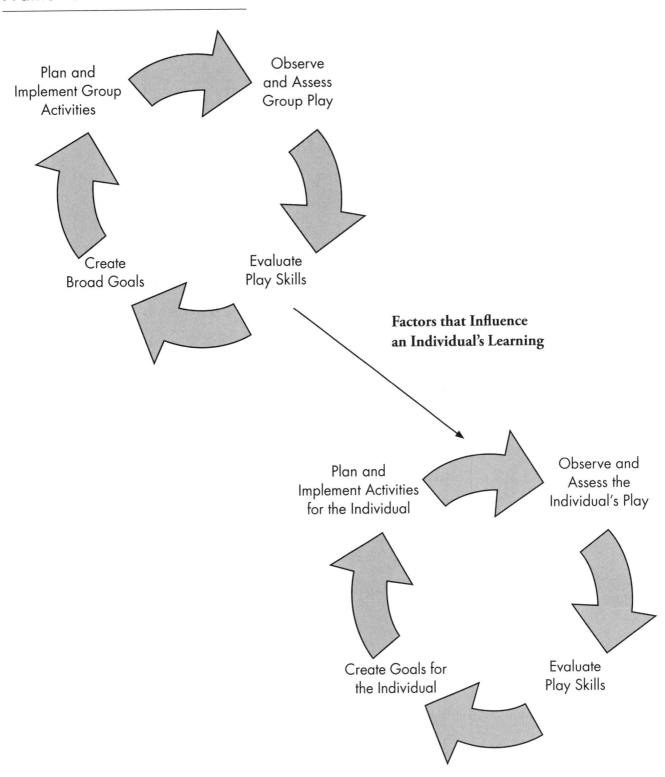

Plan and Implement Group Activities

Observe and Assess Group Play

Create Broad Goals

Evaluate Play Skills

Factors that Influence an Individual's Learning

Plan and Implement Activities for the Individual

Observe and Assess the Individual's Play

Create Goals for the Individual

Evaluate Play Skills

Because we want to include both boys and girls, we have chosen to use the pronouns *he* and *she* in alternating chapters. We use the terms *teacher, caregiver, adult, early childhood educator,* and *provider* to describe the wide variety of people working with children. Typically, we refer to the caregiver as *she,* because most of those currently working in the field are female. Occasionally, we use *he* to acknowledge the important contribution of men and the role they have in early childhood settings.

We hope that learning more about play, how children develop play skills, and how to give them support as they learn to play with others will inspire you to keep learning more. This new edition reflects how much we continue to learn about play and how it enriches the lives of children. By increasing our skills of observation, planning, and evaluation, we can give children playful success.

Reflection Questions

1. What do you consider to be the greatest challenges facing the field of early childhood education today?

2. What is the greatest challenge you face in your early childhood setting?

3. What do you consider the greatest value of play?

Play Is the Main Event: Valuing Play

It was the beginning of the school year, and Sabrina was getting her classroom ready for the children. She had to change her daily schedule for a new curriculum and health guidelines. How was she going to fit everything in her half-day program? She had to make sure there was time for two meals, tooth brushing, large-group time, gathering time, small group, and, oh yes, free play, when the children could choose to play in interest centers. She rearranged the times over and over and finally cut ten minutes from free play. Now it was down to twenty minutes; it didn't seem like enough, but she had to meet all of these other mandates. Then she remembered a particularly wonderful play sequence last year when one child began a wedding. Soon the whole group was putting on a wedding. The children made invitations, found dress-up clothes, and assigned roles. The literacy mentor joined the play by exclaiming, "I want to come to the wedding. Can someone give me directions?" The bride immediately stopped, grabbed a piece of paper and a pencil, and wrote down the directions. Sabrina had facilitated the play by finding the right props and asking questions about roles and script, and the children were carried along in a spirit of enthusiasm and pure joy. Sabrina looked at her daily schedule again. It was time to go back to the drawing board. She realized the importance of play and vowed to find more time for play in her schedule.

Within the last five to ten years, you may have faced similar questions about the role of play in early childhood settings. In many settings, time in the schedule for play has been cut back or split into smaller chunks so children don't have extended time to develop themes. As expectations for young children have mounted, you have had to wrestle with how play and standards intersect, how academic content like literacy and math can be integrated into your current practices, and where school readiness fits with your beliefs about how young children learn. Play is in danger of becoming a side attraction, not the main event. In this chapter we discuss the following topics:

Theories of play
Play in the twenty-first century
What children learn during play
Advocating for play

Theories of Play

Since the nineteenth century, theorists have observed children as they play and have attempted to understand the function of play and how it contributes to children's development. Many of the early classical theories continue to inform our beliefs and practices concerning play in the classroom. Early on, some observed that play served to release excess energy, something that teachers and parents certainly continue to believe. Teachers often state, "It's time to go outside," when children start to run around and play more roughly. Theorists also observed that play was a way to renew energy after stressful periods. This function of play can be observed today as teachers structure their days with periods of more quiet activity alternated with more active times. Philosopher Karl Groos believed play was a way to consolidate and practice vital skills for survival (Johnson, Christie, and Yawkey 1999). We all observe ways that children practice roles and experiences during play episodes, such as pretending to be parents in the housekeeping area or pretending to look up a recipe in the cookbook.

In the twentieth century, theorists moved beyond philosophical reflection to actually describe how play contributes to a child's development. You can go into any early childhood classroom and see evidence of these theories at work. The way we encourage play, provide props, set up environments, and document children's language comes from the theorists' observations and later research.

Theorists have given us a complex picture of play and its benefits. On the following pages, we explore theories that fall into two main categories: psychodynamic theory and cognitive theories (Johnson, Christie, and Yawkey 1999). Within psychodynamic theory we examine Sigmund Freud and Erik Erikson as they consider how play affects emotional development. We discuss the cognitive theorists Jean Piaget, Lev Vygotsky, and Jerome Bruner as they look at how play furthers language, symbolization, creativity, and thinking. In addition, we analyze the research on play training, and academics and play.

Psychodynamic Theories

Psychodynamic theorists have laid the groundwork for much of what we understand about children's emotional development. Their theories about stages in children's emotional development were developed from their observations of children as they played and learned.

Sigmund Freud

Sigmund Freud was an Austrian psychiatrist who practiced psychiatry in the late nineteenth and early twentieth centuries. He is the founder of psychodynamic theory and believed that play assisted children in dealing with their anxieties, fears, and traumas. He noted that these anxieties and fears are often unconscious and that play provides a way for children to bring them out into the open. As children act out a trauma, they change their roles in the story and gain some sense of control (Freud 1961). For example, they can be scolded by a parent and then pretend to be that parent as they scold a doll or a playmate. They also can repeat difficult experiences over and over in play to reduce their anxiety.

Erik Erikson

Erik Erikson, a German-born American twentieth-century psychologist, built upon Freud's observations by outlining how children form the foundation for social and emotional health as they accomplish emotional tasks at several stages of development. One example is the first stage of a child's emotional development: trust versus mistrust. Children develop trust through consistent, responsive care. If they do not receive that kind of care, they may become mistrustful and carry that mistrust into the next stage. According to Erikson, children use their play experiences to explore and incorporate frustrations and conflicts inherent in emotional tasks (such as developing trust) and the ongoing reality of their lives (Erikson 1950).

The following example illustrates how Freud's and Erikson's theories become real in children's lives: Makisha had a traumatic experience and used play to express her feelings about it. She was in her bed one evening when the police burst in the door and told everyone to lie down on the floor. They thoroughly searched the house for drugs and weapons. Makisha watched the raid from a doorway. The police took a couple of people away in handcuffs. Makisha's mother shared this with her teachers, but the teachers saw no evidence that Makisha was more anxious at school. A couple of months later, Makisha replayed the events of that evening in great detail. She yelled, "Everyone get down," and threw herself on the floor. She acted out the police looking for drugs in various parts of the house and demonstrated how police handcuffed people she knew. This play was repeated over and over again and eventually subsided when she became more able to integrate the experience.

Losses such as family deaths or temporary upsets, like new siblings or family moves, become part of play scenarios children use to help cope and gain more control over their frustrations. Even disturbing movies can bring on reenactments that play out themes of fights, rescue, doctors, and healing in which the child plays the hero's role. Loss can also be reflected in children's play as they work through their feelings after a death. Here's an example: Darnell's father had died the previous year. Although Darnell hadn't shown overt grief in the classroom, he didn't smile or laugh very often, and he didn't show enthusiasm for activities. When the teacher brought out the play figures from a recent movie about a lion, he gravitated to them immediately. In his play, the father lion died over and over again, and the lion son rescued him, took him to the hospital, and reunited him with his family. This play continued over several months. The teacher carefully considered her role in helping Darnell with this play. She followed his lead, did not interrupt his play, and only participated when he asked her to play one of the members of the family. She sat close by in case he needed some assistance. (For more information on teachers' roles, see chapter 7.) Gradually Darnell acted out a slightly different play story. Darnell buried the father lion, and the son lion became the protector of his family. The teacher felt that Darnell was saying good-bye to his father through his play.

Cognitive Theories

Cognitive theorists are probably the most familiar to early childhood educators. Their observations have led to many of our current practices, beliefs, and values about play. This theoretical foundation has led to continued research and improved instruction in early childhood settings. Jean Piaget, Lev Vygotsky, and Jerome Bruner are three cognitive theorists who help us understand how play connects to children's cognitive growth and development.

Jean Piaget

Jean Piaget, a Swiss twentieth-century psychologist born in 1896, used his theory of cognitive development to illustrate how the play of a two-year-old looks and is different from that of a five-year-old. This is because children go through distinct developmental stages in their play that reflect the level of their cognitive understanding. When you observe children at different ages use objects to pretend, you see very different play behaviors. For example, a baby may simply lift the receiver off a play phone, mouth it, and put it on the floor. A toddler may lift a play phone to her mouth, say a few words in the mouthpiece, and then set it down again, but will not develop a theme. A five-year-old may use the phone to call her mother, write down a number, and then order a pizza. According to Piaget, their play reflects their level of development and their understanding of the function of the phone (Piaget 1962).

Piaget thought that children's play does not merely reflect their existing developmental level. Children also use play to integrate new information and grow into a higher level of cognitive understanding. Let's go back to the two-year-old with the phone. She understands adults talk into the phone. But as the five-year-old demonstrates, play with the phone changes and reflects a new cognitive understanding as the child grows older. She will learn that you need to have numbers to call someone, that you can order a pizza over the phone, or that you can talk to your mother over the phone. Piaget didn't believe children learned new skills in play but that play was a rich opportunity to practice their learning and construct a deeper cognitive understanding (Johnson, Christie, and Wardle 2005). Children reach that understanding by experimenting and integrating new information. For example, a three-year-old child enjoys building a simple tower and then knocking it down over and over again. As she learns more about the property of blocks, she learns she can make a bridge or an enclosure for toy animals. She learns the bridge will fall if she doesn't balance it just right. She has to use the right size blocks, or the pieces won't fit together. As the child continues to experiment with construction, she can put forms together to create buildings, garages, or airports. As these examples demonstrate, play helps children consolidate and practice their newly acquired skills.

Lev Vygotsky

Vygotsky, a Russian psychologist who formed his theories in the early twentieth century, believed that play helped children develop abstract thought. Unlike Piaget, who emphasized interaction with physical objects to construct knowledge, Vygotsky emphasized how adults and peers play an active role in helping children form cognitive concepts. (Piaget envisioned an indirect adult role for adults as they plan the environment and introduce new information when appropriate.) For Vygotsky, both physical interaction with objects and physical interaction with adults and peers are equally crucial for development. (For a current interpretation of Vygotsky's work, see Bodrova and Leong 2007.) To Vygotsky, play didn't just help develop abstract thought in young children; it also presented opportunities for social and emotional growth. The cognitive, social, and emotional domains are interrelated and affect each other.

According to Vygotsky, children have two levels of development: independent performance and assisted performance. Independent performance is what children can do on their own. Assisted performance is what children can do with assistance from peers and/or adults (Bodrova and Leong 2007). The difference between the two is called the *zone of proximal development* or *ZPD.* The ZPD is not static but shifts as children learn and understand more. As a child reaches independent performance, a new and more advanced level of ZPD will emerge, and the cycle will begin again. Vygotsky stated that each child is different. Some may require much assistance to learn a skill or concept, while others will require less. Sometimes a child will need much assistance with one subject area, such as math, but less with another, such as reading (Bodrova and Leong 2007).

Vygotsky proposed that adults and peers provide assistance or scaffolding to help a child reach the level of independent performance. Scaffolding consists of teacher supports, such as questioning, demonstrating, and modeling, that take the child from his current skill to a new one (Bodrova and Leong 2007). For example, James would often interrupt ongoing play experiences by knocking over the toys and then asking to play. Children would become upset and exclude him from their play. To help James become more skilled at joining the group, the caregiver sat next to the group of children and made suggestions to James as he approached the group. The caregiver was helping him move from his assisted performance to his independent performance in group play.

While she was making suggestions, she was operating in his zone of proximal development.

Vygotsky's theory establishes that scaffolding is most helpful when it targets a child's emerging skills. If a caregiver aims too far beyond a child's skill level, the child may ignore or fail to use that skill. Observing the child lets the caregiver know if the assistance is outside of the child's ZPD.

Children actually seem to perform ahead of themselves during play, stretching themselves to attain more advanced skills of self-control, language use, memory, attention, cognitive skills, and cooperation with others. Although children may not be able to demonstrate the same level of skill in more formal settings, their new level of skill becomes apparent earlier while engaged in play (Bodrova and Leong 2007). For example, Maria was a child who became very frustrated during large-group activities. She would demand to see the book, sit close to the teacher, and pout when she didn't get her way. But during free play, she would play school. When playing the teacher, she would admonish children to listen, make sure all the children could see her book, and solve any complaints. She would share her teacher role with others and cooperate fully during their turns. During play she was able to regulate her responses to be more cooperative and open. However, when she first played school, Maria would refuse to share the teacher role and stomp off in frustration. The teacher helped Maria reach her independent performance in play by coaching her when she began to argue with other children. She offered suggestions and props when Maria relented and played the student. Maria demonstrated an increasing ability to participate cooperatively during play. To help Maria translate her success during play into success during large-group time, the teacher chose to offer more assistance or scaffolding during large groups to increase Maria's ability to attend.

Jerome Bruner

Jerome Bruner, an American psychologist born in 1915, proposes ways in which play supports creativity, flexibility, and problem solving. According to Bruner, children can experiment with new and different behavior without any real-life consequences. They can try many strategies and then choose the one that is most effective. Bruner says that this flexibility can result in better problem solving and decision making. Without fear of failure, children use their imagination and flexibility to craft inventive solutions (Johnson, Christie, and Wardle 2005). This creativity and problem solving help build resiliency in young children. Maria, in the previous example, certainly tried a number of strategies as she played school. Her peers gave her immediate feedback on how the strategies were working, and with help from the teacher, Maria was able to adapt her participation in the play scenario.

Many researchers have added valuable observations and data to these theories. Two particular research areas have added to our discussions: Smilansky's research on play training and integration of academic skills into play.

Play Training

Sara Smilansky (1968) conducted a study in Israel with children from low-income North African and Middle Eastern immigrant families. She noticed that they engaged in far less sociodramatic play (play that involves make-believe, more than one child, and role-playing) than did middle-class Israeli children. Because these children were also having difficulties in school, she designed a research project to measure the effects of play training in which

adults taught children how to engage in sociodramatic play. The training involved two types of interventions: outside intervention and inside intervention. In this study, teachers used both outside and inside interventions. A teacher using outside intervention remained outside of the play episode and coached children while they were playing, using comments and suggestions. A teacher using inside intervention participated in the play and modeled play behaviors, such as pretending to drive the bus or cook in the restaurant. The results showed that both types, inside and outside of play, were effective in increasing the quality and amount of play. Further research has upheld these results (Smilansky and Shefatya 2004).

Another type of play training researchers have examined is thematic fantasy play training. In this type of play training, the caregiver helps children act out a common fairy tale or story, such as *The Three Billy Goats Gruff* or *Caps for Sale*. Research has found that play training has consistently led to social and cognitive gains (Johnson, Christie, and Wardle 2005).

Academic Skills and Play

As the emphasis on academic standards has increased, researchers have studied the effect of adding academic props and experiences into dramatic play, both inside and outdoors. They have added environmental print (print children see at home or in the community, such as print on product boxes, store signs, and road signs), introduced writing utensils, labeled objects and play things, and provided charts summarizing experiences on field trips. These additions both increased the amount of time children spent on literacy activities and lengthened playtime, both of which increased the complexity of their play (Johnson, Christie, and Wardle 2005). Although this study focused on adding literacy props, math and science props can also be included to help children both practice and gain new skills with academics.

Although various theorists and researchers emphasize different beliefs and philosophical views, they help us understand and appreciate the complexity and undisputed value of play. Taken as a whole, these various theories complement each other. They all promote play as a way for children to grow emotionally, socially, and cognitively. Yet play continues to be a controversial topic in early education. What are the changes in our landscape that are influencing this discussion?

Play in the Twenty-first Century

Edward Zigler, a well-known child development researcher and one of the founders of Head Start, writes that play is increasingly seen as irrelevant (Zigler, Singer, and Bishop-Josef 2004). As evidence that play is no longer highly valued for children, he cites the removal of recess from school schedules, the emphasis on standardized testing, and the push to introduce more academic standards in early childhood settings. In the past few years, we have also heard many similar concerns in our workshops and workplaces from teachers, directors, and other trainers. Following are some of the concerns they have expressed:

Competing curricular demands: Programs and school readiness initiatives put pressure on adults to include more and more content in the preschool day. Health, social-skills training, nutrition, and other academic subjects are added until caregivers feel the one place they can have some flexibility is during free play. When caregivers become more creative about how they address these mandates, children gain.

Separating play and academics: Early childhood practitioners sometimes set up a false dichotomy between early literacy/math and socioemotional development (development in the area of understanding and expressing feelings while also learning to relate to others). If asked to choose sides, practitioners may align play with socioemotional development. The academic subjects are more likely to be seen as drills. This false dichotomy plays out to the detriment of children, no matter which side you take. If you choose socioemotional development as the most important task of the early childhood years, you will design a class with rich play experiences but perhaps very little explicit instruction. If you choose the academic content areas, you may create a setting that is more structured and less spontaneous, with play as an adjunct activity. In either case, children lose much. Integration of academics into play brings the best for children and their learning.

Societal perceptions: Added to the field's idea of play is a society that often values purpose and task over play. Parents often expect a program to provide learning experiences and not "just playing." These pressures are complicated by other people who have a direct interest in school readiness, such as business people and politicians, who now believe that early childhood education can help children achieve success in school. However, business people, politicians, and parents may not appreciate how much children gain through play experiences. Caregivers can educate them on how children learn and how play contributes to school readiness.

Violent play: Children's play can be violent, repetitive, and unfocused. One reason may be the amount of TV, video games, and other media they have experienced. They will imitate actions of superheroes but not develop the rich themes and stories that feed their imaginations and enrich their problem-solving abilities. Caregivers can become frustrated with the noise and conflicts that arise with play that is out of control, and restrict the time for play more and more (Levin 2003a, 2003b). If caregivers can develop children's play themes beyond mere imitation, however, even superhero play can be valuable.

Assessment concerns: The emphasis on assessment leads caregivers to question how to measure play experiences. They can mark a checklist on colors, numbers, or letters, but measuring progress on play skills can be problematic. By using running records, work samples, and the Play Checklist (see chapter 5), caregivers can document children's growth.

These pressures make it more likely that play will be marginalized in our early childhood settings. However, as we increase the professionalism in our field, we will need to keep theory and current research on how children learn in front of us. Simply put, children talk more, integrate new knowledge, and are most engrossed and enthusiastic about learning while engaged in richly layered play.

What Children Learn during Play

Lists of what children learn during play abound, but we feel it would be useful to remember why play is the main event in early childhood settings. We also include charts on how play experiences connect to typical early learning standards (Minnesota Department of Education 2005; South Dakota Department of Education 2006).

Language and Communication Development

Children *communicate* during play. Language is the instrument of shared understanding as children play. With their play partners, they explore stories they have heard or read or made up. They use language to negotiate roles. When they use writing during play, they experience its function and usefulness.

Typical Early Learning Standards—Language	What You Will See in Play
Children communicate with language and gestures through play and social interactions.	Role-play in dramatic play Use props to role-play Negotiate roles Create a shared story narrative in play Act out storybooks
Children use writing and drawing to communicate.	Use pencils and clipboards in play areas Use maps and directions Fill out receipts in play areas Give out coupons in play areas Write notes and letters
Children listen with understanding during conversations.	Listen to others while playing a role Listen to suggestions about play scenarios Negotiate roles and play themes Adapt or adjust behavior based on feedback from others

Socioemotional Development

Children learn about their emotions during play. They discover what they *feel, like,* and *dislike.* They observe feelings and begin to empathize with their playmates. They learn to express their own feelings sometimes within the context of the play experience and sometimes outside of it. When a child has experienced a trauma, play can be a way to release anxiety and learn how to handle the ordeal. Children learn to regulate their responses during play so the play can continue. They work with others to create a play story.

Typical Early Learning Standards—Socioemotional	What You Will See in Play
Children demonstrate a positive self-concept and self-confidence in play.	Take risks when proposing ideas Experience success when engaged in group play
Children demonstrate an ability to understand and regulate their emotions.	Control feelings when frustrated Persist in play when others' interest is lagging
Children demonstrate social competence and participate cooperatively as members of a group in play.	Enter group play Negotiate turn taking
Children respect others and recognize and appreciate their similarities and differences in play.	Support peers during play Share leadership Increase understanding of cultures and language
Children use words to resolve conflicts during play.	Decide roles Agree on story narrative during play Agree to and enforce rules of play
Children use play to explore, practice, and understand social roles and relationships.	Assign roles Take another's perspective from a role in play

Cognitive Development

Children *think* during play. They create mental pictures in their minds about a story or actions that they then act out. They learn how to use one object to represent another. They use gestures or language to make imaginary substitutions or representations. They expand concepts based on their observations and experiences, such as those of cooking, caring for babies, driving, and shopping.

Typical Early Learning Standards—Cognitive	What You Will See in Play
Children demonstrate curiosity in play.	Explore roles, objects, and relationships Question peers
Children use problem solving and reflection in play.	Define problems when addressing conflicts Present options Agree on a solution
Children use invention and imagination in play.	Use props or imaginary objects to represent real items Make up story scenarios
Children try out various pretend roles in play.	Enact roles they observe around them Use language, gestures, and a mental picture to communicate their understanding
Children pretend with make-believe objects during play.	Substitute imaginary and similar objects for real objects
Children demonstrate ability to stay engaged in an experience during play.	Persist in play even when others' interest is lagging Offer options to reengage other children

Physical Development

Children *move* while playing. Children move while pretending to cook, clean, and wash cars. An outdoor game of monster can result in much running, twisting, turning, and jumping. Children develop their fine-motor skills by writing, stirring, and building.

Typical Early Learning Standards—Physical	What You Will See in Play
Children develop the ability to move their body in space with coordination.	Move around dramatic play area without bumping others Coordinate roles and movements when relating to each other
Children develop large-muscle control and coordination. outdoors	Climb, run, and slide while enacting play themes both inside and
Children explore and experiment with a variety of tools: spoons, pans, pencils, and keyboards.	Write on clipboards in play areas Type on keyboard while playing office or house Pretend to cook with pans, woks, tortilla grills
Children use eye-hand coordination to perform a variety of tasks.	Write menus on chalkboards Pretend to feed, rock, and carry babies using dolls, blankets, and bottles

Self-Regulation Development

Children *organize* themselves while playing. Because they are very motivated to play in a group while enacting a play theme, children will organize their behavior to flow with the group. They learn to regulate themselves as they modify their emotional reactions and plan their play scenarios (Bodrova and Leong 2007).

Typical Early Learning Standards—Self-Regulation	What You Will See in Play
Children handle feelings appropriately.	Use language to express anger when in conflict with other children during play
Children plan play scenarios together.	Take others' ideas as well as share ideas for play themes and props Change story line when other children are losing interest, and suggest new directions in play

Academic Development

In addition, caregivers can help children learn more academic content such as math, literacy, and science by integrating those experiences into the context of play.

Typical Early Learning Standards—Academics	What You Will See in Play
Children understand various family roles, jobs, rules, and relationships.	Role-play about family Role-play office, car mechanic, beauty shop, or post office
Children demonstrate increasing interest in and awareness of numbers and counting.	Count money Group or pair similar props by categories such as spoons, forks, and knives Dial phone numbers Measure the garage door so a truck will fit
Children think about events and experiences and apply them to new situations.	Play out experiences from home and neighborhood Propose scenarios to peers while playing
Children use new ways or novel strategies to solve problems or explore objects.	Combine play materials to use in a new way Suggest new roles in play so more peers can participate Act out play scenario in more than one play area, such as house and block areas Build ramps in the block area and roll down different sizes of cars Put balance scale in pretend farmers' market to weigh food
Children engage in using letter-like symbols to make letters or words.	Write menus Write grocery lists Write messages to one another Write and send letters when playing post office Write telephone numbers

Typical Early Learning Standards — Academics	What You Will See in Play
Children represent stories or scenarios they have heard or seen.	Act out stories they have seen on television or in movies Act out stories they have heard in real life

All the domains are addressed during play: language, socioemotional, physical, and cognitive, including various content areas, such as literacy, math, and language. Within play, children are learning the skills that will form a foundation for learning and social interaction in their future lives. They learn how to regulate their bodies, feelings, and attention spans. Many children learn these skills through observation and modeling. Other children need more assistance to reach a level of independent performance that will enhance their learning and social interactions.

You provide that assistance as a caregiver. Children do not learn these skills alone. They learn within the context of relationships. Vygotsky reminded us how adults and peers scaffold during play to help children become more skilled. (For a summary of Vygotsky's theory, see Berk 1994.) You set up the environment in the classroom or home, determine the schedule and the amount of time allotted to play, and gather the props you will include in the dramatic play area. But to gain these play skills, children who need more assistance due to various factors such as emotional traumas, shyness, temperament, birth of a new sibling, or special needs, require further observation and planning (see chapter 4). In this book, we give you concrete ways to observe, plan, and implement scaffolding for all children in your care.

Advocating for Play

In this chapter we have discussed the value of play, what theory and research have taught about play, and what children learn in play. Because all of us have observed and understand the power of play for children's development, we have a responsibility to advocate for play with parents, policymakers, and colleagues. In addition to discussing the research on the value of play, you should share your observations of what children are learning as they engage in play.

Develop your educational philosophy. Include statements on how play helps children learn. Community Action Partnership Head Start of Washington and Ramsey Counties in Minnesota (2007) included this belief statement in their printed educational philosophy:

> We believe children learn through play. Children develop language, cognitive, socioemotional, and physical skills, as well as creativity, through play.
>
>   Therefore we
>   • keep play experiences fresh, relevant, and fun.
>   • provide children opportunities, materials, and time for free play within the daily schedule.

Parents may also come to you with concerns about children's play. They are anxious for their children to achieve school success and worry that encouraging children to play in school will slow their academic progress. They worry their children will enter kindergarten without the literacy and math skills needed to ensure their future achievement. Here are some ways you can address these concerns:

- Acknowledge the validity of these concerns, and reassure parents that you also want the best for their children.
- Ask them to come to your setting and observe a playtime with you.
- Point out the ways children are learning specific skills while you are observing them. For example, list the ways children are learning literacy skills as they play restaurant with menus, paper, and pencils in the dramatic play area.
- Ask the parents what they are observing during the child's play, and tie those observations to the areas of development.
- Refer back to the joint observation during parent-teacher conferences, and show how the child's skills have continued to develop.

At the beginning of this chapter, Sabrina struggled to define her priorities. Should she cut time from free play so all her mandates could be covered? Not only did she have to decide the value of play for children in her care, but she also had to define her own philosophy and beliefs about play. Theorists can help us think about play and its components, but caregivers and parents are the ones who actually give children opportunities to play.

We believe that Sabrina did find a way to increase the amount of time for play in her classroom. By remembering the wedding in her classroom, she

---

How to Advocate for Play

- Examine and define your own values, philosophy, and beliefs concerning play.
- Improve your communication skills so you are able to share your beliefs about play while listening to others' concerns.
- Document concrete examples of what children are learning in play. Post children's writings created during play for others to see.
- Link these observations to what you see children learning in all areas of development. Point out how they express themselves through language, demonstrate their thinking as they solve problems, become more coordinated as they write down orders in their play restaurants, and learn to share ideas and toys.
- Identify and write stories about what children are doing in play and what they are learning. Share these stories in a variety of settings: meetings, parent conferences, workshops, and conferences.
- Write an article on play for your newsletter.

(Adapted from Oliver and Klugman 2004)

realized how play opens opportunities for children to learn literacy, mathematics, and social skills. She knew play had to be the main event in her classroom. As a result, the children in her care will experience not only developmental gains but pure, playful delight.

In this chapter, we discussed several theorists of play, tied what children learn to early learning standards, and gave suggestions for how to advocate for play. In the next chapter, we consider more deeply how children learn to play with objects and with others. As these two types of play unfold, children move to a more complex type of play: sociodramatic play. By deepening our understanding of play, we can more easily help children develop play skills.

Reflection Questions

1. Write down observations of children during free play, and connect them to your state's learning standards or the ones we have presented here. What do you see children learning?

2. Did one or more of the theories of play resonate with you? Which one(s)? Why?

3. How have you settled the play versus academic debate in your setting? Are you satisfied? What more can you do, or what more needs to be done?

4. How do you advocate for play with parents and colleagues?

Props and Peers:
Learning the Basics of Play

ANDREA, A FOUR-YEAR-OLD, busily arranges boxes, clothes, and blankets as she lets others know, "This is where we keep our money and other things too." Timmy uses a sweet, high voice and answers, "I'll get the babies over here." He hands a doll to Luisa. She lays it on a blanket and declares, "This is where we change the diapers." Andrea quickly moves the doll off the blanket and says, "No! This is a mattress—not a changing pad."

Timmy hands another doll to Luisa as he explains, "Uh, oh! I left my baby out here. You take her." Once free of the doll, he spins in a circle and shrieks, "I get some magical powers and can fly. When you're up here, you just turn around."

Andrea ignores Timmy, looks over her house, and states, "Our house is turning out nice." Luisa agrees: "Andrea knows how to clean up a mess. Don't you think so, Timmy?" Timmy stops spinning and suggests, "Let's pretend it's night now." The three of them settle onto the blanket and close their eyes.

The animated and imaginative play of Andrea, Timmy, and Luisa is woven together as they create their story. They are engaged in complex play in which they combine the use of objects, actions, verbalizations, and interactions into a sociodramatic play scene. You probably have your own examples of play scenes: a child sitting in a sandbox patting mud pies, a couple of children putting on dress-up clothes to go out, or a group of children gathering blocks, pegs, and puzzle pieces as the ingredients for the soup they have bubbling on the stove. Despite many observations and theories about play, we sometimes have a difficult time defining it. Some point out that play involves make-believe or pretend and that the child is actively engaged. However, the quality most often mentioned by caregivers and children themselves is that it is fun.

The foundations of play begin in a child's infancy as he interacts with his parents and learns how to explore objects. As the child matures, he builds upon this foundation. He becomes more skilled at pretending with objects, playing a role, and cooperating with others. By age four, most children engage in sociodramatic play, which combines all of these skills and leads to complex thinking and interactions with others. Because of the intricacies of play, adults have spent many hours discussing and researching it. From this work comes an impressive body of knowledge that helps us learn about children's play. In the first chapter, we examined theories and research about play. In this chapter, we look deeper into the fascinating world of play to understand how children's development progresses while they are gaining play skills. We review and define types of play and add reflection questions:

Play with objects
Social play
Sociodramatic play

Play with Objects

Play with objects begins as soon as children can explore them physically. The ways children play with objects change with their maturity and ability to pretend. When a baby or toddler first plays with a new toy or material, he spends time exploring the object physically. He uses his senses to discover how the object works and what he can do with it. A child turns a brightly colored Lego over and over to examine all of its sides. He may stick his fingers in the holes of the Lego or feel its bumps. After exploring it, the child may use the Lego to play hiding games or bang it on the bottom of a pan. When he is capable of fitting them together, he may begin to build by stacking Legos on top of one another. With practice, his ability to build will become more skilled, and he may try to make one of the cars pictured in the Lego pamphlet. At another time, when he is pretending to be in a rock band, he may return to the box of Legos to look for something that can become a microphone. Yet another day,

Legos may become the place markers for a game of hopscotch. When he begins learning letters, he may use the Lego letters to write out words or his name.

Children tend to use materials in the ways described above. First they use their senses to explore and learn about the object. Then they see how it fits with other objects and how to build with it. In toddlerhood, objects become props for pretend play and represent or symbolize something else. Finally, materials are incorporated into the games children play. The types of play in which children engage while using objects include sensori-motor, constructive, and dramatic play, as well as games with rules. Each type of play is described below.

Sensorimotor Play

In sensorimotor play, children learn to use their muscles through repetitive movements to explore the properties of objects. Infants spend many of their waking hours in sensorimotor play. You see them explore objects by turning, pressing, poking, mouthing, and prodding them. They use all of their senses: taste, touch, smell, sight, and hearing. They learn what objects feel like, smell like, look like, and sound like. Toddlers demonstrate their sensorimotor skills when they dump toys on the floor or practice jumping. Preschoolers engage in this form of play when stirring sand, patting playdough, or pouring water.

Constructive Play

Hunter, a bright five-year-old boy, took several chunks of playdough the size of robin's eggs and began rolling them into balls. He asked for toothpicks, which he stuck into the balls at various places. Finally, he connected the balls with drinking straws and announced he had built the "borf molecule." Hunter is engaged in constructive play by using materials to make or build things.

Construction may begin at a very simple level—for example, when a twelve-month-old learns to place one block on top of another. You might see a toddler stack ten blocks in a tower. As the child's skills improve, he can combine forms like bridges, enclosures, and towers to create a building or a molecule, as Hunter did. Constructive play involves imagination, creativity, and sustained problem solving. Other materials, like Tinker Toys, Legos, playdough, and magnet blocks, might be used by a child to build things.

Dramatic Play

Dramatic play involves two skills: (a) representational skills, in which a child begins to use objects to pretend, and (b) role-playing, in which the child takes on a pretend role. In the opening vignette to this chapter, we have examples of how children use these two dramatic play skills. Andrea uses a blanket to represent a mattress. Timmy takes on the role of a superhero as he pretends to fly. Both of these skills help children develop a shared play scenario.

Representational Skills

The ability to have one item represent another, referred to as a representational skill, is closely related to a child's cognitive development (Vygotsky 1976; Golomb 1979). As a child matures, he is able to think more abstractly (Piaget 1962). A symbol or a replica of an object can take the place of the real object in the child's mind. The ways in which a child uses objects to represent other objects correspond to this cognitive maturation. Children also use actions, such as pretending to sleep, drink, eat, or talk on the phone, to represent the real behavior. Symbolic or representational skills become even more elaborate when children pretend that a doll or plastic animal is eating or drinking.

Children around the age of eighteen months to two years often need to use a real object or an exact replica of the object when they pretend. For instance, in pretending to diaper a doll, a toddler is likely to prefer a real diaper or a real-looking diaper. Shortly after a child turns two, he may be able to use a substitute or a similar object to pretend. A replica of a diaper, such as a doll diaper, might be used by a child at this level. When a child becomes about three years old, materials further from the real object may be substituted in play. In this diapering example, a child at this level may use a facial tissue as a diaper. At

four years, a child may be capable of pretending to diaper with no diaper at all. This demonstrates that he is able to think more abstractly than before, since he is now able to use actions in place of a real object.

Role-Playing

Role-playing is an extension of representational skills. Children role-play when they use not only materials and objects but also voice and actions to represent others during play. Infants and toddlers begin to play a role when they imitate adults' language, dress, or actions. For example, a child may take an adult hat and put it on his head. An older child expands on this role by imitating familiar roles, such as a parent or doctor. The child uses gestures and language to communicate his understanding of what this role represents. He uses the doctor kit or kitchen playthings as props to support his actions while he plays. For instance, he may use a cylinder-shaped block as a syringe when pretending to be a doctor. As he becomes familiar with other people and their roles, he may imitate them with the actions and verbalizations of a grocer, waiter, or firefighter. Playing fantasy characters, such as a monster, Cinderella, or a superhero, become common once a child is able to engage in more abstract thinking.

Games with Rules

Children play games with rules at all ages. The games and rules change as the child grows older. Infants play games like Peek-a-Boo or drop their toys off the high-chair tray. Even at this early age, the adult and the baby have a shared understanding of the game. If one or the other loses interest or doesn't adhere to the rules, the game falls apart. Toddlers enjoy games of chase, and preschoolers begin to do well with simple board games.

At all ages, games have rules that are agreed upon by all players. Rules help to organize play and allow it to continue. Sometimes the rules develop as children play; other times, the rules have been predetermined by adults or commercial games. Play is more or less cooperative between a pair of players or within a group of children. Simple games with rules you know include Pat-a-Cake (in which the child follows the adult's lead and attempts to imitate actions), lotto, and tag. More complicated games with rules are Candyland, Chutes and Ladders, and Ring-Around-the-Rosie. Even in dramatic play, children set rules about dress, language, and actions for a certain role, props to use, and the shared story of the play. In all games, if the rules are not agreed upon and followed by all the players, the game quickly becomes a source of conflict or may fall apart.

Games with rules are only one type of play with objects in which children participate. They also use objects in sensorimotor, constructive, and dramatic play. Understanding the many ways children use materials in play is vital to understanding their play. An early childhood educator can encourage different types of play with objects by setting up the environment with materials that encourage all types of play. On the following page, we have charted examples of how children use objects in play.

Type of Play	Use of Object	Examples
Sensorimotor	Explores properties of object by banging, stirring, touching, shaking, rolling	Banging pots and pans Rattle
Constructive	Uses materials to make or build things	Unit blocks Cubes Snap-together blocks Cardboard blocks
Dramatic	Uses objects to pretend Begins with real-looking objects Acts out roles using real, substitute, and imaginary objects	Playing house, restaurant, doctor
Games with rules	Games are played with rules that are shared Rules can be unspoken or formally stated	Peek-a-Boo, chase, Go Fish, lotto games

Social Play

As children learn to play with objects, they also learn to interact with other children and adults. Object play and interacting with others develop together, moving from simple to more elaborate play. Playing with others requires that children learn to coordinate their behaviors so play can continue in a cooperative manner. Children must learn to take turns with ideas and materials. Mildred Parten (1932) lists five characteristics of social play that are helpful to review as we examine interaction patterns. We have chosen to use the categories Parten first proposed in 1932, even though others have expanded her work beyond these five. Parten's classic categories are simple, straightforward, and easy to observe as we work with children. These five interaction patterns are

- play with adults
- solitary play

- parallel play
- associative play
- cooperative play

Play with Adults

Play with others usually begins with adult/child interactions. Very young infants play games with their parents as they coo back and forth to one another. Or the adult may begin an interaction by blowing a soap bubble and pausing for a response. The child laughs, pops the bubble, or blows a bubble too and the game starts over again. The interactions are usually repetitious. This rhythmic interaction between the adult and the child helps to establish a conversational pattern and can be seen as the beginning of turn taking. Other examples of typical play between infants and adults include So-Big and Pat-a-Cake.

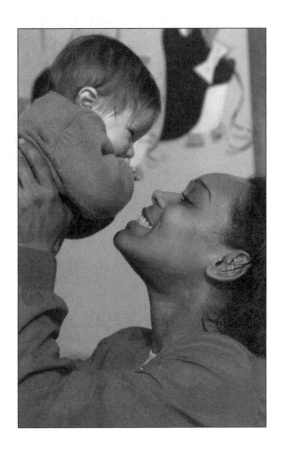

Solitary Play

José brought his caregiver blocks to stack. He watched expectantly as the tower grew taller and taller. After about ten blocks were stacked, he could stand it no longer and gleefully kicked them over. Gabriel was nearby. He picked up snap-together beads and put them in a carton. He glanced frequently in José's direction but did not attempt to join his play. This type of solitary play is what you see when watching twelve- to eighteen-month-old children. Children this age usually play alone rather than with their peers. They watch and enjoy the activity of others. However, they have not yet learned to coordinate their behaviors so they can play together. When infants do interact, they usually do so very briefly. Most often, the interaction comes about because both children want the same toy at the same time. Infants may also interact with one another by touching, poking, or prodding. Usually children are trying to learn about this other creature in the same physically explorative way they learn about the rest of the world around them. You need a watchful eye at these times because the exploration can all too quickly become hair pulling or pinching.

Children continue to engage in solitary play throughout their childhood. Whether building with blocks, writing a story, or putting a puzzle together, children can use play as a satisfying way to express their individuality. Solitary play is not a problem unless the child seems left out and distressed about it.

Parallel Play

Between the ages of two and two and a half, play changes, and children start to play nearer to one another. Parallel play is characterized by the way the children play side by side but with very little exchange of materials or conver-

sation. At this stage, the activities of the children are likely to be unrelated. For instance, while sitting next to each other, one child may be talking on a toy telephone while another is building with blocks. You may also see parallel play when a number of children are playing in the housekeeping corner, and even though they are all pretending to cook, they are not exchanging any ideas or conversation. Children engaging in parallel play like being near each other but are not ready for much exchange.

Associative Play

A group of children were seated at a table, and all were using playdough. Ernie rolled ropes, Theresa used the rolling pin to flatten out pancakes, and Destry patted the dough until it was flat enough for a cookie cutter. When Theresa saw Ernie use a scissors to cut his rope into pretend pieces of candy, she abandoned her rolling pin and began to roll ropes too. A few minutes later, she searched for a scissors and cut her ropes in small pieces.

These children are engaging in associative play. At two and a half or three, children begin to like playing in a group that is involved in the same activity. The children tend to watch one another and to imitate the actions of their peers, but verbal exchanges are limited. They borrow materials and ideas from one another, but they do not work together in order to create. A child may look over to see what his neighbor is building, and before long, he may build the same thing. Their creations, however, remain separate.

Cooperative Play

Cooperative play begins with the simple back-and-forth play of two children. They attempt to coordinate their actions so they can roll a ball back and forth or take turns talking on a toy telephone. In these early interchanges, children practice the turn-taking pattern of "first me, then you." In their preschool years, children develop their interactional skills further, and some group play begins to form. They learn to play together, deciding what to play and what roles to take.

In cooperative play, all the children involved take part in the same activity. They may pretend to take a trip to the library by setting up a scene with a librarian, people reading books, and the computer system to check out books. Their conversation may sound something like this:

Joe: I'm going to be the librarian, so I'll go get the books. You be the customer and come to my checkout.
Sam: I've got all these books here. I want to take them home.
Joe: No, you can only take a few of them, not all. Where is your library card? You got to have a card. Here—you can use this for your card.

Another place you may see cooperative play is in the block area. A small group of children decide what to build and what props to use. They may build roads, garages, fences, or elaborate buildings. They add cars, plastic animals, and signs.

Generally children move through the stages of social play as they progress through the developmental stages. Babies play with adults, young toddlers tend to engage in solitary play, and older toddlers begin associative play. Three-year-olds can engage in cooperative play for short periods of time, but usually only older preschoolers display rich and multilayered cooperative play. Sometimes we have seen children begin parallel play, associative play, and cooperative play even earlier when they enter group settings at an early age.

Sociodramatic Play

When we study play, we tend to separate play with objects from play with people. But when we observe play, we see that the two are interrelated. The skills needed to manipulate and pretend with objects in dramatic play and the social skills required in cooperative play are both needed. The two types of play overlap whenever we see groups of children working together to construct a building, pretend to be teachers, or play restaurant. *Sociodramatic play* is the term used to describe how these two types of play, dramatic and cooperative, come together. When children are playing restaurant, they role-play the servers, the people coming to eat at the restaurant, and the cook. They often use props like pencils and order pads, cooking utensils, pretend food, and cash registers.

Children use language to communicate from within their roles. When the play is going well, they tend to agree on how the roles are played, the next part of the scenario, and how props fit into the ongoing play experience. If they are in conflict, they may suspend play to disagree, discuss, and plan together. Social skills such as problem solving and turn taking, and dramatic play skills like pretending with objects are needed to keep the play going smoothly.

Sociodramatic play is recognized as the highest level of dramatic play because it requires this combination of social and dramatic play skills (Christie 1982). Smilansky (1968) describes six components that must be present in order for play to be considered sociodramatic. The components are listed below:

- Imitative role play
- Make-believe in regard to objects
- Make-believe in regard to actions and situations
- Interaction
- Verbal communication
- Persistence

Sociodramatic play prepares a child for many of life's experiences. The representational skills practiced in sociodramatic play are essential to a child's ability to understand many of the things taught in school. Pretending with objects, or representation, helps children recognize other symbol systems, such as numbers and words, as they grow older. To read, you need to comprehend the meaning in the letters and words; to add numbers, you need to recognize that the numeral 2 signifies two objects. Both Vygotsky and Piaget theorize that children begin this representation in the early years through play with objects (Vygotsky 1976; Piaget 1962). Likewise, the interactions demanded during play prepare children for the give-and-take of social relationships. During play, children learn how other people may experience the world as they play out new roles that may lead to more empathy and generosity. In the first chapter, we learned that Jerome Bruner believed children develop creativity through play (Johnson, Christie, and Wardle 2005). Their creativity is strengthened as they learn a variety of ways to solve dilemmas that arise. They expand on situations they have observed or experienced and play them out in new ways.

Competent sociodramatic players have gained the necessary skills of creativity, representation, and social interaction. Before they attain these skills, they have experienced solitary play, parallel play, associative play, and cooperative play. By understanding these developmental stages, you can help children gain skills while playing with objects and playing with others. These skills can lead to more exciting, participatory, and affirming play.

Many preschoolers learn the skills needed for sociodramatic play by watching others and by playing in groups. For these children, the ideas set forth in chapter 3 give them support while they learn to play with others. We help you set the stage for group play in the next chapter by discussing classroom environment, time for play, and materials that help all children gain success in play.

Reflection Questions

1. Watch how the children in your group play with objects. What level of play are you seeing? Watch how the children play with others. What categories of social play are you seeing?

2. List one activity or material that encourages each of these types of social play: solitary, parallel, associative, cooperative, and sociodramatic.

3. What types of play (solitary, parallel, associative, cooperative, or sociodramatic) do you remember as a child? Did you have preferences?

Setting the Stage: Organizing for Play

AMY, MIKE, AND DARIUS are playing at fighting fires by the climber. They have created houses with the large blocks. Amy shouts excitedly, "Oh, no! Our house is on fire!" The caregiver has put out a clear plastic tube, and the three children are excitedly aiming the pretend hose at the blocks. Amy says, "Oh, I think the fire is almost out." Mike yells, "Oh no, that one over there is on fire!" They quickly pull the pretend hose to the climber. Darius leaves the group to put down a block and beckons: "Come on, let's go in our fire truck now to the station." The climber becomes the station, and the play goes on, much to the enjoyment of all.

Scenes like this are witnessed over and over again in schools, centers, and homes. In the example above, the caregiver had offered opportunities throughout her room for various types of social play. She also made many different materials available so the children could engage in various types of play with objects. Amy, Mike, and Darius used a similar-looking object, a clear plastic tube, to represent their fire hose and were able to build on each other's ideas to play cooperatively.

The play looks effortless and goes so smoothly that the caregiver may simply appreciate the children's enthusiasm and forget what she did to prepare for this play. Nevertheless, before Amy, Mike, and Darius began playing, the caregiver did several things that contributed to the success of their play. The things done to set the stage by adults often determine the quantity and quality of the play.

In this chapter, we discuss what things adults do to influence children's play in the classroom. We cover the following topics:

Time
Space and play materials
Types of play encouraged by play materials
Planned experiences
Continuous cycle of improvement

In the course of growing up, many children acquire play skills easily and naturally. Adults provide supports that increase the likelihood that children will succeed in their play together. In the example above, the caregiver made available equipment like the tube and the climber. She also provided enough time so that play could develop. She watched carefully for any indications she should offer suggestions or more props while Amy, Mike, and Darius developed their scenario. When play is going smoothly, these stage-setting tasks are the kinds of supports children need. The caregiver, acting as the stage manager, greatly influences the type of play, the amount and duration of play, as well as the quality of play. In theatre productions, the stage manager ensures the success of the play by having props available, actors ready to begin, and lights set at the right color and brightness. In a similar way, teachers help children's play by setting an optimal environment for play. Researchers have documented four ways in which adults can encourage high-quality play (Johnson, Christie, and Yawkey 1987):

- Provide an adequate amount of free time
- Design space that invites play
- Provide a large variety of props and materials
- Provide planned experiences that are related to play

Time

It is vital that children have enough time to plan and carry out sociodramatic play. It often takes a while to set up the play, choose the roles, work out conflicts, and get other children involved. Play periods should last at least thirty to forty minutes (Johnson, Christie, and Wardle 2005). If play periods are shorter than this, children may choose simpler forms of play, begin to organize a scenario and need to quit, or not get started at all. In our example at the beginning of the chapter, the teacher provided forty-five minutes of free play. The exciting firefighting didn't occur until thirty minutes into that time.

> ABOUT TWENTY MINUTES INTO one teacher's fifty-minute free play, the children seemed to need help getting settled into an activity; they were wandering and looking around the room and not making play choices. The teacher called this a "twenty-minute slump." Some teachers might be tempted to say that the change in play indicates that free play was too long. But because this teacher was aware of the time needed for sociodramatic play to develop, she recognized the slump as a time when she needed to become more involved. Some days she offered a new prop, some days she helped children make new play choices, and some days she became engaged in the play to help them expand their play ideas.

In chapter 1, we discussed the time pressures that early childhood educators juggle in every setting. If you are not able to provide enough time in your schedule for play to develop, consider the following (adapted from Johnson, Christie, and Wardle 2005):

- Build support for extended play periods by developing an educational philosophy that emphasizes play's benefits for children. By sharing that philosophy with parents, administrators, and funders, you help them see that the choice is not either/or but both/and. Children need both time to play and time to learn skills. And by combining the two, you help children learn more.
- Limit the number of times children are pulled out of the play periods for special events or services. All children need consistent access to group play. By breaking up playtime, you limit children's ability to participate with a group of children.
- Combine several shorter periods of play into one longer period. For example, if you let children play when they arrive and during transitions, reconfigure your schedule to lengthen these times, or eliminate a couple of shorter ones and combine them to create a longer play period.
- Shorten whole-group learning times to provide more time for play.
- Keep your schedule somewhat flexible so you can extend playtimes that are especially exciting and productive for the children. If a play theme is particularly involving for the children, consider extending it into the next day.

Space and Play Materials

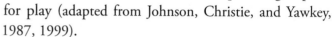

Planning an appropriate space for play is one of the most powerful ways an adult can influence children's play. An environment that is well planned draws children in, while an environment that is haphazard and too open can actually increase aggression and disruption. When you plan and set up an environment for play, you are putting in place one of the basic building blocks for successful involvement. Here are some considerations when planning a space for play (adapted from Johnson, Christie, and Yawkey, 1987, 1999).

- Arrange the room so children can see the toys and materials when they enter it. Include play areas that encourage solitary, parallel, cooperative, and socio-dramatic play. Both block and housekeeping areas encourage more social play. Housekeeping play results in more language than other areas. Children learning a second language seem to take more risks with language when playing in a group. Puzzles encourage more solitary play.

- Plan play experiences outdoors as well as indoors. Many teachers do a great job of planning indoor dramatic play experiences but miss opportunities for outdoor pretend play. Studies have shown that boys and children from low-income homes actually play longer and with more complexity outdoors. Bring play props such as trucks, blocks, and even house-area toys outside to encourage dramatic play.

- Include both housekeeping and block areas in your space. If you place them close together, children can use both to build their themes. For example, the block area can also be used as a bus for going home from work. Children leave the bus and go home to eat supper. The play becomes more complex and multilayered.

- Create an opening between the housekeeping area and the block area so materials can be used together or moved back and forth. This can result in more boy-girl play and use of blocks as props by older children.

- Use a separate room for a play theme occasionally, if possible. This heightens interest and excitement.

- Keep the housekeeping corner when adding separate play theme centers— post office, fire station, or doctor's office—to your setting. Such arrangements lengthen the time children play together because children have more options to explore. As they expand their play, they use the housekeeping corner as a base for their activity.

- Set up learning centers that are well-defined, enclosed, and visible. Well-defined spaces increase play more than wide open spaces.
- Keep in mind that the size of the interest area affects how children play. If an area is too small, children may fight over props and space. However, if a space is too large, running, rough play, or aggression may result. It may take some experimentation to learn the right size for your group, but avoid very small spaces or wide open spaces for dramatic play.

- Include literacy and math props, such as writing instruments and child-sized clipboards, in all interest areas. You can also add a cash register and receipts for playing store and charts in the science area. Including these props in learning areas helps children understand that literacy and math are used in everyday life and have functions in their lives. They can practice the skills they are learning during other times of day and weave the skills into their pretend play. Literacy and math props increase play activity, and play activities increase involvement with literacy and math.

Theme Centers

The following chart lists play theme centers and possible props you can include in your setting. By adding a theme center to your dramatic play area, you enliven children's interest and involvement. We recommend introducing a new play theme center at least four to six times a year. New play theme centers give children opportunities to learn about new roles, try out unfamiliar props, and create fresh, new story lines. By keeping the play theme centers available for longer periods of time, children are able to practice and deepen their knowledge and understanding of these new themes. Theme center props can be organized and placed in prop boxes, then stored for later use. In chapter 8, we give more examples of props you can include in a prop box.

Theme	Props
Library (with book making)	Paper, pencils, pen lights for checkout, books, puppets, bookmarks, small rectangles of cardstock for library cards, book bags, paper folded into books, long strips of paper for due-date slips
Doctor's office	Doctor's kit, lab coat, ace bandages, prescription pads, appointment book, magazines, x-rays, telephone, telephone book

Theme	Props
Veterinarian's office	Veterinarian's kit, stuffed toy animals, ace bandages, x-rays, prescription pads, empty pet food containers, books on pets, telephone, telephone book
Flower shop	Silk flowers, baskets, plastic vases, cash register, seed packets, foam rectangles, books on flowers, receipts, signs, play money
Farmers' market	Bags, toy fruit and vegetables, baskets, cash register, play money, signs, receipts
Message center or post office	Pocket-on-pocket chart (long pieces of fabric or plastic with transparent pockets attached) labeled with each child's name, paper, writing tools, stamps, inkpads, recycled greeting cards and postcards, recycled envelopes
Gas station or car wash	Tube and box for gas pump, vehicles or pedal toys, soft sponges, rags for wiping, books on cars, receipts, signs, play money
Repair shop	Toy tools and tool box, repair order forms, writing tools, items to repair, cash register, golf tees for pounding into foam blocks or pumpkins, play money, receipts
Ice-cream shop	Colorful cotton balls, ice-cream scoops, paper ice-cream cups, construction paper shaped into waffle cones, sign for the shop, menu, empty topping containers (chocolate, strawberry, butterscotch), cash register, play money
Take-out restaurant	Sign, menu, empty containers, cash register, play money, toy food, donated napkins, cups, and carryout bags
Pizza restaurant	Sign, menu, tablecloth, centerpiece, donated boxes, cardboard circles, felt shapes for toppings, strips of yarn for cheese, cash register, play money
Grocery store	Empty food containers, bags, cash register, play money, paper, writing tools for lists, toy food
Dinosaur land	Toy dinosaurs, cardboard mountains (use cardboard separators from packing material), felt shapes for lakes and rivers, blocks, construction paper, scissors, tape (children can cut leaf shapes and tape on cylinder blocks for trees), books on dinosaurs
Submarine	Large cardboard box, dials, recycled headphones, walkie-talkies, treasure box, colorful "gems," liter-bottle air tanks, goggles, treasure map, toy tools, toy ocean animals, books on underwater life

Theme	Props
Spaceship	Cardboard box control center, dials, recycled headphones, walkie-talkies, liter-bottle air tanks, toy tools, ice-cream bucket helmet, books about planets and the moon
Ice fishing	Fishing poles with magnet, construction paper fish with paper clip, bucket to store fish, mittens, scarves, books on fish
Shoe store	Variety of old shoes and boots, cash register, play money, ruler, shoe boxes, purses
Skating rink	Leotard to put on over clothes, medal on necklace, hard plastic rectangle (the type used under office chairs) for skating rink, large blocks around the edge, sports books, props to play knee hockey (knee hockey is hockey played on your knees with a plastic puck, foam blades on miniature hockey sticks, and miniature hockey goals)
Zoo	Plastic zoo animals, visitors' train and train tracks, signs for zoo and animal cages, felt for water and habitat, play money, tickets, animal books

Book-Related Play Themes

Below we offer a chart of props related to favorite books. These props can be used in thematic fantasy play training (see chapter 1) or placed in the literacy corner for children to use during free play.

Book	Props
I Went Walking	Stuffed toy animals featured in the book, additional animals to expand the pattern
The Three Bears	Three bowls, three chairs, three towels for beds, three stuffed bears, dolls, or puppets
The Three Billy Goats Gruff	Troll, three goats, cardboard mountain, block for bridge

Book	Props
The Mitten	Large mitten, small toy animals featured in the story, additional animals to expand story
The Carrot Seed	Gardening tools, seed packet, plastic watering can, sign
Jump, Frog, Jump!	Plastic animals featured in the story, netting, basket
Five Little Monkeys Sitting in a Tree	Monkey puppets or toy stuffed animals, alligator puppet or plastic toy alligator, CD of the song, CD player
Abiyoyo	Paper bag masks, dress-up shirts, play guitar/ukulele and other musical instruments, cardboard houses/stores in village (refrigerator boxes) or houses built with hollow blocks, CD of song and CD player

See appendix C for further information on the books cited in this table.

Types of Play Encouraged by Play Materials

Caregivers need to provide a large variety of props and materials to encourage all types of play. Children's play changes according to the play materials available. For instance, dress-up clothes or other theme-related props encourage more sociodramatic play than puzzles or playdough. Children playing with puzzles often engage in solitary play; children playing with playdough often engage in parallel play. The greater the variety of props available, the more options children will have during free play.

The following chart outlines types of play and the toys or materials associated with each type. With this chart, you can observe children's choices in play materials and identify which types of play individual children prefer. When you expand their choices, children gain more experience in all types of play, both social play and play with objects. Sometimes materials can be used with several types of play. For example, children can build with blocks alone or in a group with others. Observation helps you determine when and how to expand children's choices.

Social Play

Parallel and Solitary
    Blocks
    Puzzles
    Writing tools and paper
    Books
    Art materials
    Clay and playdough
    Sand and water
    Lego blocks and other manipulatives

Cooperative
    Housekeeping toys
    Theme centers
    Plastic animals
    Blocks
    Vehicles
    Story or book-related props

Play with Objects

Sensorimotor Play
    Snap-together beads
    Stringing beads
    Clay and playdough
    Glurch
    Silly Putty
    Sand and water
    Shredded paper
    Foam peanuts
    Art materials

Constructive Play
    Blocks
    Puzzles
    Art materials
    Bristle blocks
    Magnet blocks
    Snap-together manipulatives

Dramatic Play

Furniture and props related to housekeeping area
Theme-related props
Dress-up clothes
Dinosaurs
Cars and vehicles
Blocks
Lego blocks and people

To help children move from pretending with real objects to pretending with imaginary objects, caregivers should offer a mixture of realistic and more unstructured materials. For example, a house corner can have a cradle, stove, and refrigerator, all of which look real. Pretend vegetables, steak, and potatoes can be used in the pots and pans. Also include some unstructured materials like cardboard boxes, scraps of materials, and paper that can be used for any number of play themes. Younger children, ages two and three, need real-looking objects to maintain pretend themes. Older children, ages four, five, and six, feel comfortable incorporating cardboard boxes, featureless dolls, and blocks, as well as real objects, into their play. Children with cognitive, language, or behavioral delays may need real objects for a longer time to encourage pretend play. Caregivers should look at the ages and skills of the children in their care to determine how many props should be realistic.

At times, group pretend play seems to get stuck and becomes repetitious. Repetition in play can be helpful in working out feelings, processing traumatic events, and gaining understanding. Repetition becomes a problem when play lacks creativity, spontaneity, and flexibility. To help children move beyond a single play idea, try one or more of the following suggestions:

- Add new props to the area.
- Make a play suggestion that is related to the theme yet expands it.
- Encourage the children to make a prop that supports their play.
- Join the children's play and make suggestions.
- Ask questions that may give the children an idea about what can come next.

EACH DAY FOR THREE weeks, the teacher watched three boys rush to the large plastic building blocks at the beginning of free play. Each day, they constructed a tower four blocks high and climbed on top. They revved up their motors and began their daily motorcycle trek. The teacher was becoming concerned because the same theme was repeated over and over. The children didn't vary the props, the sequence of events, or even the language, which consisted of making loud motor sounds. She had tried to introduce a new concept, like stopping to get gas, driving to the grocery store to get some groceries, and driving the kitty to the vet. Each time, her suggestion was rejected, and the trio just revved their motors further in response. Finally, she hit upon an idea that matched their interest. She brought some plastic tools to the area and asked, "Do you hear that?" The boys said, "No. What?" She said, "I hear a funny clanking noise. Your motorcycle must be broken. You better fix it." The boys quickly clambered down from their perches, grabbed the tools, and began their work. The next day, she added some paper and pencils so they could write up work orders. A few days later, she brought in a cash register so they could pay for their repairs. And finally, she suggested the boys make a sign for their repair shop.

The teacher was relieved that the boys had been able to expand their play theme. And the boys were practicing some new, valuable skills without leaving their play behind.

Caregivers should provide enough props so that children are not always competing for toys, thus reducing the number of fights and conflicts between children. Some props must be shared because caregivers cannot afford to buy one for each child. No early childhood setting, for example, can provide a trike for every child. But some props do not involve that much expense. Caregivers can provide more of these toys. Younger children, especially, need more duplicate materials and props.

For example, one teacher saw that the three-year-old children were constantly fighting over the plastic phones. She thought about several solutions and discussed them with her supervisor. Most of the solutions focused on teaching the children to share. The supervisor suggested buying three more phones. Once the extra phones were bought and added to the environment, fighting over phones stopped.

When you are deciding how many of a certain toy to include in your play space, look at the ages of the children in your group. Younger children need more of each type of popular toy because they have less ability to share.

Literacy and math props in all interest areas and theme centers can build academic skills through fun and involvement. Putting small clipboards, cookbooks, and phone books in the housekeeping area; menus, cash registers, and receipts in restaurants; and computer keyboards, envelopes, and stationery in the office make literacy and math skills real to children. Add paper and pencils to the block area so children can label their buildings and put up signs in the area.

Include props and materials in your environment that reflect the cultures of the children in your care. Talk to the parents about the things they do at home, and include these activities in the children's play props. Invite parents and community leaders in to share cultural interests. By doing this, you encourage more play, give a sense of inclusion to all children in your setting, and teach respect for differences. Go beyond the cultures of children in your care, and expand the children's awareness and understanding of other ethnic and racial backgrounds. Survey your environment to see if the toys and materials reflect diversity of experience, race, culture, and language. For example, housekeeping utensils, puzzles, books, dolls, and pictures must reflect diversity. Include different types of bread, dishes, and cooking utensils from many cultures, such as woks and comals, and empty food boxes in several languages when you set up the housekeeping area to help all children feel included.

Offering children opportunities to develop themes from their own experiences can bring unexpected surprises. One teacher placed a square of colorful fabric on the table in the housekeeping area and topped it with a centerpiece of flowers. A child approached the table, took the fabric, and placed it on the floor. She placed a doll in the center and raised the doll to her back and asked the teacher to tie the knot of her baby carrier.

Consider how to adapt materials to best suit children with special needs. For example, if a child has fine-motor delays, be sure to set out puzzle pieces with big knobs and larger writing instruments, like chubby pencils. If a child has sensory sensitivities, be aware of which textures are uncomfortable for the child, and set out more choices. Children who use wheelchairs require wider aisles and designated places at tables and in whole-group areas. Individualizing your attention to all of the children's needs brings more opportunities and choices for all.

Planned Experiences

Children tend to play what they have experienced or observed. Movies, television, and environments at home, school, and neighborhood shape the roles they play and the play scenarios they develop. When children have no direct experience with a play theme, they may need planned experiences to successfully act out the unfamiliar roles in sociodramatic play. All children have some idea of roles within a household, but work-related roles may be difficult for them to act out unless they have observed them. This means that adults may need to give children additional experience when introducing a new theme center. These experiences can include field trips, classroom visits by people in different occupations, and books and DVDs about different jobs. In the beginning of this chapter, we mentioned a group of children thoroughly engrossed in putting out a fire. The week before, the teacher had taken her class to the fire station on a field trip. The children were able to get on the truck, walk around the station, and see the hoses and other equipment. Later, they could act out fighting a fire using props that represented this equipment.

Little did Amy, Mike, and Darius know as they became engrossed in fighting the fire that the teacher had done a great deal of behind-the-scenes work. She had set the stage for play by planning how much time she would allow for play, how she would arrange the space, what props and materials she would include in her environment, and what kinds of experiences she would plan. Provide these same supports, and many children will enthusiastically join the group in play.

Once you have put all of this in place, observe the children's play. You will learn how the whole group interacts, how your space and props work, and which children need more help to become involved with others. Sometimes groups of children need adult assistance to move out of unproductive play experiences. The chart that follows summarizes possible patterns and what strategies teachers can try.

Play Challenge	What It Looks Like	What You Can Do
Children getting stuck on one theme	Children play the same scenario over and over again without variation until it seems stale. Children may appear to be bored or to disagree more about the play scenario.	Add props; suggest new ideas related to the current scene to help play develop more depth.
Children getting stuck in one role	Children insist on playing the same roles day after day with the same people. Everyone has his role, such as dad, mom, dog, and child. Any proposed variation causes conflict.	Suggest varying the roles by adding new roles and facilitating the addition of new players. Children gain more play skills if they play out different roles. It helps them adopt the perspective of others.

Play Challenge	What It Looks Like	What You Can Do
Children leaving peers out	The same group of children plays together every day and excludes others trying to join in. Such groups may consist of two or more children.	Make sure play scenario has enough roles for others to join; if not, suggest more. Create a new play theme center with new play scenarios, and add roles so other children can join in.
Children scapegoating another child	Children make fun of a child and exclude him from play because of language differences, color of skin, gender, disability, or an unknown reason. (See Entrance into a Play Group, in chapter 8 for more information about rejection.)	Conduct group discussions on differences, and support children as they honestly speak about their differences. Affirm all in your classroom. Make sure you have books, tapes, songs, and toys that reflect differences and build affirmation. Intervene if you see exclusion, and talk with children about it. Do puppet plays and discuss.
Overly agressive play	Children run in the play area. Children may start out playing together without conflict but soon are running, wrestling, arguing, or hitting one another.	Assess the size of your play area. If overly large, cut down the size to reduce the running and wrestling. If it is too small, consider removing some furniture or increasing the size to accommodate more children. Teach children problem-solving skills, and reinforce these when conflicts arise during play.

Play Challenge	What It Looks Like	What You Can Do
Superhero play leading to conflict, aggression, and running	Play quickly gets out of control when children are playing superheroes.	Move superhero play outdoors, where running is safer. When playing indoors, add props and/or new themes. For example, if children are playing Spiderman, add a hospital or doctor area with an ambulance, doctors, and doctor's props to attend to the villain's victims.
Isolated and fleeting play scenarios	Children introduce play scenarios but do not develop them. The scenarios are short and often disconnected.	Help children connect themes by pointing out similarities. Suggest new roles, and add new props and ideas to build enthusiasm for the play. Plan an experience that gives children more ideas for roles and scenarios, such as a book, story, or field trip.

Continuous Cycle of Improvement

Early childhood educators engage in a continuous cycle of observing and evaluating play skills and creating goals, followed by planning and implementing activities. The following illustrates the cycle.

The Continuous Cycle

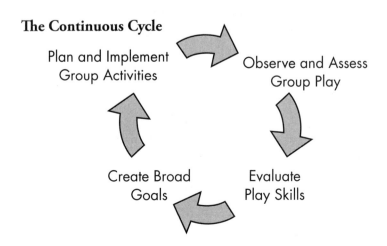

Plan and Implement Group Activities

Observe and Assess Group Play

Create Broad Goals

Evaluate Play Skills

This cycle is familiar to caregivers. Informally, you have been observing, evaluating play skills, and changing what you do to make your schedule go more smoothly or to help individual children. Use this cycle to support continuous progress in children's play skills as well as in other developmental areas; it can guide your observations, plans, and activities.

For example, one teacher begins to get to know the children by watching them work and play together. She may notice that many of the children gravitate toward the large colored pegs she has placed on the table. She analyzes what she sees and determines that some children are not only stacking the pegs but matching them too. She uses what she knows about widely held developmental expectations and standards to set goals about matching objects. She plans a number of activities to give the children practice in matching. She offers a variety of matching activities over the next few weeks. After many opportunities to match objects, she observes again to see if the children are grasping the concept and which children, if any, are ready to start sorting objects.

Another teacher looks at her group and recognizes they are having trouble agreeing on a play theme and coordinating their play ideas. She decides to concentrate on helping the children learn to play cooperatively with one another. This teacher continues to observe the children in her group so she can provide props for play themes that bring the children together. She plans experiences that children are interested in and with which they have some experience. She creates spaces that invite children to participate and helps them feel comfortable playing near each other. She chooses materials that they have in their homes and introduces them to new ones. She allows plenty of time for free play so the children can fully develop their play ideas. She encourages cooperative play by suggesting how their ideas can work together. She takes part in play when she is invited and when the children need additional support to solve problems. While she works with the children, she keeps her goals in mind and is alert to teaching opportunities. As she implements her plan, she evaluates how it goes and then repeats the process. From there, she plans new goals and activities and repeats the cycle continuously during the year.

As the early childhood educator uses the cycle, she asks a number of key questions:

Observe and assess	What do I see?
Evaluate	What do I think?
Create goals	What will the child do?
Plan and implement activities	What will I do? When will I do it?

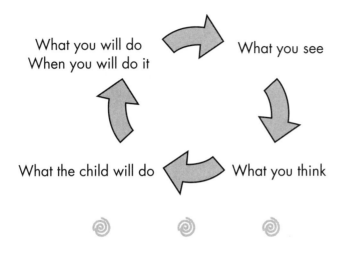

When you set the stage for play, you give all children in your setting an opportunity to succeed in playing with others. You design your daily schedule and plan your space. By adding materials and props and providing experiences to enrich the play, you influence the quality and quantity of play in your setting.

Sometimes individual children or a small group of children may hold back from joining in, initiate conflict when they do, or lack social or pretend skills to participate with others. In the next chapter, you will learn more about factors that influence a child's development of play skills. By adding the extra supports we suggest for individual children, you give every child in your care the opportunity to experience the benefits of play.

Reflection Questions

1. What props can you add to the block area? To the housekeeping area? What might you observe in the children's play with the addition of these props?

2. Describe a play theme you could add to the housekeeping area. What planned experience would you provide to help develop the play?

3. Rearrange an area of your setting. Observe and reflect on how the children react.

4. Have you experienced any situations in which groups are having difficulty with play? What did you try? Did it work? What else might you try in the future?

5. Brainstorm ways you can incorporate opportunities for language and literacy development in each area of your setting.

Play Environment Quick Check

Complete the Play Environment Quick Check below. After completing the checklist, write down one or two ways you will improve your play environment.

Put a check on the line by the items you are doing.

_____ I provide at least thirty to forty minutes a day of play in interest areas.

_____ I plan for dramatic play outside.

_____ My interest areas are in well-defined, enclosed spaces.

_____ I have provided space for at least four to five children to engage in dramatic play at the same time.

_____ I have a mixture of realistic and more unstructured props.

_____ I have enough play props in my dramatic play areas.

_____ I have props relating to theme centers and/or the housekeeping area.

_____ I have math and literacy props included in the dramatic play areas.

_____ When I set up an unfamiliar theme center, I plan related experiences for the children.

_____ I set up at least four to six theme centers during the year in addition to the housekeeping area.

I will improve the play environment by:

1.

2.

It's Not Always Easy: Recognizing Influences on Play Development

A GROUP OF FOUR children are playing post office. They are addressing envelopes, writing notes, and putting them in the play classroom mailbox. Anjelica watches the group at a distance. She inches closer, but when she notices the teacher watching her, she moves back. Again she inches closer to the action and then moves to the periphery of the group. She picks up a pencil and stands there. One child, José, notices her, shakes his head, and grabs the pencil away—"I need that." Angelica looks at José, backs away, and goes to work on an art project at another table. She keeps looking over at the group of children playing.

Many children gain play skills much the same way as they progress in cognitive, socioemotional, language, and motor areas of development. The teacher in the example above set up the post office play theme by providing envelopes, note paper, pencils, and a mailbox. The children had enough time to develop the theme and enough space for a group of them to play comfortably. With this opportunity, many of the children seemed to naturally play together, to pretend, and to verbally interact during play.

Children's development of play skills can be highly variable. If Anjelica were in your setting, you might be concerned if you saw her stay away from a group of children who were playing, even when she seemed to be interested. Anjelica started to join the play, but she was unable to join on her own. With observation and increased understanding, you can form plans to assist Anjelica and others. Observation provides a more complete picture of a child's play skills and the adult help she'll need.

Some children like Anjelica may need more adult assistance as they learn to play with others because of their individual experiences and challenges. It isn't always clear why some children find it so difficult to play with others, but we can examine some of the factors that influence the development of children's play skills. In this chapter, we look at the following topics:

Culture and language
Gender
Temperament
Lack of experience with play
Exposure to violence
Gifted and talented
Special needs

Goodness of Fit

Your observations of a child help you learn about his unique characteristics, his strengths and challenges, and his special temperament. To encourage each child's strengths and help him learn new skills, a caregiver needs to match her responses and strategies to the individual child. This means the caregiver must recognize her own styles and modify them to meet a child's needs. To do this, a caregiver must develop a variety of strategies and mannerisms from which to choose. When these are matched to a child, a caregiver is creating "goodness of fit" (Croft and Hewitt 2004). For example, if the caregiver is usually outgoing and boisterous, she recognizes that this approach may overwhelm a child who is shy. Instead, she approaches the child slowly and perhaps without words. Similarly, the adult can adapt her style to that of a child who needs firm, clear direction. Perhaps with this child, she needs to say in a firm voice, "Kameron, pick up your coat and hang it in your locker before you play." Thinking about this "goodness of fit" can help a teacher select the most appropriate type of support for each child (Gillespie and Seibel 2006).

All children come to our early childhood settings with unique temperaments, home experiences, languages, cultures, and strengths. As caregivers, we need to understand typical developmental processes and accommodate all the variations we see before us. As we write this chapter, we hesitate to make broad general statements. For example, boys tend to gravitate to more active play, but we recognize that not all boys choose active play, nor do all girls avoid it. Yet understanding how tendencies like these might affect children's play can give us valuable information from which to observe and plan. While keeping such tendencies in mind as we observe, we also want to accommodate each child's unique situation. Whatever each child brings to our setting, he can use his experiences in play to gain social and cognitive skills, practice literacy and math skills, and have pure fun with others. Understanding when the child can use assistance helps you stimulate his growth through play.

Culture and Language

Culture is embedded in the play of children. Their play can reflect their home culture, the larger society, media culture, or distinctive parts of a neighborhood. Culture can influence choice of play topics, themes, interactions, language, and play patterns. For example, a child immigrates to the United States from India. In the beginning, the language, the props, and the play themes he chooses during play reflect his life in India. As he becomes part of the American culture, he retains some of his home culture and language while he learns to speak English and gravitates toward a wider variety of props. Play allows the child not only to express his cultural experiences but also to deepen his understanding of culture. A child may reflect his culture during play by choosing play food and cooking instruments that he sees in his home and adding some he sees reflected in other cultures.

Children benefit when you

- respect and value all cultures, being sure to focus initially on the cultures of the children represented in your early childhood setting.
- reflect the cultures of the children in your care by providing culturally diverse play props, dolls with a variety of skin colors, and inclusive posters, pictures, and bulletin boards. Give children additional exposure to cultures they have not directly experienced through books, pictures, stories, and props. Discuss differing skin colors openly and without judgment.
- address directly any child's exclusion because of culture, race, or language. Problem solve how to accept and include everyone.
- communicate openly with parents about their language, culture, and traditions. Ask them to share with the children, if they are willing.

Children who attend early childhood programs are linguistically as well as culturally diverse. Many speak a non-English home language while also learning English. How this affects the development of play skills remains somewhat unclear, but from our observations, children who speak a language other than English find it more difficult to participate fully in group play, particularly when the other children in the group are speaking English. In some situations, children who speak the same language may group together and play primarily with each other, choosing to speak their home language, which then becomes a barrier to English-speaking children. Bridging these differences in language becomes a challenge in early childhood settings, especially during play.

For some children who are learning English, your setting is their first exposure to peers and adults who speak a language other than what is spoken in their home. Following are the stages of second-language acquisition through which children often move:

1. Uses home language
2. Is nonverbal or silent
3. Uses individual words and short phrases in new language
4. Uses new language productively
(Tabors 1997)

Each child progresses at his own individual rate as he acquires English language skills. A child learns language through many experiences, but play helps him learn English because play is highly motivating: the child wants to learn to communicate with his peers. Play encourages children to talk about the here and now of a play scene, teaches them new vocabulary, and allows them to practice their new language skills in a nonthreatening play environment.

Stages of Language Development	Child's Experience of the Stage	Teacher Tips for the Stage
1. Uses home language	Uses home language in the early childhood setting	Use parallel play (see chapter 7).
	Begins to realize he doesn't understand others and they don't understand him	Use parallel talk to describe what you and the child are doing (see chapter 8).
		Take regular breaks from language because listening and responding can be stressful for the child.
		Offer directions in a variety of ways—gesture, model, use pictures, and rephrase.

Stages of Language Development	Child's Experience of the Stage	Teacher Tips for the Stage
2. Is nonverbal or silent	Recognizes the home language isn't working/being understood in this setting May lose confidence as he wonders why skills he possesses aren't working May practice some English privately Communicates through gestures, through facial expressions, or by showing you May cope by watching others and copying their actions	The child may understand some simple words or phrases in English before he is able to produce words on his own. Match questions you ask to the child's level—phrase questions so the child can respond with a nod or a single word, choose from two words, or say a short phrase. Be patient and encouraging. Invite a response or participation without requiring it.
*3. Uses individual words and short phrases in new language	Takes risks each time he tries a word or phrase in the new language May learn to name objects, name colors, or count Can use simple social speech like, "Hello, teacher," or "Come see" May mix or combine languages Works hard to understand and be understood	Expand words or phrases. Model phrases for the child to repeat.

Stages of Language Development	Child's Experience of the Stage	Teacher Tips for the Stage
*3. Uses individual words and short phrases in new language (cont.)	Learns language best by using it to communicate May count on supportive adults for help during play	

*Can give the impression that he knows a lot of English because he has ability to converse socially or use basic communication skills. Social language precedes academic language. Academic language uses more abstract vocabulary and takes four or more years to develop (NAEYC 1996).

4. Uses new language productively	Becomes more competent in using new language Begins to put phrases together to build sentences	Expand child's phrases into sentences. Introduce academic concepts like more or less, near or far, same or different, etc.

Learning a new language can be stressful for children; they may exhibit the following behaviors as they progress through the stages:

- Children may be more frustrated if they can't make themselves understood. Some children demonstrate their frustration by becoming aggressive, others by leaving the situation, hiding, or giving up.
- Children who can't communicate may be on the outskirts of group play.
- Children who can't communicate may manipulate the props for sociodramatic play but may not be able to take part in the story.
- Children may choose others who speak the same language as their playmates.

Although learning a second language may hinder some participation in play initially, children can enhance their learning by playing with others. Play is a motivating activity, and children work to reach success. Their language use is often at a higher level as they try new words, the number of words increases, and they link words into phrases.

We would like to add one more word about culture. Sometimes we think of culture as what comes from another country. However, we all have culture, and its many variations are reflected across our country. It includes language as well as the gestures we use, the food we eat, regional practices, and even the way we think. If children and parents feel their culture is not supported by those around them, they may become less invested in school. As caregivers, we must honor, value, and give attention to all the cultures of the children in our care.

Gender

Gender is a powerful influence on development and consequently on play, although research gives us a mixed picture on exactly how it influences play. Research has shown that boys tend to engage in more dramatic play outdoors than indoors. They gravitate more to construction themes, active play, and vigorous exploration (Johnson, Christie, and Wardle 2005). Girls tend to be drawn to more traditionally female activities, such as the housekeeping and library areas and puzzles (Tokarz 2008). Whether girls and boys are born this way or are socialized into such roles remains somewhat controversial, but gender preferences during play present a challenge to us as caregivers. We want to offer activities and experiences that are attractive and motivating for children while encouraging them to move beyond initial preferences to more diverse choices.

Every caregiver has observed a range of gender differences when children are playing in a classroom or a family childcare home. One year a teacher noticed that girls were drawn to the housekeeping area every day, while boys ran to the block area to build ramps and race the little cars. She tried everything she could think of to encourage boys to seek out the housekeeping area and to encourage girls to enter the block area. She put up pictures of female mechanics and construction workers in the block area and pictures of males as fathers and chefs in the housekeeping area. She put props in the block area that she thought would be attractive to girls, such as families of plastic people and plastic animals. She read books about fathers taking care of babies and women as firefighters. The girls nevertheless continued to choose dramatic play in the housekeeping area, while the boys continued to build ramps, roads, and buildings in the block area. She noticed the children themselves were enforcing their own rules. When a girl started to enter the block area, boys would say, "Girls can't play here." The teacher was disturbed by this and reminded the group of the rule they had discussed: "You can't say you can't play" (Paley 1992). She went on to ask the boys, "What can she do? How can she help?"

The teacher in this anecdote did not resolve the dilemma quickly. She tried a number of strategies, such as encouraging play in all areas, setting up the dramatic play area next to the block area, and building themes that were interesting to both boys and girls, such as post office and pizza shops. Slowly she noticed that the boys and girls were playing more together and trying out new areas of interest.

Many children do not fit within strictly defined gender categories. For example, a girl may love active, outdoor play; a boy may prefer dress-up in the housekeeping area or love to complete puzzles. In both of these cases, you want to support their choices.

Understanding how gender influences play requires a look at the combination of how children are taught and the tendencies they inherit. Although we cannot change inherited tendencies, we can address the stereotypes children bring with them to our settings. By the time they reach preschool, children often have set ideas about what boys and girls can or cannot do. You can challenge these ideas by planning a wide variety of activities that boys and girls can choose and then working to broaden their interests and skills.

High-energy boys who are kinetic or total-body learners are uncomfortable when asked to sit for long periods of time; often, they have few opportunities to move around (Gartrell 2006). We would add that this is equally true for highly active girls. Ask yourself the following questions as you assess how well your setting matches the needs of active learners. After reflection, think about what you can change to fully address their needs.

- Do you give children the opportunity to learn concepts through active movement?
- Are your small- and large-group times too long (more than fifteen to twenty minutes), requiring active children to sit or else be admonished?
- How do you channel the boundless energy of some children? Do you use humor, physical affection, and redirection?
- Do you have sufficient time for outdoor and large-muscle play?
- Do you plan dramatic play themes for outdoors?
- Do you have sufficient time for play (at least thirty to forty minutes at one time)?
- Do your play themes achieve balance between boys' and girls' interests?

Encourage both boys and girls to experience work life and home life. By encouraging diverse choices, you offer boys the opportunity to experience nurturing behavior and girls to engage in more active play with building and exploring.

Gender differences can pose other challenges to caregivers. Gartrell (2006) cautions early childhood professionals to be sensitive to the needs of young boys in particular. Because the field of early childhood education is predominately made up of women, many caregivers feel more comfortable with the kinds of play traditionally preferred by girls. They may not seek out or encourage the rough-and-tumble play so often seen within groups of boys. Trying to channel boys' energy may be frustrating to caregivers, and this frustration may be communicated to the children. By planning for and embracing the various activity levels of both boys and girls, caregivers can communicate acceptance for all types of interactions.

Temperament

Children come to us with their own temperaments. Their differences in temperaments show up in play as they learn to work together to create themes and play experiences. Researchers Alexander Thomas, Stella Chess, and Herbert Birch have defined nine behavioral characteristics that either are inborn or develop very early in life. Children tend to fall on a continuum for each of these characteristics. For example, a child may have a very active temperament, a quiet temperament, or more commonly one that is somewhere between these two. Temperaments are neither good nor bad, but they do affect how a child experiences and responds to people and situations. The child's task is to learn how to manage various behaviors associated with his temperament. Sometimes these behaviors may get in the way of developing relationships or adjusting to life's experiences. Learning to manage or handle these behaviors happens over time. The nine characteristics are

- activity level
- regularity
- adaptability
- approach/withdrawal
- physical sensitivity
- intensity of reaction
- distractibility
- positive or negative mood
- persistence

(Thomas, Chess, and Birch 1970)

Most of the time, children fall somewhere in the middle of the continuum for each characteristic. When their temperament falls at either end, it can pose particular challenges affecting the children's behavior and relationships. Parents and caregivers can encourage changes in these characteristics, but real change requires patience, practice, and consistency (Crary 1993). We discuss how the caregiver can provide assistance during play to help modify these characteristics. A chart on how each of the nine temperaments affects play follows this discussion.

Activity Level

Children range from the very active to the quiet. On both ends of the spectrum, play experiences can be affected. When a child is too active, he can become disruptive to others' play by knocking down block structures, running into play areas, or initiating fights over props. A child's individual play can be affected by his short attention span and his inability to develop play themes. By helping the active child moderate his activity level during play, the caregiver can improve his interactions with others. An active child may concentrate more when he is engaged in sensorimotor activities. The caregiver can try to combine dramatic play and water or sand.

When a child is too inactive, he may only observe play, be reluctant to join in, or not participate fully when he does join a play group. The quiet child can be encouraged to join in a dramatic play experience by playing a less demanding role. When the group is playing restaurant, the quiet child can be a cook behind the scenes until he feels more comfortable. This child may be more likely to plop down in a chair and concentrate on one activity throughout free play. Help him join group activities. Encourage him to run and jump in the gym or outside.

Regularity

Infants can be very regular or irregular in their sleeping and eating patterns and schedules. Older children also reflect these large differences. Some children adopt new routines and schedules easily, while others vary greatly in their ability to accommodate caregivers' routines. A child who tends to be regular likes a consistent schedule and responds well to having free play occur at the same time each day. Sometimes this child may become upset when a routine or schedule is changed and needs sufficient warning to adjust.

A child who is irregular may seem resistant to routines and schedules, but he may just find it hard to regulate his system to a predictable timetable. Although he appears to dislike regularity and routine, he may actually develop play themes in more depth if you can provide consistency and predictability to his participation. Provide the same toys and materials in the same area each day to encourage his play skills.

Adaptability

Children who are adaptable adjust easily when confronted with changes in routine or schedule. Although they may notice changes in their environment, such as a new play theme or a substitute teacher, they tend to adjust quickly. Children at the other end of the spectrum, who are slow to adapt, find change very stressful. They may reject new children, room arrangements, and play themes. A change in caregivers causes upset or anxiety. By providing children who are less adaptable with warnings about upcoming changes, offering a bridge between an old play theme and a new one, giving them opportunities to move into new environments more slowly, and allowing choices of activities, you can help them learn to adapt successfully to small changes within play.

Approach/Withdrawal

Some children approach new experiences with enthusiasm. Whether forming new friendships or attending a new school, these children tend to approach these experiences openly rather than withdraw from them. Other children may be temperamentally shy or cautious and withdraw from new experiences. These children may be onlookers for a much longer time and approach other children only when they become comfortable. They often become very quiet in larger groups. They tend to move with caution and become even more withdrawn when attention is focused on them. These children commonly become less restrained if you encourage them to play physically by running, throwing balls, or playing chase. Their play skills tend to develop more quickly when you try techniques like assigning the child a play partner or adjusting your approach to ensure "goodness of fit" as discussed previously in this chapter.

Shy children sometimes behave very differently at home than they do at school. For example, Tineja's mother was very quiet during the fall parent-teacher conference when the teacher described Tineja's behavior at school. At one point, Tineja's mother got a very confused look on her face and asked, "Are you talking about Tineja Wilson? My daughter is never shy or quiet at home." At home, Tineja felt comfortable, accepted, and willing to take risks. If the teacher continues to encourage Tineja, the teacher may describe a more outgoing child in the spring parent conference.

Physical Sensitivity

Children's physical sensitivity can be quite variable. Even on a daily basis, children's physical sensitivity can vary because of illness, stress, or injuries. Children on either end of this continuum can find their play affected. A child who is too sensitive will be aware of temperature changes, noises in other areas, and the physical closeness of his peers. This can disrupt his concentration while playing and cause emotional distress as well. Even background music may be challenging for him. While trying on dress-up clothes, the child may react strongly to different textures and fabrics. Help this child adapt to various noises, temperature changes, and sudden touch by teaching him how to breathe and relax when anxious and tense. Provide places in the classroom that are more quiet and secluded so he can go there when too stimulated.

A child who is not as sensitive may seem oblivious to textures, sounds, and peers. Although his concentration during play may be unaffected, he nonetheless may be unable to attend to the needs of his playmates when developing play scenes and stories. Encourage him to notice his peers and their ideas and questions when playing. Help him notice changes in the environment by pointing out new textures, activities, and areas. Provide several cues when introducing cleanup or changes in routines, because he may miss those signals on his own.

Intensity of Reaction

As with physical sensitivity, children's intensity of reaction can vary greatly, depending on their health, stress level, and how rested they are. Children demonstrate a range of intensities of reaction from high to mild. Some children react strongly to frustration or excitement with immediate and boisterous emotions. They show us by jumping, crying, screaming, or yelling. Their reactions can overwhelm any play scene that is occurring and upset their playmates. Because these strong reactions can be hard to predict and come quickly, without much buildup, caregivers may behave reactively themselves, moving quickly to respond to emotional children or raising their voices. If you can slow down your reaction, respond calmly to help the children problem solve their frustrations with play or playmates, you can teach the children by example that they can learn to moderate their reactions.

Some children react mildly when angry or excited. Caregivers may overlook mildly reactive children because they seem to just accept and adapt to situations. But their play can be greatly enriched by learning to express excitement at new play ideas, defend possessions or props, or put forth their own play themes.

Distractibility

Children who can focus and who are not easily distracted tend to be more successful at developing play scenarios with other children. They are not distracted by stimulation and suggestions from others. Unlike them, children who are distracted by noise, other children, new toys, and colors in your setting cannot concentrate long enough to maintain a play scenario with others. They tend to wander around the room, trying many activities for brief periods of time. All children are distracted occasionally by illness and worries, but you should be concerned when children are consistently wandering around the room without engaging with materials or other children for substantial amounts of time. Cutting down stimulation in the environment, such as noise, materials, wall hangings, props, and adult conversations, helps such children concentrate for longer periods of time.

Positive or Negative Mood

Even as infants, some children seem to present a positive, cheerful mood to events around them, while others may present a persistent negative reaction to those same events. Caregivers may prefer the more positive child because the child with negative reactions can appear moody, angry, disappointed, and difficult. Even though the child with a more cheery disposition can be easier to care for, both can use help to moderate their moods. You can see how a child's negativity affects his participation in play: he may give up easily when interacting with peers, become upset when disappointed, and complain about how others are playing or sharing. Help this child problem solve when he is upset and develop a sense of humor about temporary setbacks.

The child with a positive outlook may get along well when playing with others but may need your encouragement to express anger at his peers, stand up for himself when another child takes away a toy, and or recognize other children's sadness and discouragement. Developing more sensitivity to his own feelings and the feelings of others helps him interact better with others during play.

Persistence

Each child brings a level of tolerance for frustrating tasks and for how long he will persist when trying to solve a problem. Some children persist for long periods of time, and some give up quickly. Persistence is closely related to attention span and tolerance for frustration. It is easy to see how persistent a child is when he is learning to tie his shoes, ride a bike, or write his name. You can also see his level of persistence while playing. Does the child stay with a play theme, even when its direction isn't clear or other children are leaving the area? If other children disagree about the direction of the play theme or the use of a prop, does the child work to solve the problem or to find a compromise? Does he give up or come back after trying another activity? When you help a child persist for a longer time, you help him develop richer play themes and more rewarding relationships with peers.

Although a child with a long attention span can persist during play, he also may need your encouragement to change play themes when other children are becoming restless or to notice when other children would like a turn with a prop or play role.

Now that we have looked at the characteristics in more depth, we include a chart that labels the behavior of the nine temperament characteristics at each end of the scale and presents an example illustrating how this behavior may be problematic when a child participates in play. We offer a few suggestions to help this child.

Behavior in Play	Temperament Characteristic	Behavior in Play
Active The child wants to run, jump, and climb. During dramatic play, he may knock over props or jump onto other children.	ACTIVITY LEVEL	*Quiet* The child watches play of other children and rarely speaks in groups when spoken to.
Suggestion Provide times for active play. Combine active play and dramatic play. Help the child slow down by teaching relaxation techniques.		Suggestion Try parallel play. Allow the child to watch others; then gently encourage him to stand near the group. Try not to bring attention to the child or ask too many questions. Use descriptive statements (see parallel talk and self-talk in chapter 8).
Regular The child learns schedule and routines easily and seems to enjoy following them. She may become upset when routines are changed. Sometimes the child becomes attached to a play theme and doesn't want to move on with a group decision.	REGULARITY	*Irregular* The child has a difficult time learning the daily schedule and forgets or ignores routines. Transitions to new activities in the schedule become stressful and the child may be resistant or defiant. Sometimes the child's reaction is unpredictable and children avoid playing with her.
Suggestion Give warnings about upcoming changes in schedule. Use a visual calendar or picture schedule to help the child see change concretely.		Suggestion Be very consistent with routines, transitions, and your schedule. Use pictures and enjoyable, motivating transition activities and verbal reminders. Continue to help the child moderate her reactions, express feelings to peers, and listen to peers' thoughts.

Behavior in Play	Temperament Characteristic	Behavior in Play
Adaptable The child adapts to changes fairly quickly. Once he understands the new routine, he consistently follows it. He doesn't seem overly anxious when asked to change play themes and use new props.	ADAPTABILITY	*Slow to Adapt* The child may become anxious when there is a change in routines, caregivers, or new play themes. When asked to use new, unfamiliar props, the child may leave the area or show anxiety by crying, complaining, or clinging to the caregiver.
Suggestion Give warnings when you know there will be changes so the child can adapt.		Suggestion Give many warnings when you expect changes. When changing a play theme, stay close to the child. Demonstrate, model, and suggest ways to use props and play roles. Give the child time to get used to changes in environment.
Initial Approach The child approaches new situations easily. When you introduce a new theme, the child will enter the area and experiment with props and roles. She may enter too quickly, before she has learned about the new theme and its possibilities.	APPROACH/WITHDRAWAL	*Initial Withdrawal* The child tends to remain apart from group play. When a new play theme is introduced, the child may observe but not enter the area. She may withdraw further if given too much attention.
Suggestion Demonstrate new props and roles during whole group time. Encourage experimentation.		Suggestion Play next to the child and comment but do not direct questions at her. If the child is observing a dramatic play area, sit close by. Show the child some of the props and let her handle them. Enter in the play, drawing the child with you. For example, you play the parent and ask the child to pretend to be your child.

Behavior in Play	Temperament Characteristic	Behavior in Play
Not Sensitive	PHYSICAL SENSITIVITY	*Very Sensitive*

Not Sensitive

The child seems almost unaware of slight differences, noises, or textures. Sometimes he may be unaware of the differences affecting other children and ignore their requests or discomfort. He may not be aware of peers' space before he enters or their legitimate claim on props when he grabs them.

Suggestion

Gently point out when peers are upset by his actions. Suggest ways he could be sensitive to the feelings of others.

PHYSICAL SENSITIVITY

Very Sensitive

The child is very sensitive to any differences in temperature, noises, or textures. The child may become overly anxious or demanding about addressing the differences. For example, he may become distraught and unable to concentrate if there is noise from excited play in the block area.

Suggestion

Encourage him to express his discomfort, then brainstorm ways to solve the problem. For example, he may feel too hot after running in the gym. Talk about ways he could become cooler: take off his sweater, sit and rest, fan himself, or drink water. Help him find a quieter space to play, and/or remind all children to use quieter voices.

High Intensity

The child reacts to frustration/joy/anger with intensity. Her reactions are sometimes surprising because they are loud and immediate. In play, she may be in more conflict than other children because she reacts in anger to requests to share or to changing roles. When she is excited, other children may be attracted to her enthusiasm.

Suggestion

Help the child solve problems without reacting so quickly. Encourage the child's leadership qualities to bring out her enthusiasm.

INTENSITY OF REACTION

Mild Reaction

The child seems to have little reaction to frustration/joy/anger. Although this child may be easy to care for, her mild reactions may make it harder for her to interact with others in play. The child may not express excitement at peers' play ideas or defend possessions when other children take them.

Suggestion

Remind the child to defend possessions when it is her turn. Point out good ideas of other children and suggest she imitate and play next to them.

Behavior in Play	Temperament Characteristic	Behavior in Play
Very Distractible The child wanders the room, rarely engaging in play. He picks up props but does not play with them. He enters play groups but does not stay to develop a play theme. Suggestion Cut down distractions, such as noise, too many materials, or too many wall decorations. Encourage the child to explore the play theme through the props.	DISTRACTIBILITY	*Not Distractible* The child can concentrate on task even with distractions. The child enjoys developing the theme with props. However, the child may become immersed in pretend play and ignore other children. Suggestion Suggest that the child notice the play theme as it evolves and moves on. Encourage him to move along with it.
Positive Mood The child tends to be cheerful and enjoys playing with other children. The child may not express sad or angry feelings when she has hurt feelings during play. Suggestion Comment on the child's mood in a positive way. Encourage the child to express disappointment or anger with peers.	POSITIVE OR NEGATIVE MOOD	*Negative Mood* The child may cry easily, fuss when told to wait for materials, and complain when children won't cooperate with her play idea. Suggestion Help the child express feelings appropriately with peers and adults. Problem solve together when the child is upset. Choose a solution, ask her to try it, and then ask her how it worked. Comment positively on all attempts to address the problem. Note: Although it may be easy to become frustrated with a child's consistently negative reactions, remember they are probably innate or were developed early on. Help the child see a more positive picture while commenting on her good problem-solving skills.

Behavior in Play	Temperament Characteristic	Behavior in Play
Long Attention Span The child can attend to activities, play experiences, and peers for increasing periods of time. Occasionally the child's attention span won't match those of his peers and he becomes disappointed that play is not continuing.	PERSISTENCE	*Short Attention Span* The child loses interest quickly when playing, especially with other children. He may move quickly from area to area.
Suggestion Suggest that the child find other activities when peers are done playing. Remind him that he can play again the next day, and maybe other children will join him then.		Suggestion Add new props or make new suggestions when the child begins to leave the area. Try the adult role of parallel player (see chapter 7) to help the child attend. Plan play themes that combine sensorimotor play and dramatic play.

Lack of Experience with Play

Children may simply not have been exposed to dramatic play, play materials, or play themes. When it is time to pretend, they don't know how to join in. Sometimes this lack of exposure is to a particular play theme, such as playing office or riding in an airplane. Other times, children may not have received much stimulation or encouragement to play in their homes. Children from differing cultures and languages may not understand what to do with some of your props or themes. They may not comprehend the language of their peers and therefore find it more difficult to follow the play. If you suspect that the children need more experience, you can provide field trips, modeling, and books to encourage play (see chapter 3).

Exposure to Violence

Children become aware of violence through television, video games, movies, toys, and sometimes their own experiences. Their awareness, fear of, and attraction to violence are expressed through play. They draw their play themes from superheroes, television, and video games. Children often work out their understanding of these experiences through play.

Children have played good guys versus bad guys long before video games were invented. They want to feel powerful and strong, and their play behaviors reflect this desire. Some characteristics are common across the range of violent play:

- The game always has good guys and bad guys, with no gray areas.
- The game has conflict between the two: good guys fight the bad guys.
- Control and power is an issue. Who will win?
(Reschke 2002)

These observations remind us that children play out these themes in part because of their developmental stage. Preschoolers are learning how to judge right from wrong and think in simple categories, and they still become confused between what is real and what is pretend.

Whether children play out these violent themes because of their developmental issues, the violent media, or violence they observe in their homes or neighborhoods, caregivers often become disturbed by this type of play. Concern occurs when children stereotypically play out themes from television, movies, and media-derived action figures. Children can become particularly obsessed and difficult to redirect away from violent themes when their exposure to media violence is coupled with personal experiences of violence. Teachers worry about safety when children explore violent themes. Yet the very children who seem most determined to play out the most violent themes are probably the ones who most need to work out their own questions, fears, and worries about violence. Banning this type of play does not seem to work well (Levin 2003a, 2003b). You can help children in a number of ways (adapted from Levin 2003a, 2003b):

- Reduce the amount of violent play by accepting the original theme and expanding it to something less violent. Suggest new ways to explore the play theme that move beyond scripted play and help children find more creative and imaginative explorations. For example, children have been engaged in a pretend fight with a dragon. The teacher can suggest, "Now that you won the fight with the dragon, maybe we should have a party to celebrate. What should we eat at our party?"
- Develop rules for physical play, particularly indoors. Emphasize both emotional and physical safety.
- Encourage children to write, draw, paint, and tell stories about their experiences and their feelings when they are distressed by violence or violent images around them.

Gifted and Talented

Some children devise unusual and imaginative play themes that are unfamiliar to other children. Their flights of fancy may indicate high intelligence and imagination. Often these children are ignored because the rest of the group does not know how to play along. You can connect the children by explaining or modeling the different roles in the play scene. It is important to support children who think up new play themes because doing so shows great creativity, and other children may learn new words, have new experiences, and become more curious. Playing these themes may result in a fun adventure for your whole group. For example, a child may suggest, "Let's say you are all animals in the circus and I am the Ring Master and I teach you to do tricks." You can use this suggestion to set up a circus with rings, play animals, tickets, and costumes. Another child may suggest playing Weather Girl. This is an opportunity to set up a television station with a map, pointer, microphone, and dress-up clothes. Add cameras and an audience; children can choose their roles.

Here's how you can help gifted and talented children communicate their play ideas:

- Ask them to talk about their ideas so you can understand the play theme.
- Suggest roles and props to other children.
- Provide props to act out their idea.
- Comment on the good ideas of all the children, especially when they are making suggestions about this particular play theme.
- Become a play partner occasionally to draw other children to the theme.
- Keep the play theme going over a number of days so the children can develop and deepen the theme.

Special Needs

Children diagnosed with special needs often face challenges when participating in play events with other children. To effectively assist children with disabilities, learn more about how their special needs may affect their play skills. By understanding each child's particular strengths and difficulties, you can design a plan that is individualized and more effective. Planning moves the child toward successful inclusion in a regular setting. In this way, you can build on what each child can do and provide assistance to make it happen.

Physical Disabilities

Injuries, birth defects, cerebral palsy, and other conditions can affect how children move physically during play. Children with physical disabilities may have a hard time moving around furniture or may be unable to handle the play materials. If they have cerebral palsy or other motor problems, they may have difficulty expressing themselves in speech. Working with an occupational or physical therapist to design adaptations can greatly improve these children's participation. Sometimes the adaptation needed is as simple as removing a chair from a table to make room for a wheelchair.

Hearing and Vision Impairments

Hearing impairments can affect how children communicate during play, especially sociodramatic and cooperative play. Children with hearing impairments may be unable to pick up the cues from other children that indicate a desire to engage in play and consequently look indifferent to other children's overtures. Visual impairments can affect how children manipulate objects, especially during constructive and exploratory play. Visually impaired children may not imitate others or explore objects in the same ways. Both conditions can block progress in play skills. By working with special education teachers and other professionals, you can help these children overcome barriers to social play (Johnson, Christie, and Yawkey 1999).

Neurobiological Disorders

Pervasive Developmental Disorders (PDD) and Autism Spectrum Disorders, Attention Deficit Hyperactivity Disorder (ADHD), Attention Deficit Disorder (ADD), Obsessive Compulsive Disorder (OCD), Tourette's Syndrome, depression, and other conditions can greatly affect how children interact and play with others.

Children with PDD and autism often play in repetitive ways that may exclude other children. They may seem unaware of others' invitations to play, and other children may start to leave them alone. Children with PDD and autism may also have sensory sensitivities that make them very uncomfortable with light touch, clothing, and textures—and these sensitivities in turn may affect the children's reactions to materials and activities.

Children with ADHD can be very active and unaware of other children's discomfort. In their enthusiasm to be part of play, they may alter or even put an end to the play episode they wanted to join because they move too quickly, knock things down, and disrupt the play. They may knock down buildings or brush the dishes off the table in the housekeeping area. Children with ADD may not be as physically active as children with ADHD, but they may lack concentration and focus. In play, they lose track of how the play scenario is developing and may feel left out and frustrated.

Children with OCD may become overly engaged in hand washing, touching, or counting and ignore invitations from their peers to play. Children with Tourette's Syndrome may have unusual tics that other children notice and point out. Children suffering from depression may show little emotion but demonstrate heightened sensitivity to slights from their peers. These behaviors decrease the positive interactions that children with neurobiological disorders have with peers and adults.

Caregivers need to understand how these conditions affect children's perceptions and behavior and then help them in playing with others. Professionals such as doctors, psychiatrists, psychologists, and special education teachers can help you design plans to address many of the behaviors that impede development of play skills.

Language Difficulties

If a child has difficulty expressing thoughts and feelings, he finds it hard to enter or participate in play. Descriptions of play scenarios seem impossible to express even if he knows what he wants to say. Other children don't understand and start moving the play in other directions. If the child has a disagreement with another child over props or ideas, he may simply use force because of his frustration and his inability to express his anger verbally. Because he cannot effectively communicate his ideas or frustrations, the child may be reluctant to initiate play and holds back even when invited. Some children who have experienced repeated breakdowns in communication may express their frustration in the form of aggression or tantrums. Use speech and language techniques (see chapter 8) during the day to encourage language development and help the child express anger and frustration with a combination of words, gestures, and sign language.

Socioemotional and Behavioral Difficulties

Any trauma—such as the death of a parent or loved one; separation from a parent because of travel requirements for work, military service, or divorce; chemical abuse in the family; a natural disaster; domestic violence; or abuse and neglect—can result in a child's diminished ability to play. Loss of self-esteem and control, along with overwhelming feelings, can impair a child's ability to open herself to new experiences and other people. This may occur for only a short time or can extend throughout childhood. When a child has experienced a trauma, her play may reflect her experiences and overwhelming feelings. Here are some of the ways stress can affect a child's play:

- The child chooses play themes that are violent or strange in nature. For example, a child may use small toy people for food or hit dolls excessively. These behaviors may drive other children away rather than draw them in.
- The child has behavioral difficulties in the context of play, such as hitting, poor impulse control, or low tolerance for frustration.
- The child has reduced ability to carry on pretend themes or use objects to pretend. Delayed language or cognitive abilities as a result of multiple stresses may slow down a child's acquisition of representational skills. Some children may become very quiet and slow to interact.
- The child has heightened anxiety around certain play themes or areas. For example, if the child has been abused in his family's kitchen, the housekeeping corner may be a reminder of that pain.
- The child blanks out during play. When the child comes out of a trancelike state, the play has moved on and it is difficult for the child to reenter.
- The child may have little flexibility in conflict resolution and an impaired ability to empathize with others.

Children with multiple stresses need consistency, routines, ways to express their feelings in a productive fashion, and individual help with their behavior. Play is an excellent way to create positive experiences for them when they interact with others.

Cognitive Delays

The quality and amount of play can be affected by cognitive delays. A child's cognitive delays can be biologically based, as in Down Syndrome, or caused by environmental factors, as in cases of brain injury or fetal alcohol syndrome. Some studies suggest that children with special needs may go through the same developmental sequence as other children, only more slowly (Heidemann, unpublished data; Federlein 1979). They may have difficulty with abstractions in sociodramatic play and complex constructions. They often use less language or language that is not as complex as their peers. Some children with severe cognitive delays demonstrate rigid play behaviors. Taken together, these characteristics affect the level of these children's play development.

Slower development and/or rigid play sequences can isolate children with cognitive delays from other children. Only with adult modeling and/or interaction with other children can associative or cooperative play develop. Children need this help to move beyond exploration to more advanced forms of play.

You may be working with children who have an Individualized Education Plan (IEP) addressing cognitive delays or the other special needs we have discussed here. Some of the children you work with may have delays that have not yet been formally diagnosed. If you notice that a child is consistently left behind or not joining in and he has not been diagnosed with special needs, you must look at other areas of development: language, cognitive, emotional, and motor. If you observe a delay and the child is not already receiving special services, refer him for a developmental screening. Work with the parents to locate resources in your community, and offer to arrange an observation or an appointment.

Your involvement does not end with that referral. You can still help that child learn to play more successfully in your environment. Some of the children you initially have concerns about may have special needs. Others do not. All of them benefit when you use the suggestions and strategies from this book.

In this chapter we explored how various factors influence children's development of play skills. When you observe the children in your care, you may find that several reflect one or more of the factors. Recognizing children's difficulties is only the first step in determining how to help them. In the following chapter, we present our Play Checklist. It will help you observe and intentionally plan for a child who is experiencing challenges.

Reflection Questions

1. What are several things you can do to help a child who speaks a second language feel more comfortable in your setting?

2. Think of children in your early childhood setting. As you read this chapter, did the descriptions remind you of any of them? What are the factors that affect their play, and how do the children exhibit these in their play?

3. Have you ever learned a second language? What was your experience? How could someone have helped you?

4. If you have children learning a second language in your setting, how do they participate in play? What stage in their second language acquisition do they exhibit in play? In other classroom activities?

Finding Out More: Observing, Evaluating Play Skills, and Using the Play Checklist

WILLIE'S PROVIDER STEPPED TO the counter for just a moment to get the food ready for snack. While she was there, she heard familiar sounds: "No, I'm going to be the baker and you have to be the customer. Now get in line. You say that you want a cake and I'll say we only have these cookies." She recognized the voice and the situation immediately. It was Willie, directing everyone's play again. Most of the time, Willie had pretty good play ideas and the children liked playing with him. Sometimes it got to be too much for the others, as it did today.

The next thing the provider heard was Jackson saying, "I want to be the baker or I'm not playing." Willie said, "I'm the baker and you're the customer." Jackson responded, "Come on, Mehdi, let's get out of here." The provider was still in the middle of preparing snack and couldn't leave, but she could imagine what was taking place. Jackson and Mehdi were stomping off to another activity.

Pretty soon she heard Jackson say, "Let's make a big ramp and race our cars down it." She could predict what she would hear next. She was right: Willie was pleading with them to return by saying, "Come on, you guys, you can put the money in the cash register."

Many caregivers observing this scene would be perturbed by Willie. Some might even label him *bossy*. When we observe him systematically, though, we find a lack of play skills underlying his behavior.

In the previous chapter, we discussed possible factors that can influence the development of play skills. One of the factors we discussed was special needs, but not all challenges are related to special needs. We don't always know why a child experiences challenges in play. She may experience temporary frustrations, difficulty learning to coordinate behaviors in a new group of children, or changes at home, such as a new sibling, that create vulnerabilities affecting play. In this chapter, we begin to look at how a teacher assesses an individual child who has difficulty in sociodramatic play. We discuss assessing the child's play and use of our Play Checklist, including these topics:

Observing and assessing a child's play
Using the play checklist
Explanation of the play checklist
Evaluating play skills
Willie: A case study

It is very important that you read the entire chapter before you use the Play Checklist. With complete information, it is easier to accurately match the child's skill level with the checklist items.

Observing and Assessing a Child's Play

To understand a child's play, you must observe. By watching her, you will learn

- what she most frequently likes to play
- what toys and materials she prefers
- what areas of the room are most attractive to her
- her ability to control her emotions
- how much she talks to herself and others
- who her favorite playmates are
- her skill level for playing

As you look at the children in your group, you may notice that one child has difficulty sticking to an activity for any length of time. A second child may display some sociodramatic skills, like pretending with objects or playing a role, but does not interact with her peers. You may notice that a third child does not pretend with any of the materials.

In order to gain a true understanding of a child's play, you need to systematically observe and assess her play skills. Early childhood educators engage in an ongoing process of assessing children's skills and planning activities to further their development.

Assessment

Assessment is the process of gathering data in order to make evaluative statements. Evaluation is the process of judging how closely something comes to a standard (Rebus Planning Associates 1995). You need to gather data to evaluate how closely a child's skills come to widely held developmental expectations.

Assessment information is commonly used in four ways (McAfee, Leong, and Bodrova 2004):

- To gauge a child's development and growth over time
- To plan for an individual and group(s) of children
- To inform educational decisions about who may benefit from additional screening for special services
- To talk with others about a child's skill development

The assessment process is similar to that used by a doctor. When you go to the doctor, you first see a technician who takes your blood pressure, temperature, weight, and pulse. She is gathering data. The doctor looks at this data, along with other data collected while examining you, analyzes it, and develops a plan for treatment. As you follow the treatment plan, you and the doctor track your progress.

As an early childhood educator, you do the same thing. First you gather data. You watch the child to find out who she plays with, if she plays by herself or joins others, and if she is able to solve problems she encounters during play. Next you analyze the data by looking for patterns, determining what she can do independently and what she needs help with. Then you evaluate or gauge if she would benefit from individualized instruction in play skills or if typical classroom experiences are adequate to help her learn the next level of skills. If you find she may benefit from extra help, your next steps are to write a goal and develop learning activities that will move her along the path of development. You offer the activities and continue to observe the child. You make note of changes in skill level and behavior and start the process once again.

This continuous cycle of improvement includes several steps:

1. Observe and assess.
2. Evaluate play skills.
3. Write a goal.
4. Plan and implement activities.
5. Repeat the process.

Continuous Cycle of Improvement

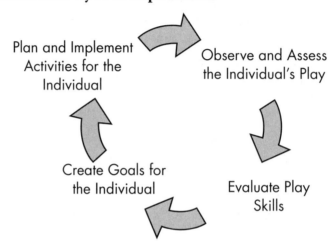

Most early childhood educators have come to agree that it is important to assess young children in an authentic manner. This means that assessment (gathering data) is part of everyday activities. Authentic assessment provides you with rich information about each child. In this type of assessment, familiar adults observe a child's performance while she engages in everyday activities within a familiar setting. Assessment relies on many sources of information, such as observations, work samples, and parent reports. Authentic assessment is helpful in working with children who may have special needs because it focuses on progress. Authentic assessment is ongoing.

Recording Techniques

In authentic assessment, you gather data throughout the year and in a variety of ways. To help keep track of the information you glean, you can use a number of different methods to record what you see. Commonly used recording techniques include the following:

Frequency tallies: This involves counting how often a behavior or skill is demonstrated. Be sure to clearly define what you are counting before you begin. For example, if you plan to count how frequently a child shares an object, determine if you will count the times a child offers a toy to others as well as when she agrees to share if someone else asks.

Running records: To observe and record in this way, separate yourself from the group. Explain to the children that you are going to watch them play for a while. Write down everything that is taking place. You may need to develop a shorthand of sorts or codes for certain names and words in order to keep up with the action.

Anecdotal records: These are short stories that you record about a single event. In one anecdote, you might describe how one child joined a group of children already at play. In another, you might describe the way a child suggested using a stick with a ball of tape on top to represent a microphone as they played Rock Star.

Language samples: If you are trying to gather information about a child's ability to use words in play settings, recording a language sample would be helpful. In this recording technique, you simply write down or record what a child says during a play episode. You examine it later to look for ways that she used language to create play scenarios or to instruct others in their roles.

Work samples: Work samples can provide helpful information about a child's level of development. If a child goes to the writing center, cuts a strip of green construction paper, draws numbers on it, and then takes it to the ice-cream parlor theme center, you can ask for a sample of this work. It demonstrates her ability to create props and to represent a pretend item for a real one. You can also use it as part of your larger assessment to gauge her fine-motor control, awareness of numbers, and emerging writing skills.

As part of your classroom assessment, record a sample of a child's language when she is playing with others or when she talks to herself. Periodically record the child's language in similar play situations. Keep this record in the child's portfolio as a way to track her language development and growth over time. The growth noted can be truly dramatic for children who are monolingual English speakers as well as for English-language learners.

Early each school year, one teacher took a photograph of every child at play. She showed the photograph to the child and asked her to tell a story about what she was playing. As the child spoke, the teacher took a language sample, writing exactly what the child said.

One photograph showed Pa Ying playing with a bear puppet, doll furniture, and little bowls. This is what Pa Ying said about her picture in October: "I play bear. Him play toy." Pa Ying was shown the same picture in April and asked to tell a story about it. This is what she said in April: "I play teddy bear, and the three bears eat the bowl. Papa bear bowl is too hot. Momma bear bowl is too cool. The baby bear eats, and it is just right, and the baby bear eats it all. That's it."

Checklists: Checklists can range from informal, teacher-made checklists to formal developmental checklists that help determine if a child is developing skills at an age-appropriate rate. Both rely on teacher-planned activities and teachers' observations to check items off the list. The Play Checklist introduced here includes a number of skills a child needs to be successful in group pretend play. The progression of skills outlined in each section can be used as a guide when you assess, evaluate, and plan activities to strengthen each child's play skills.

When you gather data about a child's play skills, use a variety of observation and recording methods. Make sure you have information from more than one source recorded on more than one day. To gather data, you might directly observe, count behaviors, and collect samples of a child's work. Observe the child at play, both indoors and outdoors. Record information about how well and how often the child engages in a behavior or skill. When you look at both types of information, you will better understand the behaviors the child exhibits and if she engages in them very often. You will also learn if the skill is something the child uses by herself or only with help, if she performs the skill consistently, or if the behavior was a fluke. Gather information about how well a child is performing the skill or behavior. For example, when you look at a sample showing how a child writes her name, you can look to see how well she forms the letters, if her strokes are smooth or jerky, and if she includes all the letters.

Gathering data about how often the child demonstrates a skill or behavior is also helpful. For example, you can tally how often the child initiates play with others. Or you might record a language sample and then count how often the child starts a conversation or responds to someone else.

When you record your observations, be careful to write down only the facts. Include only the observations that all people who are watching would agree have taken place. Use only objective terms to describe what you see. It is objective to write, "Sally's head was down. She made no eye contact. She frowned." Anyone looking at Sally at the same time would record her behavior in a similar manner because it clearly describes what anyone watching would see. Avoid subjective statements. A subjective statement would be "Sally is unhappy," which is your personal interpretation of her behavior. There may be other explanations for her behavior. Someone else may look at the same behavior and explain it by saying that Sally is shy.

As you record, keep the following in mind:

- Avoid judgmental comments.
- Use descriptive terms.
- Avoid personal opinions about what the child may be feeling.
- Don't try to guess what the child might be thinking.

An objective running record of a play scenario that focuses on Sally might read something like this:

[*Four children at the water table, washing dolls.*]
[*Sally leans over table. Pushes doll's stomach.*]
Gavin: Sally, watch.
[*Sally glances briefly.*] **Sally:** Her taking a bath.
[*Kari pulls at Sally's arm. No response.*]
Kari: Move it, Sally! [*No response.*]
[*Sally twirls doll on head. Picks up doll, looks at doll's face. Smoothes doll's hair.*]
Sally: I need a towel.
Teacher: I hear you, Sally.
Sally: I need a towel. [*After a short pause.*] I need a towel.

From this example, you can see that correct grammar and complete sentence structure are not necessary when recording observations. In fact, you would probably abbreviate further and find a way to identify the children without writing out their names each time. The important thing to remember is to record information accurately in a way that enables you to describe the situation to others or to re-create it in your own mind's eye. You should strive to record children's actual words accurately, though, because doing so will help you evaluate the information later.

The information gathered can provide you with what you need to evaluate a child's play skills and can become part of your overall assessment system. The data you gather should provide you with examples of a child's social and representational skills. Language samples can be used to analyze the child's skills in play situations and to look at her expressive language skills in particular. Any writing samples gathered while playing restaurant, for instance, may document the child's emerging writing skills as well as how she uses props to support her play ideas. Examples of her ability to solve problems in play situations may also provide evidence of her newly emerging leadership skills.

In this chapter, we introduce our Play Checklist. It is intended to be used with children who appear to be having difficulty with sociodramatic play skills, but it may be a tool you choose to use as part of your classroom assessment for all children. There are many ways you can use the Play Checklist. Here are a few:

- Complete the Play Checklist for one or two children you are concerned about.
- Complete the Play Checklist for all children in your classroom.
- Complete a few sections of the Play Checklist for one or more of the children.
- Share a summary of the Play Checklist with parents to help them understand the value of play, what skills are challenging for their child, and what their child is learning.

A FAMILY CHILD CARE provider recognized that a number of the children in her care cried whenever they needed to share with each other. She had done the entire Play Checklist on one of the children in her care, and she wondered what she would learn if she did the turn-taking section for all of the children. She was surprised by what she found. Although the children ranged in age from two to four years old, most were at the lower end of this section on the Play Checklist. She found that two of the children would put down toys but protested if others picked them up, and three took turns but only if she arranged it. She decided to focus her attention on helping the children learn to take turns by reading books and doing role plays at group time. She also decided to invest in a few duplicates of the favorite toys. And she committed herself to giving the children more reminders during play, such as, "If you leave, it means you're done with the toy, and someone else can play with it."

Using one section of the Play Checklist helped her focus her attention on a situation that was frustrating her. She used the information she gathered to come up with some positive steps to improve the situation. Her efforts did not eliminate the situation overnight, but they greatly reduced the amount of crying and helped the children begin to learn to share.

Finding Time to Assess

Finding time to assess is never easy in a busy, demanding early childhood environment. Early childhood educators have been very creative in finding ways to make time for this important aspect of their work with young children. Some providers arrange for an additional person to be in the room so they can take time to observe. This could be a volunteer, the center director, or a high school student looking for community involvement hours. Many providers include their plan for observation in their lesson plans. They know what they want to look for and link it to the best time of day to see it. Free play and outdoor play will be the ideal times to see the skills on the Play Checklist. Other caregivers decide on whom they will observe or the work samples they will gather and write it in their calendars. Some providers stagger when they change the materials in interest centers because they know some centers will be familiar to the children and children will be able to work in them independently. This frees up the provider to observe in the areas on which she wants to focus. Find the process that works best for you.

Making Recording Easier

Before you observe, be sure to identify what you want to look for or learn about. Then determine what time of day, week, or activity you are most likely to see that skill or behavior. If you want to know about the child's ability to join a group in play, you obviously want to observe during indoor and outdoor free play sessions. Problem-solving skills can be observed in many situations throughout the day. Make sure the tools and materials you use for recording are handy. Some providers place a clipboard in each learning center throughout their room. Others prefer to carry a self-adhesive notepad with them. Still others use large, self-adhesive mailing labels to record their notes during play. The value of the self-adhesive paper and the labels is that you can transfer the information to a child's notebook or folder without having to rewrite it. To do a behavior or skill tally, you need an easy way to record the number of occurrences. Some people use golf counters (handheld device used to count golf strokes, or in this case, behaviors), while others place a supply of checkers or plastic chips in one pocket, and each time they see what they want to count, they transfer a chip to the other pocket.

Using the Play Checklist

The Play Checklist has been developed to help adults understand children's sociodramatic play skills. It can be used to write goals and as the foundation for planning. The Play Checklist consists of ten sections. The first six are an adaptation of Smilansky's Play Inventory (Smilansky 1968; Christie 1982) and the seventh is adapted from Hazen, Black, and Fleming-Johnson (1984). The next four take a closer look at social skills needed to succeed in socio-dramatic play.

The Play Checklist includes these categories:

Pretending with objects
Role-playing
Verbalizations about the play scenario
Verbal communication during a play episode
Persistence in play
Interactions
Entrance into a play group
Problem solving
Turn taking
Support of peers

Preparing to Complete a Play Checklist

Thoroughly familiarize yourself with each item on the Play Checklist before you try to use it. Read through the explanation of each item that is provided over the next few pages. Think of and look for examples of each item as you work with the child.

Observe the child during a time and in a place that offers an opportunity for sociodramatic play. To give the child an opportunity to demonstrate this high level of play, you must make certain that the materials she has available are conducive to role-play and that other children are around to engage with in group play. Dolls, puppets, costumes, and many types of building materials promote sociodramatic play (refer back to chapter 3 for charts showing types of materials, themes, and settings that encourage sociodramatic play). Painting or putting puzzles together are not activities that are likely to bring about the type of play you want to observe. Some children may be more comfortable pretending during outdoor play. Be sure to observe children in both indoor and outdoor play settings.

Make sure that the child you are observing knows the other children. When she is familiar with the children, she is more likely to exhibit sociodramatic skills. Give children who are new to your setting a few weeks to adjust and get to know others before observing them.

Observe a child three or more times. To get a true picture of the child's skill level, collect a variety of work samples and observations. If you obtain only one sample or observation, you may watch the child on a day she isn't feeling well or when her usual playmates are unavailable. Or you may collect a sample of work with which she received a lot of help. This would greatly influence the results you get.

The information you record in your observations, as well as other data you collect, will be used as the basis for completing the Play Checklist.

The Play Checklist is a tool you can use for each child in your group, but it was designed to be used with the child who is having difficulty with group pretend play. You may be able to quickly pick out the child who needs help. However, if you have trouble deciding whether or not to do a Play Checklist, use the following questions as a guide. Consider the frequency, the severity, and the number of areas in which the child is having difficulty to determine whether you will do an entire checklist or only one section of it.

- Does the child consistently have trouble interacting with a small group or with a particular individual?
- Is the child rejected when she attempts to join group play?
- Does the child appear anxious when others are playing and she is not included?
- Does the child become aggressive when playing with others?
- Does the child manipulate objects rather than pretend?
- Is the child silent or does she talk only to herself during play?
- Does the child refuse to take turns?

If you are troubled by the child's lack of interest in play or feel she is ready to move to a new level of development in play skills, use the Play Checklist to pinpoint her present skills and how you can help.

Instructions

To use the Play Checklist, decide which child you will observe. Observe her during free play. Focus on this child, and do a minimum of two or three running records of about ten to fifteen minutes in length. Observing an entire play scene can be very helpful, even if it runs longer than fifteen minutes, but this may not be possible, given the needs of your group of children. Use other observations and recording techniques as described earlier in this chapter to gain further information.

After gathering your data, it's time to analyze it. Your data will help you understand the child's play and be more intentional as you plan to meet her needs.

Look at the data to see

- what the child can consistently do on her own
- when the child needs assistance
- noticeable patterns
- signals that this child is becoming anxious

- other factors that may be influencing the child's performance, such as time of day or special needs
- if you notice anything you weren't expecting

Use the information you glean from your observations and analysis to check the highest skill on the Play Checklist that the child consistently performs. The individual items under each section heading have been listed in order from easiest to most complex skill. You may find that the child is capable of a higher-level skill on occasion but seems to use a lower level of play skill more consistently. If this is the case, check the one the child uses most often. (After the checklist, we explain each item.)

Play Checklist

Child's Name: _____ Date: _____

Date of Birth: _____

Check the highest level skills you consistently observe:

*1. Pretending with Objects
❏ Does not use objects to pretend
❏ Uses real objects
❏ Substitutes objects for other objects
❏ Uses imaginary objects

*2. Role-Playing
❏ No role play
❏ Uses one sequence of play
❏ Combines sequences
❏ Uses verbal declaration (for example, "I'm a doctor")
❏ Imitates actions of role, including dress

*3. Verbalizations about the Play Scenario
❏ Does not use pretend words during play
❏ Uses words to describe substitute objects
❏ Uses words to describe imaginary objects and actions (for example, "I'm painting a house")
❏ Uses words to create a play scenario (for example, "Let's say we're being taken by a monster")

*4. Verbal Communication during a Play Episode
❏ Does not verbally communicate during play
❏ Talks during play only to self
❏ Talks only to adults in play
❏ Talks with peers in play by stepping outside of role (for example, "That's not how mothers hold their babies")
❏ Talks with peers from within role (for example, "Eat your dinner before your dad comes home")

*5. Persistence in Play
❏ Less than five minutes
❏ Six to nine minutes
❏ Ten minutes or longer

*6. Interactions
❑ Plays alone
❑ Plays only with adults
❑ Plays with one child, always the same person
❑ Plays with one child, can be different partners
❑ Can play with two or three children together

**7. Entrance into a Play Group
❑ Does not attempt to enter play group
❑ Uses force to enter play group
❑ Stands near group and watches
❑ Imitates behavior of group
❑ Makes comments related to play theme
❑ Gets attention of another child before commenting

8. Problem Solving
❑ Gives in during conflict
❑ Uses force to solve problems
❑ Seeks adult assistance
❑ Imitates verbal solutions or strategies provided by adults
❑ Recalls words or strategies to use when reminded
❑ Initiates use of words or strategies
❑ Accepts reasonable compromises

9. Turn Taking
❑ Refuses to take turns
❑ Leaves toys, then protests when others pick them up
❑ Takes turns if arranged and directed by an adult
❑ Asks for turn, does not wait for a response
❑ Gives up toy easily if done with it
❑ Gives up toy if another child asks for it
❑ Proposes turn taking, will take and give turns

10. Support of Peers
❑ Shows no interest in peers
❑ Directs attention to distress of peers
❑ Shows empathy or offers help
❑ Offers and takes suggestions of peers at times
❑ Encourages or praises peers

Note: The developmental progression outlined in each segment of the Play Checklist can be used as a guideline when assessing most children's development. However, not all children will go through the same steps in development nor through the same developmental sequence.
*Smilansky, Sara. 1968. *The effects of sociodramatic play on disadvantaged preschool children.* New York: Wiley.
** Hazen, Nancy, Betty Black, and Faye Fleming-Johnson. 1984. Social acceptance: Strategies children use and how teachers can help children learn them. *Young Children.* 39(6): 26–36.

Play by Sandra Heidemann and Deborah Hewitt, copyright © 2010. Redleaf Press grants permission to photocopy this page for classroom use.

Explanation of the Play Checklist

The following is a detailed explanation of each of the individual sections of the Play Checklist. Remember that the individual skills under each section heading have been listed in order from the easiest to the most complex.

1. Pretending with Objects

Pretending with objects is one of the first skills a child acquires in play. At around twelve to eighteen months, a child begins to use objects in a dramatically new way. Instead of simply exploring the object's physical properties, the child begins to use the toys and materials to pretend. The child not only picks up and puts down the telephone, she talks when the receiver is near her mouth. Now she is beginning to symbolize. The smooth transition between these two stages underplays the truly dramatic and exciting beginnings of pretending.

It may be difficult to always interpret accurately how a child is using an object. Because you cannot see inside the child's mind, you need to observe her behaviors and listen to her language. Most of the time, if you understand her frame of reference, you can see how she is pretending with objects. For example, the child picks up a string and drags it on the floor. She says, "Here, Spotty, here, Spotty." You are probably safe in assuming that she is pretending to walk her dog.

Checklist Items

Does not use objects to pretend: This means that the child simply uses objects to bang, roll, drop, or push. All the action is done to explore physical properties, not to pretend.

Uses real objects: By eighteen months, most children begin to use real objects or child-sized replicas to pretend. For example, a child may use a bottle to feed a doll or may pretend to cook by stirring with a spoon in a pan. At this level of development, the child almost always needs an object that looks like the real thing to pretend. If given substitutes, she may ignore them.

Substitutes objects for other objects: A child uses increasingly more dissimilar objects to pretend. For instance, a child may use a block as a bed for the doll and a few months later use a blanket or rug as a bed. A child who cannot do this seeks out a more realistic prop to use.

Uses imaginary objects: By age four, most children no longer need an object to pretend with, although they still may enjoy playing with realistic toys. They use action and words to indicate imaginary objects. In our experience, many children do this first with imaginary food or imaginary money.

Gradually, they learn that even if they don't have an object, the play doesn't have to stop. They can pretend to have the object. Acquiring this skill is important because it gives children so much flexibility in play.

2. Role-Playing

This section highlights a child's ability to act out a role in play. Certainly, most children find role-playing delightful. They quickly don the white doctor's smock and stethoscope to help a peer pretending to have a stomachache. Doing so requires a complex understanding of how the role is played. Children use voice, dress, body language, and props to communicate that understanding.

Checklist Items

No role play: The child uses no props, language, or actions to play a role. She may lack the cognitive understanding of what a role is or may be afraid to risk role-playing in a group.

Uses one sequence of play: In early role-playing, toddlers pretend just one incident. For example, a two-year-old may pick up the telephone, say hello, and hang up. Or she may put a bottle to a doll's mouth for a few seconds and then throw the bottle and the doll aside.

Combines sequences: As a child matures, she learns to combine play events so they become more complex. For example, Pa Quazi stirs a spoon in a pan at the stove in the housekeeping corner and then sets the table. Combining these distinct and separate events into one continuous flow forms the basis for a role played in an elaborate and unique style.

Uses verbal declaration (for example, "I'm a doctor"): A child may verbally indicate she is the mom or a firefighter. However, this may or may not be supported by dress, actions, and language appropriate to that role. If the child does not elaborate beyond the verbal declaration, she may need help to further play out the role. For example, Ali would run into the doctor play area and say, "I'm a doctor." He would then run out. His caregiver helped him perform the actions of a doctor by encouraging him to put on the white coat, take a blood pressure reading, and give a shot.

Imitates actions of role, including dress: The child has the ability to imitate roles in play, such as doctor, parent, superhero, or baby. She uses dress, actions, body language, props, voice, and words to play out her understanding of what others in that role do. Sometimes a child demonstrates that she can imitate the actions and voice of a role by using a plastic figure, such as a toy elephant. The child bangs the elephant on the ground to show how it stomps through the jungle, uses her voice to trumpet its call, and says "Sssssshhhh" to pretend to spray water through its trunk. A child learns what each role requires by watching adults, television, or movies and reading books. Unless a child can succeed in role play, she will have real difficulty with sociodramatic play in a group. She will be quickly left behind the ongoing action.

3. Verbalizations about the Play Scenario

Children use language during play to let their play partners know where the play is going. Without words, children lose track of the collective play theme, and play disintegrates. In this section of the Play Checklist, we look at the words children use to build the pretend theme. These words may or may not be spoken to others in play.

Checklist Items

Does not use pretend words during play: If you check this item for a child, she probably is not talking much during play. A child who has a language delay, who speaks a language other than that spoken by playmates, or who has a shy temperament may have difficulty with verbalizations.

Uses words to describe substitute objects: The child uses words to communicate what a substitute object represents to other children or adults. For instance, she may put a piece of paper in another child's hand and state, "Here's a rock for the wall."

Uses words to describe imaginary objects and actions (for example, "I'm painting a house"): The child uses words to communicate what an object or action is. She possesses a mental representation of an object or an action, and the only way someone else can know what it is would be for her to tell you. For example, she may hold out her hand and say, "Here's the money." She may stand in front of the wall and move her arm up and down it, saying, "I'm painting now."

Uses words to create a play scenario (for example, "Let's say we're being taken by a monster"): This is the most difficult skill of all. The child uses words to create a scene. You may see her outlining a scene that a group of children will then enter. For example, Sarah says loudly, "Let's say this is an ocean, and we are on this boat, and there's a whole bunch of sharks after us." The group of children may agree to this scene or add to it, and the play begins. This shared understanding of the play scenario allows the play to become more complex as it develops.

4. Verbal Communication during a Play Episode

Children not only use words to create agreement on actions and themes but also use language to direct or communicate with others during play. Unless this verbal interaction occurs, children play their roles alone, with little communication between them. Gestural language, such as sign language, can perform the same function. Language or gestural communication becomes the glue that holds the play together.

Checklist Items

Does not verbally communicate during play: The child does not speak during play episodes. Sometimes she is an onlooker. At other times, she may be in the middle of a play group but does not attempt to communicate verbally. This child may be in the nonverbal stage of second-language acquisition in which she recognizes that her home language is not working, so she does not use language to communicate in this setting. (See stages of second-language acquisition in chapter 4.)

Talks during play only to self: The child may talk, but her words aren't directed or intended as communication. The child may simply be talking to herself. This skill is used by many children to further their individual play, but it doesn't help them integrate into group play.

Talks only to adults in play: The child talks with an adult to ask for toys or materials or to describe what she is doing. She may ask for help with sensorimotor tasks like buttoning the buttons on a doll's shirt. Or she may tell the teacher, "She won't give me the cookbook," without having asked the other child.

Talks with peers in play by stepping outside of role (for example, "That's not how mothers hold their babies"): The child directs comments to others but steps out of a role temporarily to do it. When a child does this, she may tell another child how to play a role or correct the other child's actions. For example, Calli stops feeding the baby long enough to tell Wyatt, "No, Wyatt! That's not where the daddy sits."

Talks with peers from within role (for example, "Eat your dinner before your dad comes home"): The most sophisticated way to verbally communicate during play is to talk from inside of the role. A skilled child is able to give suggestions or direct others in respective roles by playing the mom, teacher, or doctor. In the example above, if Calli had learned this skill, she could say in her mommy voice, "No, dear, you sit over here." When this skill is achieved, there are fewer breaks in the play.

5. Persistence in Play

How long a child may play in a group as part of a sociodramatic play theme has implications for the child and the play. A child with a short attention span has difficulty staying in one place, much less playing with a group. While she may persist in playing alone longer than in a group, you should use this section to measure the amount of time she remains engrossed in a group play episode. Playing with others is an important skill to observe more than once. Even children who are typically capable of maintaining attention during play may be interrupted easily if they are playing in high-traffic areas with many distractions.

Checklist Items

Less than five minutes: Toddlers flit from activity to activity, but most three-year-olds should be able to join in group play for as long as five minutes.

Six to nine minutes: Four-year-olds should increasingly expand their group play times to nine minutes.

Ten minutes or longer: Most five-year-olds can sustain a sociodramatic play episode with other children for ten minutes or longer.

6. Interactions

In sociodramatic play, a child interacts with at least one other child. The children exchange ideas, conversation, and materials as they work together to create playful scenes.

Checklist Items

Plays alone: The child who plays alone is sometimes thought of as a loner or a withdrawn child. English-language learners often remain on the outskirts of the group's activities until ready to risk some of their new language skills. Some children may isolate themselves further by choosing activities and materials that are typically used by one person at a time, such as easel painting or working with beads.

Plays only with adults: Adults can become a child's primary play partners if the child is uncomfortable with her peers. She can be quite demanding of adult attention and unsure of what to do with herself when the adult is unavailable to her. She may look to the adult to provide play ideas and to keep play going. For example, Nakita preferred to be with one caregiver and followed her around the classroom. When that caregiver was unavailable, Nakita was at a loss for appropriate play ideas and went to the water table to play alone.

Plays with one child, always the same person: Some caregivers consider this child to have only one best friend. This child has learned to get along adequately with this best friend but seems unable to transfer her interaction skills to playing with other children. A common language may bring children together.

Plays with one child, can be different partners: A child interacting at this level plays with a number of different children, but she needs to play one-on-one. She may switch partners from day to day or from activity to activity. At this point, she is still unable to play in groups of three, so she may reject others by saying, "You can't play with us."

Can play with two or three children together: Playing with two or three others in a group is the most sophisticated level of interaction. The child who knows how to do this pays attention to the other children and is capable of some give and take.

7. Entrance into a Play Group

This skill differs in a subtle way from the interactional skills already discussed. It refers to the child's ability to enter into a group of children who have already established a play scenario.

Checklist Items

Does not attempt to enter play group: A child who does not attempt to enter a play group may be somewhat disconnected from the others. She may not attend to others' behavior or verbalizations. This child plays alone frequently and may decline the play invitations of other children.

Uses force to enter play group: Many types of force may be tried as a way to enter the play of others. The child may initiate contacts with others by patting them on the back, poking their arm, wrestling them to the ground, or using verbal threats—for example, "I'm not going to be your friend anymore." These attempts to join play are rarely successful.

Stands near group and watches: Sometimes standing near the group and watching established play can be an effective method of gaining entry. The child becomes integrated into play as the group surrounds her.

Imitates behavior of group: The child stands near the group and begins to perform the same type of activities. She is usually on the outskirts of the group, but instead of only watching, she imitates their behaviors. Again the play of the group surrounds her.

Makes comments related to play theme: Using this strategy to enter play, the child comes into the group and says something related to what the other children are doing. When Marie approaches a group of children playing school, she says, "How about we go on a field trip to the zoo?"

Gets attention of another child before commenting: The most effective strategy a child can use is to call another child's name, establish eye contact, or tap his shoulder to get his attention before making a comment that is related to the existing play. For example, Marie may say, "Josh, how about if we go on a field trip to the zoo?"

8. Problem Solving

For many preschoolers, conflicts occur because they don't agree on who should play with a toy or what they should play. If problems cannot be resolved in a way that is acceptable to all those involved, play falls apart or individuals become left out.

Checklist Items

Gives in during conflict: Some children respond to conflict passively. A child who gives in leaves the area or goes on to another activity when someone takes her toy. Sometimes this child looks very surprised that another person would take her toy, and she may look as if she doesn't know what to do in such a conflicting situation. Others choose not to respond or do not have the language skills with which to respond.

Uses force to solve problems: Preschoolers often try to solve problems through the use of force. Force can involve physical or verbal aggression, manipulation, or physical intimidation. Preschoolers with poor or newly emerging language skills may use aggression to get a toy because they have difficulty making themselves understood verbally. Others may threaten their peers by saying, "Give me that truck or you'll be sorry." A child may even try to bully someone by standing over him and puffing out her chest while showing her clenched fist.

Seeks adult assistance: When a child has little problem-solving ability, she relies on an adult to solve her problems. She may start crying when she has a problem and look toward the adult, or she may come to the adult for help with a situation that she doesn't know how to handle. Most often the adult must accompany the child to assist her in solving the problem.

Imitates verbal solutions or strategies provided by adults: At this stage, the child may not be able to solve the problem by herself but can use the words that an adult gives her. The adult must provide the child with the appropriate words to use in the situation. The child is responsible for going back to the situation and imitating the words given.

Recalls words or strategies to use when reminded: A child at this level still goes to the adult for help when faced with a problem. The adult reminds her how to solve the problem by offering a directive, such as "Tell her what you want." She can then go back to the situation and use some of the words she recalls having learned in the past.

Initiates use of words or strategies: After much practice, a child learns to use words or strategies to solve conflicts on her own. She needs no reminders or help in formulating the words to use. But she may need help in getting the other child to listen to her or to follow through with her request.

Accepts reasonable compromises: Children who are able to accept reasonable compromises in solving problems know how to use words to get their needs met and can sometimes do as another child asks.

9. Turn Taking

In early childhood settings, we ask children to learn to share at a very early age. Because of a limited number of resources, children must learn to take turns with toys and equipment. In order to successfully take turns, a child must understand give-and-take. She must learn to temporarily delay her own satisfaction in order to coordinate her behavior with that of others. In addition, she must know how to negotiate a trade or a deal and sometimes accept the suggestions made by others. These skills are closely related to the child's ability to problem solve.

Checklist Items

Refuses to take turns: It is not uncommon for a child to refuse to take turns. If she is forced to share a possession, she may prefer to leave the area rather than share something she is not ready to give up. A young child may have a tantrum when asked to share an item. An older child may say, "I'm not playing if I can't have the one I want."

Leaves toys, then protests when others pick them up: A child leaves a toy she has been playing with but still feels it is hers. She may become upset and demand back a toy that someone else has picked up. Nancy has been using the yellow truck in the sand but has left the area to greet another child who has just arrived. When Nancy returns, she finds that Larissa has picked up the yellow truck and is driving it around. She yells, "Hey, I was using that."

Takes turns if arranged and directed by an adult: Some children need an adult to structure turn taking. The adult may tell the child how to judge when another child is finished using an object, set limits on the number of children using a material, or divide up toys among those who want to play. Whatever type of adult intervention is used, a child at this level can agree to the terms of turn taking.

Asks for turn, does not wait for a response: When a child starts learning to ask for a turn, she asks but sometimes leaves out the pause that gives the other person a chance to respond. She doesn't understand that she needs to wait for the other person, so her words and her taking occur simultaneously. For example, when Jackie asks for a towel, she says, "Can I have a towel, Tamika?" At the same time, she takes it from Tamika's hand.

Gives up toy easily if done with it: As a child matures, she gives up a toy she is finished with. She understands that if she is no longer using it, someone else can.

Gives up toy if another child asks for it: Even when the child is still engaged with a toy, she shares it when asked. A typical response is "Sure, I'm going to play with the dump truck now."

Proposes turn taking, will take and give turns: Play can proceed smoothly when a child has successfully learned to share a piece of equipment. Learning to share means being able to give up a toy at times, offer a toy at times, and ask for a toy at times.

10. Support of Peers

Being able to support your peers is important to starting and maintaining friendships. This is a difficult set of skills for many younger children to acquire; they may be at a very egocentric stage in their development. A child needs to be able to look at a situation from another person's position and to empathize with his feelings. She needs to know how to offer others comfort or help when they need it. She needs to establish a balance between giving and taking suggestions that help play to continue. She also needs to develop positive attitudes toward others (Kostelnik, Stein, Whiren, and Soderman 1998).

Checklist Items

Shows no interest in peers: Some children do not notice the actions and expressions of others. An impulsive, active, or distracted child may have difficulty showing interest in her peers.

Directs attention to distress of peers: A young child pays attention to others in the room who are crying or upset. She stops what she is doing momentarily and looks in the direction of the other child. She may even move closer to the child who is upset.

Shows empathy or offers help: Not only does this child pay attention to another child in the room who is crying or upset, she also tries to help. She may hold out a cuddly stuffed animal or a blanket to provide comfort. She may try to hug or pat the back of a child who is upset. Her actions suggest that she understands how the other child feels and wants to help her feel better.

Offers and takes suggestions of peers at times: When two or three children are playing together, they must share in the planning and leadership roles of play. A child capable of doing this goes along with the suggestions of others and may say something like "Yeah, let's do that" or "That's a good idea." At other times, the child offers play ideas, saying, "Let's pretend . . ." or "How about if we . . . ?" Some English-language learners become skilled observers and follow the lead of others as well as suggest play through their actions. There should be some balance in suggesting scenes to play and accepting those of others.

Encourages or praises peers: A child who can do this is able to recognize the strengths of other children and comment on them or notice and say something about a child who is working hard or doing a good job. For example, as Jack arrived at child care, Damon says, "That's a neat sweatshirt, Jack."

> DAVID, A CHILD IN the silent period of second-language acquisition, was playing with others at the sand table. They were using rakes, shovels, containers, and funnels. David purposefully crashed his rake into the rake of another child and then looked up at the other child's face with an expectant smile. When the other child frowned and said, "Hey!" David tried something else. This time he got a funnel and poured sand through the funnel onto the other child's hand. Again, he searched the other child's face to see if this idea worked. This time the other child smiled, grabbed another funnel, and poured sand on David's hand.
>
> Although David didn't use any words, his keen awareness of the nonverbal and verbal cues of others helped him gauge if his play ideas were being accepted.

Evaluating Play Skills

Now that you are familiar with the Play Checklist, remember it is not intended to diagnose developmental delays. Instead, it should be used to assess, evaluate, plan, and assist in monitoring growth. When you use the Play Checklist, you notice that there are no age ratings on it to indicate when a child should be performing a particular skill. In general, young preschoolers, ages two and a half to three, are expected to demonstrate the skills and behaviors at the lower end of each section, while older preschoolers, ages four and a half to five, are expected to demonstrate the more sophisticated skills at the upper end.

After analyzing your observation notes and data, mark the highest level of skills the child is consistently performing on the Play Checklist. By doing this, you are establishing the child's level of independent performance. When you interpret this information, you may discover that in some cases a child's level of independent performance doesn't create a concern. That child may only need your continued encouragement and an appropriate play environment to learn more complex play skills.

However, other children in your group may be having difficulty performing even the most basic skills. These children may not be gaining play skills in the ways other children do. You must use the information from your observations, other sources of data (such as writing samples), the Play Checklist, knowledge of widely held developmental expectations, and your professional judgment to evaluate whether or not the child needs individualized help with play skills. Consider the following guidelines. If any of them ring true, develop an individual plan.

- The child demonstrates a low level of play skills on two to three sections of the Play Checklist.
- The child demonstrates a very low skill level on one of the sections of the Play Checklist. For example, the child does not pretend with objects by age three.
- The child shows signs of anxiety when others are playing and she is not included, or the child is consistently excluded from group play.
- The child often becomes aggressive when playing with other children.
- The child remains an onlooker for longer than six months.
- The child can't sustain play for an extended period of time.
- The child does not engage in role play.
- The child isn't communicating with others during play by age four and a half.

Willie: A Case Study

At the beginning of the chapter we learned about Willie, a boy three years and eleven months old, who has been in family child care for three months. Let's look more closely at how analyzing Willie's records helped his provider complete the Play Checklist and gain a better picture of his play skills.

Willie's schedule at child care is sporadic, and he is absent frequently. When he is present, he is usually in a good mood and easily occupies himself with appropriate play ideas. He plays with a variety of materials, although he most frequently plays with blocks or housekeeping toys. After using a running record to note her observations of Willie, his caregiver looked for patterns in her notes.

She recognized the following pattern and highlighted the examples in her notes.

Note # 1:

Willie playing with Mehdi in blocks. Mehdi has a pile of blocks in front of him. W. says, "Can I have this?" while pulling it from M.'s pile.

Note # 2:

Jackson and Willie in the sand. J. puts the shovel he has been using down next to his leg. W. says, "I'm gonna make a mountain. Can I have the shovel to build the mountain?" W. reaches for the shovel as he says it.

Note # 3:

Willie is putting books away after story time. He says, "I'll put them in the shelf." He takes Denise's from her hands before she has a chance to close it.

She hadn't recognized this before, but the caregiver's notes showed that Willie seemed to know the words to use when asking for toys, but he said the words and grabbed the toy at the same time. This upset the other children. When she marked the section on turn taking in Willie's Play Checklist, she marked that Willie was at the level of "Asks for turn, does not wait for a response."

Another thing his caregiver found in her observation records was that Willie was very helpful with the younger children. He would offer one of the toddlers a toy if the child was crying, and he would run to get a diaper if she asked him. During free play, however, he often insisted that play go his way. (We saw this in the example at the beginning of the chapter, when Willie wanted to be the baker.) When other children refused, the play fell apart and Willie was left to play by himself. This wasn't what he wanted, so he begged the other children to come back. Having had enough, they shrugged off his pleas. On the Support of Peers section of the Play Checklist, his provider concluded that Willie was able to show empathy or offer help, but he had difficulty with taking the suggestions of peers.

This is the Play Checklist she completed for him:

Play Checklist

Child's Name: __Willie__   Date: __December 12__

Date of Birth: __January 10 (three years and eleven months old)__

Check the highest level skills you consistently observe:

*1. Pretending with Objects
- ❑ Does not use objects to pretend
- ❑ Uses real objects
- ☒ Substitutes objects for other objects
- ❑ Uses imaginary objects

*2. Role-Playing
- ❑ No role play
- ❑ Uses one sequence of play
- ❑ Combines sequences
- ☒ Uses verbal declaration (for example, "I'm a doctor")
- ❑ Imitates actions of role, including dress

*3. Verbalizations about the Play Scenario
- ❑ Does not use pretend words during play
- ❑ Uses words to describe substitute objects
- ☒ Uses words to describe imaginary objects and actions (for example, "I'm painting a house")
- ❑ Uses words to create a play scenario (for example, "Let's say we're being taken by a monster")

*4. Verbal Communication during a Play Episode
- ❑ Does not verbally communicate during play
- ❑ Talks during play only to self
- ❑ Talks only to adults in play
- ❑ Talks with peers in play by stepping outside of role (for example, "That's not how mothers hold their babies")
- ☒ Talks with peers from within role (for example, "Eat your dinner before your dad comes home")

*5. Persistence in Play
- ❑ Less than five minutes
- ❑ Six to nine minutes
- ☒ Ten minutes or longer

*6. Interactions
☐ Plays alone
☐ Plays only with adults
☐ Plays with one child, always the same person
☐ Plays with one child, can be different partners
☒ Can play with two or three children together

**7. Entrance into a Play Group
☐ Does not attempt to enter play group
☐ Uses force to enter play group
☐ Stands near group and watches
☐ Imitates behavior of group
☒ Makes comments related to play theme
☐ Gets attention of another child before commenting

8. Problem Solving
☐ Gives in during conflict
☐ Uses force to solve problems
☐ Seeks adult assistance
☐ Imitates verbal solutions or strategies provided by adults
☒ Recalls words or strategies to use when reminded
☐ Initiates use of words or strategies
☐ Accepts reasonable compromises

9. Turn Taking
☐ Refuses to take turns
☐ Leaves toys, then protests when others pick them up
☐ Takes turns if arranged and directed by an adult
☒ Asks for turn, does not wait for a response
☐ Gives up toy easily if done with it
☐ Gives up toy if another child asks for it
☐ Proposes turn taking, will take and give turns

10. Support of Peers
☐ Shows no interest in peers
☐ Directs attention to distress of peers
☒ Shows empathy or offers help
☐ Offers and takes suggestions of peers at times
☐ Encourages or praises peers

Note: The developmental progression outlined in each segment of the Play Checklist can be used as a guideline when assessing most children's development. However, not all children will go through the same steps in development nor through the same developmental sequence.
*Smilansky, Sara. 1968. *The effects of sociodramatic play on disadvantaged preschool children.* New York: Wiley.
** Hazen, Nancy, Betty Black, and Faye Fleming-Johnson. 1984. Social acceptance: Strategies children use and how teachers can help children learn them. *Young Children.* 39(6): 26–36.

Play by Sandra Heidemann and Deborah Hewitt, copyright © 2010. Redleaf Press grants permission to photocopy this page for classroom use.

Once Willie's caregiver marked the current level of independent performance, she could look at his skills objectively. As she looked at his Play Checklist, she could see that he was doing well in most areas. She felt there were just two areas where she needed to help Willie make progress: if she worked with Willie to improve his skills in turn taking and support of peers, he might be able to alleviate some of the challenges and frustrations he was facing during free play. She decided she would develop a plan for him in these areas (for more information on developing a plan, see chapters 6–8).

At the beginning of this chapter, we discussed four common uses of assessment. One was to use it to talk with others about a child's skill development. Willie's caregiver was planning to update the parents of the children in her care on their skills and behaviors. As she prepared to talk with Willie's parents, she wanted to be able to summarize some of the things she knew about as well as some of the things on which she was working with him. She prepared to talk to Willie's parents by looking over her observation notes, work samples, and the Play Checklist she had completed for Willie. When she met with Willie's parents, she said something like this:

> Willie seems to be developing many important play skills. He has lots of good pretend play ideas, and he tells the other children about them. One idea that the other children enjoyed was to escape hot lava by walking on a tightrope. Oftentimes the children like his ideas, but sometimes they get frustrated when he doesn't want to play their ideas. Have you ever seen anything like this when Willie plays with others at home?

Willie's caregiver planned to share the scene described at the beginning of the chapter if his parents seemed interested in hearing an example. She continued by saying:

> I think we can help Willie learn to share play ideas, just like we are helping him learn to share toys. I plan to talk with him, as well as with the other children, about taking turns with ideas. We'll talk about playing one person's idea today and another person's idea tomorrow. Do you have other ideas that you think would help Willie learn to take the suggestions of others at times?

In this chapter, we explored observation, assessment, the Play Checklist, and evaluation. The Play Checklist breaks down ten skills essential to a child's success in sociodramatic play. These elements map a pathway from theory to practice for you and from simple to complex skills for the child.

In the next chapter, we will look at how to write a goal to guide your plan for improving the child's play skills. A well-developed goal helps you focus on what the child will gain.

Reflection Questions

1. What types of observation have you done?

2. What recording techniques have you used?

3. How have you used the information from your observations?

4. What can you do to make observation and recording easier for you?

5. When you look at the play skills included on the Play Checklist, did any children you've worked with come to mind? Which ones and why?

6. Observe a child and complete the Play Checklist. In which areas was this child struggling? What surprised you?

What Will the Child Do? Writing Goals from the Play Checklist

CHAPTER SIX

ASHELEY IS A FOUR-YEAR-OLD who rarely engages in sociodramatic play. She chooses most often to paint at the easel or to play in the water table. From time to time, her caregiver finds her in the housekeeping area. She plays with the same doll each time she plays there. When no one else is using the doll, she finds it and pretends to feed or dress it. She doesn't say a lot while playing. Asheley's play is short lived and does not involve much pretend play.

When her caregiver completed a Play Checklist for Asheley, she found that the child was having difficulty interacting, role-playing, and using language with others during play. Although Asheley is four years old, her skills are at the lower end of the checklist's items. The Role-Playing section of her checklist is presented here to illustrate her level of independent performance in this area.

2. Role-Playing
☒ No role play
❏ Uses one sequence of play
❏ Combines sequences
❏ Uses verbal declarations (for example, "I'm a doctor")
❏ Imitates actions of role, including dress

You will recall that younger children are expected to have skills at the lower end of the checklist items. Because Asheley is four years old, we would expect her skills to be more advanced. Further observation and assessment can provide information about any possible developmental delays. Regardless of her age or delays, Asheley will benefit from learning the next skill on the checklist. We have discussed observation and assessment as well as filling out a Play Checklist. Next we will look at how to use information from the checklist to write a goal as part of your plan. The chapter includes the following topics:

Developing a plan
Writing goals
Next steps

Developing a Plan

When you work with a child, planning to improve his skills is a little like planning a trip. First, you need to know where you want to go. Then you decide the best way to get there by deciding if you will drive, fly, or take a bus. You need to take various factors into consideration, such as cost and availability of funds. Next, you determine the roads or highways you will take. Finally, you pack your suitcase and set out. Along the way, you may find that you need to adjust your plan. You may run into a detour or find something interesting to explore along the way. When you reach your destination, you plan the next part of your trip, making new decisions to create a great experience.

As a reflective teacher, you do the same type of planning when you work with a child. We talk about developing a plan throughout chapters 6, 7, and 8. You will need information from all three chapters before you implement your plan for a child.

As in planning a trip, you need to determine your destination for a child by writing a goal. Then decide the best way to get there by planning the use of group activities, one-on-one activities, or home visits. Next, create activities and plan interactions that will be most effective in helping the child reach the destination. Pack your suitcase full of the materials you need for each activity, and arrange the environment. As you and the child travel toward the goal, you may notice you need to modify your plan or take a detour. Perhaps you need to select a more appropriate goal or a destination a little closer to home. Perhaps you need to plan more exciting activities for the child to explore. As you and he continue, you observe again to see if you have reached your destination. Once there, you begin planning the next stage of your work together.

You may already recognize the steps in the trip as those in the continuous cycle of improvement:

1. Observe and assess.
2. Evaluate play skills.
3. Write a goal.
4. Plan and implement activities.
5. Repeat the process.

Your next step is to write a goal.

Writing Goals

Through your observations, assessment, and use of the Play Checklist, you have decided that a child will benefit from planned activities during play. Next write a few clear, concise goals. In order to write goals, you need to decide which area(s) you will focus on. Use the child's level of independent performance (the highest level of skills he is consistently performing on the checklist) and the information from your observations to support your decision. If he has a number of areas in which he needs to improve, you may have difficulty in prioritizing them; this may be a little like determining if the chicken or the egg came first. In some cases, you may have to decide if the child needs to improve language skills in order to interact with others or to increase interaction skills as a way to improve language skills. You may want to address everything at once, but you will be more effective if you start with the areas of greatest concern and those where you feel you can have the most impact. After a few weeks of practicing a skill, if the child is not making adequate progress in the area you have chosen, you may want to change your focus to see if you can make greater gains in another area.

SMART Goals

Some say you can no longer identify who first developed the acronym for SMART goals (Cothran and Wysocki 2005); others attribute it to Paul Meyer, a top salesman (Mednick 2005). No matter who first used SMART goals, this technique is helpful in writing personal, business, and educational goals. We recommend using SMART goals to focus your work on the areas in greatest need of improvement. SMART goals are:

Specific
Measurable
Attainable
Realistic
Timely

Specific

SMART goals contain specific information. They answer the questions "Who? Does what? Where? How well or how often? By when?" Be sure to link your goals to your observations and knowledge of the child. (See chapter 7 for more information.) For example, when you decide where to work on the goal, choose a place the child routinely plays. If you plan to work in an area the child doesn't visit, your goal will not match the child's interests. State the goals in a positive way, and define what you want the child to be able to do.

Measurable

SMART goals allow you to measure how close the child is to meeting the goal. When you write your goals, include indicators to help you determine if they have been reached. When you answer the question "How well or how often?" a child needs to perform the skill to reach a goal, you have identified what you will consider to be sufficient progress.

To determine "How well or how often?" consider how often the child currently demonstrates the skill or behavior, and increase your expectation slightly. For example, if a child is not using words to describe substitute objects at all, your goal to have him use words to describe substitute objects is likely to be unattainable in the short run. It might be a more realistic goal to expect this child to start to use such words one time per week. Once he can do this, you can revise the goal and increase the expectation to one time per play period.

It is not necessary or always appropriate to expect that a child will reach 100 percent proficiency. For example, if a child is not taking the suggestions of peers during play, you do not need to expect that he would do this 100 percent of the time. Instead, you would want to determine about how often he does this now and increase your expectation by a little. Perhaps when the child is able to take the suggestions of others 40 percent of the time, he will have reached a developmentally and individually appropriate level of proficiency. In the Play Checklist item "Taking the suggestions of others," the expectation would never be more than 50 percent, because you want a balance of give and take. There are other goals for which you are looking for balance. Be aware of other situations where you would not want to expect total compliance. State your expectations accordingly.

Think about how you will document growth. Remember to use a variety of observation and recording techniques to get data about how well and how often the child is performing the skills. The data you gain will provide you with concrete evidence to determine if the goal has been met.

Attainable and Realistic

SMART goals need to be within reach and in areas that you can impact. Your goals must help the child move from where his skills currently are to the next level of difficulty. If you set your goals too high, you set the stage for failure. Setting goals too low suggests that you don't have confidence that the child can acquire the new skills.

Vygotsky describes what is attainable as the zone of proximal development (ZPD)—the distance between what a child can do independently and the skills the child is likely to develop in the near future (see chapter 1). The items in each section of the Play Checklist move in this progression. That is, once you have marked the level of independent performance in a section, the next item listed is the skill that is likely to develop in the near future. Therefore, your next goal for the child can be the next skill listed in the sequence. Because children develop at their own individual rates, you may find exceptions to the progressions outlined. It is our belief that in the majority of cases, the progressions will help you develop goals.

Timely

Set a target completion date or a reevaluation date for your goals so you remain focused and committed to working on them. Without a target date, you run the risk of losing your sense of urgency. Set your goal three or four months out. This gives you time to teach the skill and gives the child time to learn and practice it. Remember: to meet the goal, you need to see the child perform the skill independently and consistently during play.

Writing a SMART Goal

The Play Checklist can be used as a basis for writing your goals. Once you have determined the child's level of independent performance, you can use the checklist to point you to the next goal. Choose one or two areas on which to concentrate. Look at the current level of independent performance you marked on the Play Checklist; then move on to the next item. Make it the core of your next goal. Answer these questions to complete your goal:

Who?
Does what?
Where?
How well or how often?
By when?

The item that follows the child's level of independent performance answers the question "Does what?"

For example, if you were to write a goal for Asheley from our example earlier, you would note that in the Role-Playing section of the Play Checklist, her level of independent performance is "Uses one sequence of play." The next level of difficulty in that section is "Combines sequences." This becomes the core of the goal. You would write a SMART goal by answering the rest of the questions. A SMART goal for Asheley might look like this:

Asheley combines two sequences of play in the housekeeping area during two out of three free play periods by December 15.

You can see from the chart below that each question is answered.

Who?	Asheley
Does what?	Combines two sequences of play
Where?	In the housekeeping area
How well or how often?	During two out of three free play periods
By when?	December 15

Let's look at the goal Willie's caregiver (see chapter 5) wrote for him using this process. Willie's caregiver had marked his current level of independent performance in Turn Taking as "Asks for turn, does not wait for a response." The next item listed is "Gives up toy easily if done with it." This became the basis for Willie's goal. Each question was answered in the following goal:

Willie gives up a toy easily if he is done with it when playing in the block area 75 percent of the time by March 30.

Who?	Willie
Does what?	Gives up a toy easily if he is done with it
Where?	When playing in the block area
How well or how often?	75 percent of the time
By when?	March 30

As you can see, sometimes answering the questions in order does not allow the goal statement to flow very well. If this is the case, rewrite it, making sure that all the essential questions are answered.

Another goal the caregiver wrote for working with Willie was based on her observations of his skills in the Support of Peers section. Here, she marked his level of independent performance as "Shows empathy or offers help." The next item on the Play Checklist in this area is "Offers and takes suggestions of peers at times." She knew this was not happening very often at this point, and she needed to keep her expectations realistic. She decided to answer the question "How well or how often?" with a percentage that would represent growth in this area but would be attainable in the time before the target completion date. The goal she wrote for Willie in this area was this:

Willie takes suggestions of peers 25 percent of the time when playing in the housekeeping area by March 30.

Who?	Willie
Does what?	Takes suggestions of peers
Where?	When playing in the housekeeping area
How well or how often?	25 percent of the time
By when?	March 30

Willie's caregiver recognized that she might need to work on this goal for some time. If she found by the time that the target completion date arrived that Willie was taking suggestions 25 percent of the time, she could make the goal more challenging by increasing her expectation about the frequency with which he performed this skill. For the next couple of months, her new goal for Willie might be "Willie takes suggestions of peers 40 percent of the time when playing in the housekeeping area by May 28."

Next Steps

We describe each of the next steps in greater detail in the following chapters, but we introduce them here so you see the continuous cycle. Once you have written a goal, plan a number of activities that will help the child reach that goal. During the months before your target date, offer the activities so the child has many opportunities to learn and practice the new skills. Observe regularly, reflect on what you see, and modify the activities to ensure your teaching strategies and "goodness of fit" are as effective as possible. When the target date arrives (or if progress is made sooner), observe again to see if the child is performing the desired behavior.

In our example about Asheley, the target completion date is December 15. Therefore, just before December 15 you would observe again and record her progress. In this case, you might do three or more running records and, as you analyze your records, count the number of sequences she combines (like dialing the play telephone and then pretending to talk to her mother). You might write an anecdote, a short narrative describing her play, to show the quality of the play sequences she is combining. And from December 11 through December 15, you might do a frequency tally of the number of sequences she uses in her play.

Use the data to complete a new Play Checklist. Or use a different ink color on the original checklist (so you can easily compare markings) to check the new skills observed. Compare your new observations to the written goal. If you find you have not reached your goal, consider why not, and modify your plan. If the goal has been reached, celebrate your success. Then start the process over by writing new goals and developing activities that are just beyond what the child can currently accomplish.

If you have not reached your goal, reflect on the possible reasons:

- Did you focus on the appropriate goal?
- Was the goal attainable or outside the child's ZPD?
- Did you plan activities that stretched the child's skills and offered sufficient opportunities to practice?
- Does the child need more time?
- Does the child need additional, specialized help or support?
- Was there something going on in the child's life that might have affected the outcome?
- Was the child feeling ill or coming down with an illness?
- Did you base the goal and activities on the child's interests?

You may find that if you try to move a child to a new skill too soon or if the goal is too far beyond the child's abilities, he is unlikely to respond to your efforts. If this is the case, review the level of difficulty you expect from him. If you have not made too big a leap, be persistent in your teaching and creative in your approaches. Give the child time. If you have made too big a jump, revise your goal to make it more realistic and attainable.

> JAMIE FOUND SHE NEEDED to revise her goal for Raven. She knew that Raven was using real objects primarily to pretend, but she had seen her sometimes use substitute objects for other objects. She felt that since Raven could substitute at times, she could probably use imaginary objects within a few months. As she worked with Raven, she offered her things like imaginary cups of coffee and pretend money. Each time Jamie offered her a pretend item, Raven looked at her but then reached for a prop. Jamie decided her goal was too big a leap, so she revised it to better match Raven's abilities and chose to work with her on substituting similar objects.

In this chapter, we used information from the Play Checklist to provide the basis for you to complete a SMART goal. Writing a goal that includes information that is specific, measurable, attainable, realistic, and timely, is an important part of your plan.

From here, you should generate a number of lesson plans to help you reach your goal for the child. In lesson plans, you will address when a lesson takes place, in what setting it takes place, and what materials are used. In the next chapter, we continue to help you design your plan by looking at ways to make it responsive to the child's needs, considering what your role should be, and offering a planning form.

Reflection Questions

1. What personal or professional goals have you set for yourself? Have your goals included any of the elements of SMART goals? If so, which elements were helpful? If not, how could you have added one or more of the elements?

2. How do you think writing a SMART goal will help in your work with a child?

3. Describe a child you think could have benefited or will benefit from a play goal.

4. Use the information you have gained by observing and filling out the Play Checklist to write a SMART goal for a child with whom you are working. Use phrases from the Play Checklist as the core of your goals. What is one SMART goal you can write for this child?

What Will You Do?
Planning for Play Skills

Larissa is sitting on a bench. She has a steering wheel propped on her lap, and she is pretending to take a journey in the preschool van. Suddenly Larissa roars, "Vrooooom! Vrooooom! We're stuck in the mud." Selina, Larissa's caregiver, offers to push. She sees this as an opportunity to help Larissa learn to interact with others. She draws additional players in by asking other children in the area to help push. They put their shoulders to the bench, grunting and pushing, and the bench inches forward. Selina says, "There, how's that?" Larissa answers, "Not fine yet." So Selina and the children push again. Finally Larissa yells, "We're out!" The children climb onto the bench and join Larissa in her adventure.

Selina has been carefully observing Larissa and has seen an opportunity to enter the play and help Larissa interact with others. Previously she had filled out a Play Checklist, and based on that, she had written a goal for Larissa. She used a teachable moment (see Glossary) to involve other children in her play theme of driving the van. Before entering in the play, she had considered the role she would play and how she would work on Larissa's plan. Such preparations provided a way to use this spontaneous moment to achieve her goals for Larissa. Next, we'll look at how to develop a lesson plan that is responsive to an individual child's needs and that helps reach the goals you set for her. In this chapter you will find the following topics:

Developing a lesson plan
Your role
Planning your role
Which role to use

Developing a Lesson Plan

Developing a lesson plan that is responsive to the child's needs and abilities begins when you conduct regular observations. You reflect on what you have seen and make decisions about ways to help the child learn new skills. As we discussed in the previous chapter, you will write SMART goals that help you remain focused on skill development. Your next step is to develop a number of lesson plans to provide opportunities for the child to learn and practice the desired skills.

In order to write about all the aspects of planning, we must first pull apart the process. We present questions for you to consider, but some of them can only be answered once you have chosen an activity. (A list of suggested activities follows in chapter 8.) For example, you may not be able to identify your role in play until you decide on a teaching strategy. You need to use the information from both this chapter and chapter 8 to complete the planning form found in the appendix.

As you plan, consider the following list of questions; your answers to them should be based on what you have learned about the child through your observations and thoughtful consideration of the child's overall skill level and interests.

1. When will you work on the goal? Will work take place spontaneously during play, or will you plan lessons for group times? Would the child enjoy active play or quiet activities?

2. What are the child's special interests? What activities does the child most enjoy? Are those the activities you should use in your work with her? Do you want to start with an activity in which the child has had many successes and then slowly introduce a new play idea or theme?

3. Is the activity you have planned sensitive to the culture and language of the child? Is there an activity from the child's culture or family life that would be appropriate to use? What activity would be meaningful and relevant to this child?

4. Is the activity appropriate to the child's skill level? Will the activity help the child stretch beyond her current abilities? What level of assistance will the child need? Does the child have experience with the activity you are planning? Is the activity appropriate for the child's abilities? What are the child's special challenges? Are there other developmental issues you need to consider? Does the child need adaptations, adaptive equipment, or assistive technology to be successful?

5. How many children will be involved? Does this child need your one-on-one attention? Will you try to pair her with another who can help her? Is the child doing well playing with one other child in particular? Should a third child be introduced to the play group? Can you work on the skill with a small group? Can children come and go during the activity? If you work with a child individually, what will the other children do? Will they be with another adult? Will they do the same activity while you sit next to and focus on the child having difficulty? Will you arrange for an additional adult to come in to work with the others while you and the child work in another room?

6. Where will you set up the play? Will you be in your usual setting, or will you arrange a special space for the activity? Will you take the child to a quiet space away from the traffic of other children? Does the child engage in more sociodramatic play when she is outside? Would outdoors be the best place for the activity?

7. What props will be needed? Is the child still using real objects in her play? What similar materials might be substituted for those real objects? Is the child ready for more abstract materials, which can represent the real item? What materials would enhance the play? What additional materials might the child request? Are there materials from the child's culture that would support her play?

8. How will you collect data about the child's performance? Will you write an anecdote following the play period? Will you collect a work sample? Will you count a behavior or a skill demonstrated? Will you record a language sample? (Note: You don't need to collect data during each activity, but as you plan, determine if the activity provides an opportunity to collect data for your overall classroom assessment or for gauging if you have reached your play goal.)

9. Reflect on the activity afterward. How would you modify the activity if you were to offer it, or something close to it, again? What changes would you make? What worked and what didn't? How would you make it easier or more challenging? Would you use different props? Would you introduce the activity in a different way? Would you include others?

This type of purposeful planning is done before teaching most academic concepts. The same careful planning needs to be extended to include teaching play skills. All of the things mentioned above are important to the success of a play activity.

Reflection is always part of the planning process. You probably do this informally when you think to yourself, "I wish I had used props with this book." When your group time is falling apart, you must quickly reflect and change the direction. You might have noticed when you sparked a child's interest or set up an exciting play theme and have thought, "I want to remember to talk to Tina about this later." In addition to informal reflection, we recommend that you set time aside to reflect more intentionally. Reflect on the activity, the child's response, and your participation individually and with team members (see chapter 9 for more information).

Your Role

The answer to yet another question will be central to your plan: *What is your role during play?* This is a more layered question than it may appear. Young children need you to provide time, space, play materials, and experiences. You also need to act as a resource person to help them solve conflicts, expand play ideas, and cooperate with one another as they play. In addition, the child with limited play skills may need not just a resource person but an adult to play with her to move her into higher levels of play skills.

Vygotsky's theories remind us that children learn best when they interact with adults and peers. When you intentionally involve yourself in play to further children's cognitive skills, interactions with peers, or role-playing, you scaffold the learning so they can reach their optimal development. As children reach that development, adults move back and let children carry the play.

For example, when Selina joined Larissa's play, she moved from a role as an observer to that of an active play partner. She took on a role by pushing the van from the mud, and she encouraged group interaction when she invited other children to join the play. Yet the pacing of the play and the story line remained Larissa's, as she decided they were not out of the mud yet.

As a way to frame why children need adults as play partners, let's review how a baby learns to play. The first play partner a baby has is her parent. Peek-a-Boo, So-Big, and roughhousing are all ways the baby plays with the adult. The toddler learns to play house by watching her parents cook, clean, and care for her. Then, as a preschooler, the child branches out to include other children in her play. For varied reasons, children with more limited play skills do not easily include other children in play. To help children take this step, adults must become the all-important play partners.

There are a number of roles an adult can take in play. Deciding which role will be most helpful to children requires observation, assessment, and intentional planning around play goals.

Planning Your Role

Johnson, Christie, and Yawkey (1999) name six categories of adult roles in play: uninvolved, onlooker, stage manager, co-player, play leader, and director/instructor. Uninvolved and director/instructor are the least productive roles and may have a negative effect on children's play experiences. To be uninvolved with children's play gives children the message that play is not valued or important. Teachers sometimes use children's playtime to organize, do paperwork, or talk among themselves. Being uninvolved in children's play does not help children gain more skills. At the other end of the continuum lies the director's role. This, too, can be detrimental to children's play because the adult is controlling the direction of the play. Children who are capable of directing their own play often just leave or become uninterested when the adult is too involved in forming the play scenario. We recommend that caregivers concentrate on the roles in the middle of the continuum. We have adapted this list to include the four middle categories of Johnson, Christie, and Yawkey (1999) and parallel play, all of which facilitate children's engagement in play. As we list and describe the various roles, you probably will recognize them. You may have played with children in these ways in the past. Using them in an intentional way will foster more engaged play and growth in play skills. Here are the roles we recommend including in a plan:

Observer or onlooker
Stage manager
Parallel player
Co-player
Play leader

As we describe each role, remember how you have used these roles in your work with children.

Observer or Onlooker

The adult stays near the play and watches it. She may nod with approval or make comments about the play that communicate the value she places on the children's play. While observing, the caregiver can note the roles the children play, the props they need to develop their play, and how they use the space. If a particular child seems to be left out or is not following the play scenario, she can note that and devise further involvement on her part.

Stage Manager

The stage manager has already begun the work by setting the stage (see chapter 3) with sufficient time, an enclosed space, motivating materials, and experiences that provide children with concrete information about the play theme. She continues this role during play by providing props related to the theme, observing the roles children are playing, and suggesting expansions on those roles. She may provide assistance to the children during their play scenarios by making signs, lists, or menus, yet she doesn't directly enter the play experience. She may offer suggestions or comments about the play. The children can ignore the suggestions and request help, but the direction of the play remains in their hands.

The stage manager can make use of teachable moments by working within a child's ZPD (zone of proximal development—the distance between what a

child can do independently and the skills that the child is likely to develop in the near future) when she offers assistance. For example, a child with a language delay stays outside of the group in the housekeeping area day after day. The stage manager/teacher can suggest to the children that they include another role in the play, such as a pet, baby, or another sibling. She can help the child enter the play in that role.

Parallel Player

When acting as parallel player, the adult plays next to the child. For instance, he plays next to a child by the sandbox. While the child is building roads, the parallel player puts sand in containers and dumps it out. He may make comments about his own actions but not about what the child is doing.

Parallel playing can be helpful in a number of situations. It is particularly helpful for a withdrawn child who becomes more withdrawn whenever an adult gives direct attention. This way of involving himself in the play can also help children play longer. He can show the child that her play is important and that he values play. The child may also learn new ways to use materials. However, children will not learn new play skills through this kind of adult involvement.

Co-Player

In co-playing, the adult joins play that is already started and allows the children to determine the direction of the play. The adult influences the play by asking for instructions and responding to the children's actions and comments. The adult does not lead the play but offers contributions. The children can always reject any suggestion the adult puts forward. The teacher uses co-playing in this example:

The teacher is watching Alisha, David, and Antonio play together as a family. Alisha is the mother, David the father, and Antonio is the child. They are eating supper together but aren't talking very much. The teacher knocks on the cupboard and asks, "Can I come in?" David jumps up and says, "Sure." The teacher says, "I just want to come and see you. I'm your neighbor." David grabs a chair and says, "You can sit down here." Alisha laughs and says, "Here's some supper." She hands the teacher a plate and explains, "This is spaghetti." The teacher pretends to eat it and says, "This is wonderful. I was really hungry." The teacher sits for a few seconds eating and then exclaims, "I'm thirsty. Do you have coffee?" Alisha answers, "No, no coffee today." The teacher says, "Okay. What did you do today at work?" Alisha and David jump in with descriptions of their day at work. Antonio is quiet until the teacher asks about school. He smiles and talks about reading a book.

The teacher influences the play and enriches it by entering the play as a neighbor. She also asks about work to encourage more conversation. She includes Antonio when she notices he is more quiet that the others. Her involvement increases the interest in the play theme and results in more language use. She influences the make-believe play when she pretends to eat the spaghetti. When the children do not want coffee to be part of their play, she graciously goes in another direction rather than insisting on coffee.

Co-playing, like parallel playing, helps children play longer and confirms for them that play is important. The teacher can expand the play in a nondirective way. Sometimes new children can be brought into the play (as the neighbor's children, for example). This strategy works best when children already have a fairly high level of play but are bogged down or stuck in one play theme. Sometimes co-playing can be an excellent way to help children maintain newly learned play skills.

Play Leader

When caregivers become play leaders, they use their observations to more directly influence play experiences. Play leaders often have specific goals in mind and affect children's play in the following ways (Johnson, Christie, and Yawkey 1999):

- The adult often begins the play scene rather than joining one already started by the children.
- The adult exerts more influence than the children over the play.
- The adult enriches the play with new props and play themes.
- The adult models and suggests new play behaviors within that episode.

The adult play leader becomes a play partner similar to a co-player, but with the individual and group goals in mind. Unlike the co-player, the play leader assumes a more prominent role or concentrates on modeling the play behaviors with an individual child. For example, the children had been playing doctor for a week. Toward the end of the week, their play became unexciting and attracted few children. Children came into the area, took the stethoscope, listened to their hearts, then left the area. The teacher wanted to extend the time children participated, as well as add new elements to their play. He decided to take the role of play leader and entered the area as a doctor. Several curious children came over to the area. He invited them in and assigned them roles, such as patients, fellow doctors, nurses, and receptionists. He brought new props like X-rays, appointment books, and play phones. As a doctor, he modeled taking temperatures, taking and reading X-rays, and writing down appointments. Children followed his lead and sustained a much longer play period—twenty-five minutes or more.

In this example, the children were still able to ignore the teacher's suggestions or comments, but when he modeled a suggestion, doing so caught the children's attention and encouraged them to take more risks.

The role of play leader is helpful when group play is stuck and suggestions and comments don't seem to move the play along. It also can be used to introduce a new play theme, especially when children are not familiar with roles or functions in the play scenario. When an individual child lacks the skills to participate with other children, a play leader can model and suggest behaviors that fit the child's goals. Because the play leader is embedded in the play, a child learning a new language feels supported and less vulnerable to group dynamics while she works on using words to enter a group or represent an imaginary object.

Here's another example. The teacher was very worried about Doug. He often played alone even though he watched others with interest as they played together. She observed Doug and decided to try the following activity, using the role of the play leader:

Doug sat alone in the block area while several children were playing nearby in the housekeeping area. He looked over at the house while unenthusiastically piling several blocks on top of each other. The teacher entered the block area and brought suitcases, play clothes, and a few travel posters. She suggested they build an airport so the children in the housekeeping area could take a trip. Doug perked up and followed the teacher's lead while she put blocks down for the airport, helped him put up travel posters, and started to pack a suitcase. The teacher went with Doug to the housekeeping area and helped him invite the children there to the airport. Several children came over. The teacher organized the play by describing the airport, the places they could go, and how they could get tickets. She had placed special strips of paper in the writing center to make tickets. She asked Doug to sell the tickets. The other children packed their suitcases and came over to buy tickets. Doug was able to participate fully in the play scenario and responded positively to the teacher's support and influence.

The teacher in this example took an active role in the play and led the play scenario with specific goals in mind for Doug. The other children also benefited from a new play idea and fresh connections between the block and housekeeping area that expanded their play space.

Outside and Inside the Play

Another way to frame adult roles is to examine the differences between being inside and outside the play. Smilansky (1968) developed a technique called *play training* to teach children new play behaviors. She discusses two roles that adults can play to help children learn these new play behaviors: outside the play and inside the play.

Outside the Play (Observer/Onlooker and Stage Manager Roles)
When an adult interacts from outside the play, she does not join the play but sits close by, making comments and suggestions to the children. These comments

and suggestions guide the play and help the children learn the skills that the adult plans to influence. For example, the caregiver has been watching Johnny for a few weeks while he plays. Johnny consistently stays outside the group. He builds large buildings with the blocks but will leave the structures immediately if another child joins him. When he attempts to join an ongoing group in the block area, he pushes the blocks down, much to the frustration of the other children. The caregiver decides to work from outside the play to help Johnny enter a group already engaged in play.

The next day, a small group of children are building a road. Johnny starts toward the road, stops, and extends his foot as if to kick it. The caregiver gently stops him and suggests he sit close to the group and watch for a while. She comments on how the road is progressing. When the road almost reaches him, the caregiver hands him a block and tells him to say to the children that he can add it. He puts it down, and then another boy adds a block. The caregiver asks, "What do you think we will use the road for?" Several children answer, "Cars and trucks." The caregiver brings small cars and trucks from the cupboard and gives them to Johnny to share with the others. Soon the children are driving on the road with Johnny leading the way. Although it may take a long time for Johnny to truly enter a group on his own, repeated short exposures like this with an adult's support will help Johnny increasingly enjoy play with others.

In this example, the caregiver used comments and suggestions to help Johnny in his play. Following is a chart of the kinds of remarks that can be made to address a child's goal:

Type of Remarks	Remark and Goal
Comments	You're setting the table for four people. (Interactions) You have a nice couch. (Pretending with objects)
Suggestions	If you put in a door, your friends can visit. (Interactions) Here's a bed; try this. (Pretending with objects)
Questions	Are you the mom or the child? (Role-playing) Are you in the ocean or the boat? (Verbalizations about the play scenario)

Interacting in a play scenario from outside the play complements the adult roles of observer/onlooker and stage manager. The stage manager not only offers comments and suggestions but also brings in props and play clothes and offers assistance.

Inside the Play (Play Leader or Co-Player Roles)

Interacting from inside the play describes the role of the play leader or co-player. The adult takes on a role in the play and becomes an active participant. From that vantage point, the adult can model many of the behaviors she wishes to teach.

In the previous example, the teacher interacted from outside the play when she made suggestions to Johnny about building a road. If she had instead become another construction worker, she would have influenced the play from the inside. In this role, she could have introduced new pretend elements, such as signs and maps. She could have started to build a village to connect to the road. This powerful adult model can often help children gain new play skills quickly.

Caution about Adult Roles

All of these adult roles can be extremely helpful and motivating to children. The way that an adult enters into children's play is an important part of the equation: you need to be cautious about how and when to join a play scenario. Some child development experts state that adults should not take direct roles in children's play (Bodrova and Leong 2007). Others in the field recommend entering into children's play to facilitate play skills and enhance cognitive gains (Johnson, Christie, and Wardle 2005). Our experience convinces us of the value of adult participation, as long as we are responsive to children's cues and fluid in the roles we take. Be aware that the roles of co-player and play leader can be very intrusive in children's play. Too much adult participation can actually hinder the spontaneity and enthusiasm that are so central to the development of group play. Being flexible about the changes in play and play behaviors is essential to avoid becoming a controlling factor in children's play.

Because of the danger of too much adult input, you should move away from acting as a play leader as soon as feasible. After the children have learned the play behaviors, you will want to take the role of observer/onlooker. Your withdrawal should be gradual. For instance, if you have been playing with the children to increase their language in play, you may want to sit next to where the play is taking place as the next step and make comments to keep the play going.

Even during a play period, you may choose to draw back from more direct influence in play. For example, if you have taken the role of play leader to introduce a new play theme, you can draw back quickly to the role of a stage manager when children take the leadership and develop the theme.

Which Role to Use

Deciding which role to use as you play with children should be based on their needs. The more difficulty the child has with play, the more involved you must be. As the child gains more control or skill, you can move to less involvement.

A continuum of involvement applies to the adult roles we have discussed. For example, the role of the play leader interacting from inside the play requires more involvement and should be used when a child is having the greatest difficulty. As she acquires more skills, you can assume a less involved role. The following chart can guide you as you decide which role is more appropriate.

The second chart that follows will help you define roles and decide when each is appropriate.

Level of Caregiver Participation

MORE ◀——————————————————————————————▶ LESS

| Play Leader Inside Play | Co-Player Inside Play | Parallel Player Inside Play | Stage Manager Outside Play | Observer/Onlooker Outside Play |

Role of Adult	Definition	When	Why	With Whom
Observer/ Onlooker	• Adult sits near play and observes play • Occasionally makes comments or suggestions to keep the play going • Does not disrupt play	Anytime play occurs	• Acquires valuable information to plan goals and activities • Gives value to play	All children engaged in play
Stage Manager	• Adult stays near play and adds props and play materials, comments, and gives assistance as needed • Does not disrupt play unless adult involvement is intrusive or adult tries to change play themes without children's input	Is especially helpful during dramatic/ sociodramtic play	• Provides opportunity to coach individual children • Gives ways to make suggestions to groups of children involved in play	All children or groups engaged in dramatic play

Role of Adult	Definition	When	Why	With Whom
Parallel Play	• Adult plays next to child with same materials but does not address child directly • Does not disrupt play	Can be used anytime but works well with sensorimotor or constructive play	• Gives value to play • Extends attention span • Supports child initiative	• Children who are withdrawn • Children with short attention spans
Co-Playing	• Adult joins ongoing play • Allows children to control the direction of the play • Influences by asking for instructions and responding to children's actions and comments • Does not disrupt play if children retain control of play	• Can be used anytime an adult is invited to join play or asks and is given permission • Participates as long as children and adult are enjoying it	• Can give new life to worn play theme • Can extend attention span • Brings new ideas to play	• Children who are repeating a play theme endlessly and seem stuck in it • Children who already have a high level of play skill • Children with short attention spans
Play Leader	• Adult begins play • Asserts influence during play episodes • Models new play behaviors inside the play • Can be very disruptive to play because of adult influence • Switches to less intrusive roles as children's play skills develop	• Anytime adult can begin play • Can be used to introduce new play theme	• Models new play behaviors • Introduces new play theme	• Children who do not play make-believe, always play alone, or show no progress when an adult uses less intrusive roles • Children who show a need for new play skills as indicated on the Play Checklist • Children whose play is repetitious and appears to be ready to break down • Groups of children who cannot move to new play themes or new play behaviors

(Adapted from Johnson, Christie, and Yawkey 1999)

Playing with children may cause you some discomfort or embarrassment. You may feel silly or inept. But swallow hard and join in, especially when you sense that your participation can help children gain more skills. It becomes easier as you enter in more often, and consequently, you can enjoy becoming part of a classroom story.

In this chapter, we outlined a way to promote a child's growth by writing a lesson plan that summarizes needed materials, adult role(s), and time of day. The next chapter describes teaching strategies to explore as you continue to plan. The teaching strategies match up with the Play Checklist and include ideas to use during play as well as during adult-led support activities.

Reflection Questions

1. Observe children in the housekeeping area. Notice roles, relationships between the children, amount of pretend play, and how much language children use. On another day, try one of the adult roles listed in the chapter. How do the children respond?

2. Describe a time you performed the role of stage manager. What kind of assistance did you give to the children? Do you have any shy or quiet children who do not participate in play? Try parallel playing beside them. How do they respond?

The Heart of the Plan: Choosing Teaching Strategies

ALLI, A TEACHER IN the four-year-olds' room, is planning for the next day. She has observed Estella and completed the Play Checklist on her. Estella loves to play in the housekeeping corner alone. Whenever other children join her, she runs off. Alli wants to help Estella learn to play with at least one other child. As she reviews her observations, Alli notes how much Estella enjoys pretending to cook, serving food, and doing dishes in the play house. Alli knows Estella's family: they speak Spanish at home and eat a diet of tortillas, rice, and beans. Alli chooses as her first step to serve tortillas as a snack. This familiarizes all the children with tortillas. Next, Alli encourages Estella to pretend to make tortillas

with Kai, another four-year-old, during free play. If all goes well, Alli can withdraw from the play and watch from the sidelines, available if Estella needs help.

It was easy for Alli to establish a goal for Estella, but she had to plan carefully for the activities that would be interesting, fun, and encourage play skill development. You, too, may have goals and the start of a lesson plan for an individual child, but you may need activities that teach the skill and are fun. If you need ideas for activities, this chapter has suggestions to use as part of your plan. These ideas are only a few of the creative ways you can help children learn play skills. Tap into your own playfulness to design an inviting sequence of play.

We have divided this chapter into ten sections, which correspond to the sections of the Play Checklist:

Pretending with objects
Role-playing
Verbalizations about the play scenario
Verbal communication during a play episode
Persistence in play
Interactions
Entrance into a play group
Problem solving
Turn taking
Support of peers

In each section, you will find the following subsections to help you more fully develop your teaching strategy:

Getting ready: Each section includes information about a prerequisite skill or foundation that may need to be laid before working on any of the goals in the section. For example, if you observe children fighting frequently, you may need to plan a series of large-group discussions on building a classroom community before you begin to work on interaction skills.

Under the "Getting Ready" heading, you will find a brief description of the prerequisite skill(s) and some suggestions to try. For example, in "Verbalizations about the Play Scenario" in the Play Checklist, you may have marked that the child is not talking during play. Under the "Getting Ready" heading, you can find ways to help the child talk throughout the day before you try to encourage verbalizations during play.

Goals: This section includes examples of goals. The goals correspond to items in the Play Checklist. The goal is written using the item from the checklist as the core. In the Play Checklist, the item is stated as a skill or a behavior that can be observed. In this chapter, we have taken the items on the Play Checklist and stated them in language appropriate to the goal. For example, in the Play Checklist, one skill you see is "Uses imaginary objects" to pretend. If a child isn't doing this yet, it may be one of your goals for him, so we have stated it here as "child will pretend with objects." The goal language we provide answers the question "Does what?" when you write a SMART goal. (See chapter 6 for information on how to write SMART goals.)

To individualize the goals presented in this chapter, substitute the name of the child with whom you are working for "child" in the sample goals. List where you expect the child to perform this play skill, such as outdoors, block area, or housekeeping area. Identify how well the child is currently performing the skill and raise your expectations slightly. Answer the question "How well or how often?" with the frequency you hope he can achieve after a few months of practice. Remember that for many of the goals, it is unnecessary and may be inappropriate to ask a child to perform the skill all of the time. For example, it is not necessary or appropriate to expect a child to interact with others constantly. Finally, answer "By when?" with your target completion date. Remember to move a child slowly and keep your expectations realistic.

In most sections, goals correspond to the skill sequences listed in the Play Checklist. In a few sections, the goals differ from the Play Checklist when one or more of the items lead to the same goal. For instance, in "Persistence in Play," only one goal is listed: "Child will engage in sociodramatic play for XX minutes." Customize the goal to match the skill level of the child by indicating the appropriate number of minutes. Suggestions for increasing the minutes are the same whether you are trying to help a child engage for four minutes or ten. In a few places, two closely related goals are listed together. In these cases, the suggestions for one goal can be used for both.

Suggestions: In the previous chapter, we presented questions for you to consider while you prepare learning activities. Here you will find suggestions to complete your planning. These may include ways to set up the environment, words to use, and individual or group activities.

To use the activities in this chapter, find the section heading of the Play Checklist under which the child's goal is listed. Become acquainted with all the suggestions in a section. This information will help you better understand the sequence of skill development. You can also find activities under other goals that can be tailored to your situation.

Focus on the suggestions following the goal you have selected. From the ones listed, choose those that match the needs of the child and that can be implemented in your setting. Select a suggestion and complete a planning form (see appendix A). You want to create a number of lessons that teach one goal and offer the lessons prior to the target completion date. There may be times when the suggestions don't fit your situation exactly. Modify them to make them work for you and the child, or create your own activities. Respecting the child's culture, learning style, and temperament should be primary considerations in all your planning.

During play: Many of the lessons you develop will be offered during play. We have listed a number of suggestions. For example, you might work on a goal directed at improving role-playing skills by bringing in suitcases and dress-up clothes so children can pretend to pack for a trip. Work on a goal about the substitution of objects by providing cardboard boxes to be used as cars or doll cribs.

Some of your work on goals takes place as opportunities arise spontaneously during play. During these teachable moments, you need to respond quickly. For instance, when a child is having difficulty solving a problem, you may take the opportunity to teach her about the words she can use. To make the best use of teachable moments, you must know your goal for each child. Reflect on what you will do when you see an opportunity. Be ready with words you want to use, and have teaching strategies in mind. Many of the strategies offered are about teachable moments. Set up your environment and themes and then intentionally plan what you want to accomplish and how you will accomplish it. Prepared this way, you can effectively scaffold the child's learning.

During adult-led activities: Supplement your plans for teaching by including activities that help teach skills during group time, story, transitions, table times, or other structured times throughout the day. These periods usually include adult-led activities rather than teachable moments. They support your work in teaching a play skill. Some examples are a story about helping others, a discussion of ways to solve a problem, or an art project in which pairs of children share crayons and paper. These activities can help introduce a concept or skill that will be put into practice during play. For some children, several lessons and adult support are needed before the skill can be applied to a play episode.

Example: An example at the end of each section illustrates a situation in which the suggestions have been used.

Pretending with Objects

If a preschooler can only pretend with real objects, that child is limited in socio-dramatic play. Unless the child can use substitute objects or imaginary objects, dramatic play with others will proceed without him. Being able to substitute gives the child flexibility in role, play theme, and play partners. Pretending with objects is usually one of the first skills in the Play Checklist that a child acquires. If a preschooler cannot pretend with imaginary objects or is heavily dependent on real objects, concentrate on helping him develop this skill.

Getting Ready to Pretend with Objects

If a child is not using objects to pretend, you will notice that he uses toys by manipulating, stacking, and pounding them much as an infant would. There will be no pretend play with objects. The reasons you might not observe his pretend play with objects vary, from lack of exposure to the object or play theme to cognitive challenges limiting his ability to symbolize. Ways to help a child get ready to pretend with objects also vary, depending on your observations.

It requires careful observation to determine what a child is pretending. You can tell if a child is pretending by observing his actions, listening to his words, and understanding the play theme. If you have a child in your care who has delayed language, you may not be able to understand the play theme and consequently miss any pretending that happens. For example, one child was carrying around a block and periodically putting it close to his mouth. This looked like a sensorimotor activity until the teacher saw the child muttering to the block and realized that he was using the block as a walkie-talkie.

Sometimes children have no experience with a particular object and explore it in a sensorimotor way before they pretend with it. As they gain experience and observe other children's play, they begin to pretend with it. These children may require more exposure through books, field trips, pictures, discussions, and group play to get ready to pretend.

Other children with cognitive challenges tend to continue sensorimotor play with an object even after they have been exposed to pretend themes. If you stay focused on the goal, introduce familiar props, and provide adult and peer models who regularly use that prop to pretend, the child may respond. In doing so, he begins to become a part of group play, a truly inclusive experience. For more specific suggestions, refer to "Goal: Child Will Use Real-Looking Objects to Pretend" found on page 132.

Children who have been emotionally traumatized may withdraw from social relationships and show little interest in pretending with objects. If you observe such behavior, you may need to focus on building a relationship before you can address the first goal. Pretending requires taking a risk, and some children are afraid to do that without a strong relationship with an adult. By building the relationship, you are building the trust that a child needs to risk the world of play.

To build trust,

- play with the child as parents do with their infants. Use games like chase, Hide-and-Seek, or Peek-a-Boo.
- use puppets to play games with the child. Examples of simple, fun games with puppets include hiding the puppet behind your back and then popping the puppet up and singing songs.
- spend special one-on-one time with the child every day or on a consistent basis.
- move to the suggestions listed under the first goal as the child's trust in you grows.

Goal: Child Will Use Real-Looking Objects to Pretend

Children begin to pretend using real or real-looking objects at about eighteen months to two years. They will pat the baby's back, move a spoon in a pot, or pick up the receiver of a phone and say, "Hi." Start with life-sized props when first introducing real-looking objects to use in pretend play. Using miniatures, such as a small plastic horse, requires a higher level of abstraction. When working on this goal, use objects that are familiar and used frequently in the child's daily life. If you are addressing this goal with a child who is linguistically and/ or culturally distinct from the rest of the preschoolers, use props typically used in his home, such as food props reflecting his home life.

Suggestions during Play
- Observe the child closely to determine which toys are favorites.
- Collect a number of these objects and present them to the child. Demonstrate one play sequence at a time with these objects. For example,

With Dolls	With Play Food and Dishes	With Toy Cars
Feed them	Cook it	Drive them
Dress them	Eat it	Crash them
Hug them	Set table	Put people in them
Comb their hair	Wash dishes	

- Encourage the child to imitate your actions.
- Offer the child the objects and suggest a pretend sequence. For instance, say, "Amy, feed the baby with the bottle."
- Continue to scaffold the skills as the child makes progress. After Amy feeds the baby with the bottle, give her a spoon and bowl to feed the baby some cereal. Scaffold your support to her emerging skills.
- Remember that the child probably has not accomplished this goal until she can pretend with real-looking, life-size objects spontaneously, without adult assistance or involvement.

Suggestion during Adult-Led Activities
- During large- or small-group time, give each child a doll, bottle, and blanket. Talk about how to care for a baby while they act this out with the doll. For example, have them all feed the doll, wrap it in the blanket, and rock it.

Goal: Child Will Use Substitute Objects for Other Objects

This goal makes a bridge between using real objects and pretend/imaginary objects. You are gradually moving the child from using objects that look very much like the real thing to using ones that are less and less similar.

Suggestions during Play
- Collect a number of props that are similar to the real objects that the child favors. Substitute these props for the real objects in the dramatic play area. Leave some real objects in the area to encourage play. Some of the substitutions may include
  - Plastic milk bottle instead of a baby bottle
  - Box or block instead of a doll bed
  - Block instead of a milk carton
  - Paper instead of money
  - Metal ring instead of a steering wheel
- As the child plays in the area, sit close by and observe her play activity. If she seems to be looking for the real object, give her the substitute and say, "You can use this for the baby's bed."
- The child may reject this suggestion by ignoring you or picking up the substitute item and then putting it down without using it. This rejection may indicate that you are moving outside of the child's ZPD. You may want to try an object that is more similar to the real object. For example, if you are trying to encourage a child to use a block for a bed

and she will not use it, bring out a box with blankets that looks more like a real bed.

- Set up dramatic play opportunities that involve substitute materials. For example, in a pretend pizza shop, you can cut out felt mushrooms, peppers, and sausage. Strips of yellow yarn can represent the cheese.
- It is fine to go back to the real object if the child is very frustrated by your suggestions.
- Continue introducing substitutes in a relaxed manner. Do not force the child to pretend with substitutes, but continue your encouragement.

Suggestion during Adult-Led Activities
- As a substitute for a microphone, hold up a stick with a sphere on top. Ask each child to answer a question while speaking into the microphone.

Goal: Child Will Pretend with Imaginary Objects

Usually a child moves rather quickly to using imaginary objects once he has started using pretend substitutions for real objects. However, if you find that he is not doing this naturally, you can help him.

Suggestions during Play
- Set up a dramatic play area that emphasizes the feeding of food or the exchange of money—for example, cooking or buying gas for the car. Such actions are often easier for children to imagine because they see them so often.
- Continue observing the child to decide if he is adding more imaginary actions to his repertoire over time. If not, play with him and introduce imaginary actions as appropriate.
- Adopt the role of co-player and introduce imaginary actions or objects when the children have already organized their play.

Suggestions during Adult-Led Activities
- Play a modified version of charades in which you act out cleaning, cooking, washing clothes, or skating. Have the children guess what you are doing. Encourage them to perform the imaginary actions too.
- Use transition times to pretend to skate to the next room, or paint an imaginary wall as you walk.
- During movement activities, ask children, "How would you move like a robot, a baby, or a bunny?"
- Act out dramatic play themes during large-group time using imaginary actions, for example:
  - Driving a bus
  - Going swimming

- Getting ready in the morning
- Baking cookies
- Sing songs with imaginary actions like "Wheels on the Bus" and "This Is the Way We Wash Our Clothes."
- After you have played marching band with real or homemade instruments, create an imaginary marching band. Have each child make the sound and actions from an instrument and march around the room.

JENNY LOVED TO PLAY with the stove and refrigerator in the house-keeping area. However, if certain pots and pans were missing, she became quite upset. Other children were happy to use whatever was there. As her caregiver watched her, she noticed that Jenny didn't pretend with anything other than real objects. Without the pots and pans that looked like real objects, Jenny had difficulty playing and became frustrated. The caregiver decided to play with Jenny and a group of children. She brought in a bowl and used it when she cooked. In a few days, she gave the bowl to Jenny and suggested that she use it as a pot. At first, Jenny refused. The caregiver did not insist, but within the next week she tried again. After a couple of months, she noticed that Jenny was starting to substitute on her own. The caregiver then concentrated on giving Jenny imaginary food during play. For example, she gave Jenny an imaginary hamburger and said, "Here's a hamburger. Taste it."

Role-Playing

In theatre productions, actors take on the voice, costuming, actions, and words appropriate to the roles they are playing. A good actor or actress can be so completely transformed that the audience no longer sees the real person, only the role. This is what children are doing in dramatic play, and in sociodramatic play they are playing this role with others. When a child is four to five years old, he should be able to take on a role that includes a spectrum of specific characteristics: clothes, voice, speech, and physical actions. Sometimes a child can so effectively mimic the roles of a parent or teacher that it is uncanny to the observer. To learn this role, the child becomes an acute observer of human behavior and translates this understanding into action. This is a big task for a child, and one he begins very early in life. The first time a child picks up a telephone and holds it to his ear or pretends to feed a doll, he is beginning to role-play. When he can play the role of a father feeding, holding, and talking to his baby, his understanding of the role of a father has increased, as has his experience, cognitive understanding, and observational powers.

Getting Ready to Role-Play

If the child doesn't role-play in your setting, determine if he role-plays elsewhere, such as at home or with familiar friends. If he does, you know the child can role-play but is not doing it with you or in your early childhood setting. Your task is to encourage the child to risk this behavior with you and his peers. Sometimes the child may be afraid to take this risk. If you are dealing with a withdrawn or shy child who does not take risks with you, do not push or be direct in your requests. Try the following:

- Suggest a role for the child that is not central to the play. For example, the child can be a baby who has little language.
- Allow the child to observe play from outside the group for a while.
- Give the child a role in play that requires little risk. For example, in a pizza restaurant, the child can put paper pepperoni on pizzas.
- Do not bring too much attention to the child's efforts to play a role. Encourage with smiles, hugs, or indirect comments rather than direct praise.

Another reason a child may not role-play is that he does not understand the role you are asking him to play. Look at the child's experience. Does he know what happens at the health club or at the laundromat? Most likely, even if the child lacks understanding of the proposed role, he can play other, more familiar roles. If the child does not understand the role, try the following:

- Play with him, demonstrating what adults do when they take this role in real life.
- Plan a field trip so the child can observe how adults perform in that role.
- Read a book or watch a DVD about the role in the community.
- Bring people like bakers, waitstaff, clerks, firefighters, naturalists, zookeepers, and police officers to your setting to share what they do in their jobs when you introduce a related play theme.

Goal: Child Will Pretend One Sequence of Play

Usually a young toddler begins pretending a sequence of play using familiar toys like dolls, trucks, and telephones. The sequence can be short and may end abruptly. If an older child of three to four is not beginning to pretend one sequence of a role, try the following suggestions.

Suggestions during Play
- Use props that are familiar to the child, like telephones, food, dolls, pots and pans, trucks and cars.
- Use real objects rather than more abstract props. To begin with, play sessions should include just the child and an adult.
- Model the one sequence; then include the child after you have finished the sequence. For example, talk on the telephone; then hand the phone to the child, saying, "It's for you."
- Begin other sequences with new props if the child is able to pretend with one prop until you feel confident that he is ready to move to the next stage.

Suggestions during Adult-Led Activities
- Pretend to be a bird or an animal during transitions.
- Play other games with the child that encourage playfulness, like Hide-and-Seek, Peek-a-Boo, and chase.
- Act out short sequences during large-group time, like popping popcorn, growing seeds, or taking off in a rocket ship.

Goal: Child Will Combine Sequences of Play

Children rather quickly move to combine sequences, such as feeding, diapering, and rocking a doll, or cooking, setting the table, and putting food on dishes. Usually the sequences are related to each other and an overall play theme.

Suggestions during Play
- Bring props that are related to each other, like pots, pans, and dishes, or a doll, bottle, and blanket.
- Model how to combine two events or activities into a sequence as you did with the single sequence of play. For instance, feed the doll a bottle and then wrap it in the blanket. If the child does the action after you, give him praise or comment on what he is doing.
- Use different props as the child grows more confident.
- Allow English-language learners who are in the early stages of second-language acquisition to assume nonverbal roles in sociodramatic play. For example, a child can be the pizza delivery person who drives to the house, knocks at the door, and collects the money.

Suggestions during Adult-Led Activities
- Act out simple nursery rhymes. You can recite the rhymes while the children perform the actions using simple props. A number of nursery rhymes encourage acting:
  - "Jack Be Nimble"
  - "Hey Diddle Diddle"

- "Jack and Jill"
- "Humpty Dumpty"
- "Little Jack Horner"

Goal: Child Will Play Out All Parts of a Role, Including Dress, Speech, and Actions

At first when a child is working on this, he may be able to sustain the role only for a short time or use only a limited number of actions or words. As the child makes gains in this skill, you will see more complexity develop.

Occasionally, you may hear a child state, "I'm a doctor," and then run off. You may need to help him understand what a doctor does. Modeling is often very effective with such a child.

Suggestions during Play
- Play a birthday party, and have the child blow out candles, open pretend presents, and wear a birthday hat.
- The child first may enjoy role-playing an animal, such as a cat or dog, because doing so involves less language and dress-up clothing than other roles.
- Model a role with the child beside you. Suggest that he try it.
- Have different dress-up clothes and a mirror available to encourage role exploration.
- Set up a pretend bus by lining up chairs. Collect props to use with the bus, like tickets, paper money, and a map. One child can pretend to be the driver, and others can pretend to be the passengers. Other variations on this theme can be traveling on a plane or in a boat.
- Place books in the dramatic play area that are published in a child's home language. Many popular children's books have been translated into a variety of languages. Other fun books to check out include Eileen Browne's *Handa's Surprise,* Adam Jama's *Walking through the Jungle,* and Flora McDonnell's *Splash,* which are available through Mantra Publishing and are dual-language books.
- Collect a number of props that are organized into boxes and categories according to a play theme. Prop boxes can facilitate sociodramatic play. Some of these props can be stored together in boxes (prop boxes); other, larger props can be kept in a storeroom. Sorted props save time, are easy to use, and can accommodate additions and elaborations when children are ready. Possible play themes and the props that can be used for them include:

Theme	Props
Airport/Travel	Posters, suitcases, chairs for inside the airplane, tickets, trays for food, block for walkie-talkie, paper to write post cards, a flight schedule, travel posters
Pizza Parlor	Empty pizza boxes, box for delivery truck, order pads, menu, paper or play food, playdough or felt pepperoni and green peppers, stove or oven, cash register, play money, aprons
Laundromat	Doll and dress-up clothes, clothespins and clothesline, boxes for washers and dryers, play money, magazines, empty detergent box, measuring cup, laundry basket, sign with instructions for operating the washing machine
Camping	Tents, canteen, flashlight, blocks for fire, rocking boat for fishing, fishing poles, play fish, backpack, dishes, play food, sleeping bags, books to identify birds and plants, maps
Bakery	Muffin tins, stove, rolling pin, playdough, cookie cutters, cash register, numbers for customers, play money, board to write the bakery's specials on, sign for the bakery, recipe cards, cookbooks, receipts
Fire Station	Boots, coats, hoses, blocks to build houses, steering wheel, walkie-talkies, cardboard boxes for trucks, maps, paper to write addresses on, phone book
Restaurant	Menus, plates, silverware, ordering pad, pencils, cash register, play food, play money, aprons, placemats, tables and chairs, board to write the restaurant's specials on
Doctor	White lab coats, doctor's kit, gauze, ace bandages, bed or cot, medicine bottles, chairs, tables, magazines for the waiting room, clipboard and paper, pencils, old X-rays, prescription pad, sign-in sheet
House	Refrigerator, stove, cabinets, sink, dress-up clothes, dolls, doll clothes, mirror, dishes, play food, silverware, writing materials for grocery lists, fix-it books, books on different types of houses (including homes from around the world and animal homes), cookbooks, clipboards, note cards

- Set up a submarine for the children to take underwater excursions. Have them paint a large cardboard box to be the submarine. Add plastic lids and knobs for the controls. Use plastic liter bottles with straps for air tanks and inexpensive goggles for face masks. (One set of goggles for each child; disinfect daily to reduce the spread of germs.) Crumple newspaper and wrap with colorful painter's tape for the treasure. Have the children take turns hiding the treasure and making a map for the others to find it.

- Set up a moving day. Tell the children you have to move the house. Provide boxes for packing. Pack the boxes, put them in a wagon, and have children work together, moving the boxes and the furniture. Then have children join in to unpack, set up furniture, and put together the new house.

- Include at least four to six exciting dramatic play themes besides the housekeeping area throughout the year. Some children need action-packed themes, like escaping hot lava or safari. You can keep a safari fun and exciting without weapons by introducing a photo safari. Hide toy stuffed animals around the room. The children sneak up on an animal very quietly and snap its picture. Supply writing materials so the children can produce the picture of the animal they photographed. Of course, at times the animal will chase them, but that's part of the excitement.

> Introduce sociodramatic themes that are part of the experience of the linguistically and culturally diverse children in your classroom. Depending on where you live in the country, themes with which children may have had experience include
>
> - street markets
> - ice fishing
> - farmers' markets
> - pizza delivery
> - ice-cream parlors
> - drive-through restaurants
> - caring for animals
> - riding the bus
>
> For children just learning English, be sure to include pictures along with the English words on a menu at your pretend take-out restaurant and a grocery list on which children can circle the items they intend to buy at your classroom grocery store. You can also print a menu with words from other languages as well as English.

Suggestions during Adult-Led Activities

- Act out a story during large group with assigned roles for the children. First read the story to the children, and then discuss it with them. Assign the roles for the children to act out as you narrate the story. Provide props to assist them in playing out their roles. For example, if you are acting out *The Three Billy Goats Gruff*, make hats representing the goats and the troll. Help the children build a bridge out of blocks for the troll. (This is known as thematic fantasy play training, discussed in chapter 1.) Act out the story several days in a row, so children grow familiar with the roles. Let the children take on more of the roles as they grow more comfortable. Some good storybooks to use for this activity include

  - *The Three Bears*
  - *The Three Billy Goats Gruff*
  - *Caps for Sale*

- *The Three Little Pigs*
- *The Carrot Seed*
- *The Turnip*
- *The Mitten*

- Put a story corner in your environment during free play. Include props from a storybook and let children act it out during free play.
- Provide a flannelboard during free play with flannelboard figures of the stories you have acted out. The children can act out the story using the figures. Try a story like *Brown Bear, Brown Bear, What Do You See?* or a song like "Old MacDonald Had a Farm."

> RASHAAN REMAINED APART FROM the group of children that played daily in the housekeeping corner. Sometimes he would play with Legos or blocks, but other times he would just look longingly at those playing in the housekeeping area. The teacher decided to set up a pizza restaurant next to the house. The first day the restaurant was open, Rashaan came over and announced, "I'm the pizza driver man." Then he ran off and left the area completely. He went to the puzzles and sat down.
>
> The teacher realized that he might not have known what to do next. She brought him over to the restaurant and asked if he would like to play. He nodded. She gave him keys, suggested that he deliver the pizza to the house, and handed him a pizza box. He went over to the house and delivered the pizza. Rashaan spent the rest of free play delivering pizzas. The next day, the teacher drew him into the restaurant as the cashier and the pizza cook and gave him suggestions about the roles. Although he still wasn't connecting with the other children to a great extent, he was able to play out several roles within the play.

Verbalizations about the Play Scenario

Sociodramatic play cannot keep going without words or other communications between children. Language is the glue that holds the play and the players together. In this section, we discuss how a child's words communicate what he is pretending. Language brings other children into a shared vision of the play scene.

You can tell from his actions what a child is imagining. But his words provide a better picture of the child's intentions. When he uses words, other children not only understand what the child is doing but can join in and add numerous variations. Most children use words to communicate about their pretend play, but some children may use other means. For example, children who are deaf may use sign language in much the same way as children who have hearing use spoken language to label their substitute and imaginary actions. English-language learners communicate nonverbally, using gestures and actions to direct play. The suggestions we discuss involve spoken language, but we encourage you to adapt the information to your particular children.

Getting Ready to Verbalize about the Play Scenario

In order to use words in sociodramatic play, a child has to be able to use language throughout the day. If you have a child who is not using words or other methods of communicating at all during play, look closely at how he uses language during other activities. His lack of words during play may point to a more pervasive language problem. If he is not talking, is unable to express himself, or cannot understand directions, you may need to refer the child to a speech therapist for an evaluation. If you see the following behaviors in the child's home language, consider a referral (adapted from Koralek, Dombro, and Dodge 2005):

- The child does not say any words, even unclearly, by twelve months.
- The child does not speak at least fifteen words by eighteen months.
- The child is not using one- or two-word sentences to ask questions or make statements by twenty-four months.
- The child is not easily understood most of the time by thirty-six months.
- The child is not using short (two- to three-word) sentences to communicate by thirty-six months.
- The child is not understandable by forty-eight months.
- The child does not speak sentences that sound almost adultlike by forty-eight months.

A speech therapist uses speech and language strategies to help a child who has a language delay, and caregivers can also do many things in child care settings to help the child gain more skill in language. After the child has a better use of words, you can focus on language goals during sociodramatic play.

Use the following speech and language stimulation techniques with the child. These strategies are also useful when interacting with English-language learners (adapted from The Program for Infant/Toddler Caregivers 1998):

- Talk to the child throughout the day. Children learn to talk from hearing language around them. Use many kinds of sentences with simple words.
- Expand the child's statements.
  - Expand what the child says so that it becomes slightly more complex. For example, the child says, "More." You can say, "Johnny wants more juice." You are giving the child a little more than what he said. Do not expect the child to imitate you at first; this may come slowly.
- Talk about what you are doing or thinking. This is sometimes called *self-talk*.
  - Talk about what you are doing when you are engaged in activities. This can be uncomfortable at first, but it is a valuable model for the child. Remember these simple rules:
    - Keep it simple and short.
    - Articulate clearly.
    - Describe what you are seeing.
    - Describe what you are doing.
    - Describe what you are thinking.
- Stop talking at times to give English-language learners a break. Remember that the child will not often repeat after you, so you may not immediately see results.
- Talk about what the child is doing. This is sometimes called *parallel talk*.
  - Describe in short, simple sentences what the child is doing as he plays. By doing this, you are supporting his thought process. You may be watching him play with a truck. You can say, "The truck is on the road. Now it's going around the curve. Will it fall off? Uh-oh. Now the truck goes back on the road." This technique not only provides a language model but also encourages the child to increase his positive play activities.

Here are additional speech and language strategies to try.

- Reward all attempts to speak. Even if you do not understand the child, smile and respond. It is important that you do not correct him when he is attempting to speak. Model the correct sentence, but do not expect him to imitate it.
- Say the words along with the child's gestures if a child is gesturing but not speaking.
- Concentrate on language during play.
- Use all of the speech and language techniques during play as well as the rest of the day.
- Get two toy telephones and play "talking on the telephones" with the child. Let children talk to one another.

- Do turn-taking activities to encourage conversational pauses and responses. For example, perform an activity and then say, "Your turn." Or roll a ball back and forth. Use your imagination to think of other ways to take turns.
- Encourage the child to yell or call out words during gym or outside time. This will loosen him up so he is willing to take more risks.
- Play a game like What Time Is It, Mr. Fox? so children can practice repeated phrases in the safety of a group.
- Play adult-led language games that feature both speaking and listening.
    - Organize a "following directions" game. Give the child a set of one to three directions, depending on how much he can do at a time. Then have him give you directions.
    - Introduce a game of Whisper Tube in a large or small group. Collect cardboard tubes from toilet paper and paper towels. Give one to each child. Have each one whisper a message to the child next to him. Have the last child in the line report what he heard.
- Play hand-clapping imitation games. As the child learns to imitate you, clap different rhythms that he can copy.
- Clap syllables of children's names.
- Play games and activities that use sound. Part of learning to speak is learning to listen to sounds around you.
- Fill glasses with water to different levels and let the child tap the glasses lightly with a spoon. Decide together which glass sounds highest and which lowest.
- Make a recording of different sounds in your setting, such as a door shutting, people whispering, people walking. Have the child identify the sounds.
- Play a number of different musical instruments while hiding behind a wall or a shelf. Have the children guess which instruments you are playing. Another variation on this game is to have two of each instrument. Have the children guess which instruments are the same and which are different while you play them in sets of twos.
- Have the children close their eyes. Ask one child to step behind a screen or a shelf. The child who is behind the screen says, "Hello." The other children guess who is speaking.
- Using a CD or a song, encourage the children to march, play musical instruments, or do other movement activities in time to the music.
- Play musical chairs with the group. Before you play this more complicated game, do many stop-and-go games with music—that is, move to the music, and freeze when the music stops. (Don't eliminate children when you play musical chairs. Allow everyone to continue playing.)

> To play What Time Is It, Mr. Fox? one child pretends to be the fox. The rest of the children stand on a line facing the fox. They ask, "What time is it, Mr. Fox?" The fox replies with a time ranging from one o'clock to midnight. The children take the same number of steps toward the fox as the time he announces. For example, if the fox says three o'clock, the children take three steps. If the fox says midnight, the children turn and run back toward the line. The fox chases and tags the children. Any children who are tagged become additional foxes.

- Play games with the child, such as 1-2-3-Upsey-Daisy, Pat-a-Cake, Pop-Goes-the-Weasel, Ring-Around-the-Rosie, and Peek-a-Boo. Encourage the child to sing or say more and more of the words with you. During group times, ask the children to play the games with each other in pairs.
- Recite simple nursery rhymes, such as "Humpty Dumpty," "Little Boy Blue," or "Old King Cole."
- Do fingerplays, such as Five Little Monkeys, Itsy Bitsy Spider, or Twinkle, Twinkle Little Star. Rhymes with gestures allow the child who is learning English or who has language and other delays to participate and feel included, even if he can't keep up verbally. The gestures also reinforce learning the words.
- Use a pretend microphone. Ask the child a question, such as "What's your favorite toy?" Let him answer into the microphone. Look away as he answers if he is shy or self-conscious.

There are many other language games and activities listed in resource books. We encourage you to continue adding to the ideas here.

Goal: Child Will Use Words to Describe Substitute Objects

As children begin to move from pretending with real objects to substituting similar-looking objects, they use words to communicate what they are substituting. For example, the child may pick up a block, put it on the table in the housekeeping area, and say, "This is bread. Do you want some?" Although this is a separate goal from the one below, the same strategies work for both.

Goal: Child Will Use Words with Imaginary Objects or Imaginary Actions

If the child can use language at other times of the day, you can help him use words to describe his imaginary substitutions. If the child is not yet pretending with imaginary objects, the descriptions will be of the substitutions he is currently making. A child may pretend to pour into a bowl and say, "It's milk." To describe an imaginary action, he may hold an imaginary hose with both hands and say, "I'm putting the gas in the car!" Verbal descriptions are needed even more when the child is using imaginary objects or actions—words give his play partners a shared starting point.

Suggestions during Play
- Play with the child and model descriptions of the substitutions you are making. When rolling out playdough, say, "Here's some cookie dough. Do you want a cookie?"

- Model phrases for the child who is learning English to use when he is playing in the dramatic play area. For instance, hold up a stuffed animal toy to the child in the veterinarian's office and say, "His ear hurts."
- Place puppets in sociodramatic play areas. Some children who are learning to speak English or are shy sometimes use puppets to talk.
- When a child can describe substitute objects, play with him and model descriptions of imaginary objects and actions. You can pretend to feed the doll imaginary soup and say, "Baby, doesn't this soup taste good?" Or you can pretend to build a house with blocks and an imaginary hammer and nails. As you pretend to pound the nails, you can say, "I'm pounding these nails in good. This is hard work to pound these nails in with the hammer."
- Describe the child's actions as he engages in imaginary play, such as feeding the baby or driving the car.
- Sit next to the child during free play. When the child is involved in play and makes a substitution or demonstrates an imaginary action, provide the words for him. For example, you see him giving another child pretend money. You say, "Here's some money." (One precaution: The only way you know what the child is pretending is by observing his actions. You need to understand the play theme before you begin your comments.)
- Sit beside the child during play and ask him about his actions. When he is aiming the pretend hose at the blocks, say, "Tell me about your idea." Avoid questions that require only a yes or no answer.
- Sit beside the child during free play and ask questions that clarify what he is doing. When he is writing with a finger, say, "It looks like you're writing. What are you writing about?" or "Tell me about your writing."

Suggestion during Adult-Led Activities
- Perform a puppet show using a favorite play theme in your classroom, such as doctor. As the puppets act out the theme, have them talk about their imaginary actions. These should be simple statements, such as "Here are some pills. Put out your hand."

Goal: Child Will Use Words to Create a Play Scenario

This goal requires that the child already possesses sophisticated understanding of and ability to use language. He must be able to see mental pictures in his mind and then use language to create those pictures for others. A child who is already highly verbal and skilled at describing a play scene may be a great model for the child who is still working on this goal.

Suggestions during Play

- Create a play scene with props that are clearly defined. For example, set up a rocking boat with fishing poles. Ask the child what he wants to pretend.
- Pair the child with a highly verbal child to play in a room set up with a new play theme. Sit close by. Provide suggestions or ask clarifying questions, but only if needed.
- Create a scenario that draws children into the play. Begin your scene with "Let's pretend . . ." When the children add suggestions, bring in more props.
- Sit by the child during play and ask questions that help define his choice of a scenario. For instance, he may be putting a baby to bed. You can ask, "Is it nighttime or naptime?"
- Ask questions that continue the scenario. Some of these questions may include:
  - Now that you are done with the nap, what comes next?
  - What would your dad do after he set the table?
  - What else would a doctor do to help a patient?
- Adopt the role of co-player and ask the child what he wants you to do next while you play together.

Suggestion during Adult-Led Activities

- Create a puppet show in which the puppets can't decide together on a play scene. The story line can go something like this: Two puppets come out and are bored. They want to play something, but what? One puppet says, "Let's pretend we're monsters and are stomping in the snow." The other puppet says, "No." Then the first puppet describes a different play scene: "Let's pretend we are pirates on our pirate ship." But that is not agreeable either. These alternating play scenes can go on for a while and get sillier and sillier. To resolve the problem, the puppets can agree on elements from several play scenes, or the puppets can ask the children what they should play together.

ANTONIO WAS ALWAYS IN the housekeeping corner during free play and smiled as children talked about mommies and daddies and babies and cooked around him. He was in the middle of the play but not really included. He cooked at the stove or set the table, but he never said a word. Brian, his caregiver, watched him carefully throughout the day and noted that Antonio would talk a little during gym time or small-group time but was never highly verbal. Although Brian was concerned about how Antonio was left out during play, he decided to concentrate on increasing his language usage instead. He expanded any words Antonio spoke and described his actions during the day. When Antonio communicated with gestures, Brian spoke the words. Gradually, Antonio began to talk more. Brian continued using these language techniques, especially during play, confident that Antonio would use his newfound skills to communicate.

Verbal Communication during a Play Episode

Once children have begun a play theme, they require language to keep it going or to change it. This communication can take two forms. A child can communicate about play by talking to the other children from within his role. Such comments are pretend statements that fit within the child's chosen role. If he's playing a patient, he may say, "I'm really sick. My stomach hurts. Can you help me?" The second way a child communicates is from outside the role. The child breaks the flow of the play to organize the play. Here are examples of the way children communicate verbally during play (adapted from Johnson, Christie, and Yawkey 1987):

- Talk about pretend objects: "Let's pretend this block is a gate, okay? We can move it back and forth like this."
- Assign roles: "I'm the mom, and you be the dad."
- Plan where the play is going: "First we'll cook; then we go to the store."
- Correct players who are not playing the role the right way: "No, that's not what babies do."

We have one goal in this section. In addition we discuss three common situations in the Getting Ready section. First, you may observe a child who does not talk to anyone during play. Second, you may see a child who talks only to himself (this child may babble to no one in particular). Third, you may have a child in your care who talks during play only with adults. Unless the communication flows between children, the play becomes too dependent on adults.

Getting Ready to Verbally Communicate during a Play Episode

A child may be less able to verbally communicate in play if he has an overall language delay. If you have a child who is not speaking with others during play, refer to the suggestions on helping a child gain language skills. (See Verbalizations about the Play Scenario, beginning on page 141.) Occasionally a child talks easily during play but addresses his comments to no one in particular. This is called *self-talk*. The child describes what he is doing, thinking, or intending. When children are learning to talk, this skill is very valuable. Eventually such verbalizations become part of adults' silent thinking and are part of building the skills of self-regulation. However, when a child is playing in a group and talks only to himself, his words do nothing to build a bridge to other players. This child is often ignored or left behind. Self-talk is not a concern if the child occasionally prefers to talk to himself rather than to peers when playing. It becomes a concern when the child chooses to talk only to himself and does not connect with other children. Try the following suggestions:

- Sit close to the child during play. As he talks, make comments that connect him to other players. The child may be saying, "I'm pouring milk into the bottle. Be quiet, baby. I'll feed you." Say to the child, "Daniel, ask Jamie to hold the baby while you're getting the milk ready." One of the tricky parts of your role is commenting or suggesting without interrupting the flow of the group. Keep your comments short and simple. If the child ignores you, do not press your point. Just come back to it at another time.
- If the other children are ignoring this child even when he is trying to communicate with them, you can say, "Jamie, Daniel is asking for help with his baby."

Some children have excellent verbal skills but choose not to talk with peers in play. However, they immediately pull in an adult when one is near. They direct all their play comments to the adult but ignore other children. To help this child, use your central role to pull other children into his play. As connections are made between the players, you should physically distance yourself from the play to observe. If the play falls apart, you can go in again to add props or present a new play theme to the group.

If a child has articulation problems and cannot be easily understood, he may be reluctant to speak. Children may not understand him or be so busy playing that they don't give him time to finish his sentences. Sometimes children comment with brutal honesty on how the child talks. They may say, "Jerod talks funny," or, "Jane doesn't say that word right." These comments can inhibit a child from trying to communicate verbally. Although you may be uncomfortable with the other children's honesty about the child's language problems, it is best to treat the subject calmly and openly. Explain to the children that sometimes Jerod can't say the word clearly, so they need to listen carefully. Tell them that Jerod is learning to speak more clearly. Point out things that Jerod does well, like running or riding a trike. Show how everyone has things to learn and things that they do well. If they are having trouble understanding Jerod, they should come to you for help.

Children who are learning English as a second language may encounter similar questioning from their peers. When a child who is learning English or a child with a language delay comes to you with a concern that can't be understood, ask the child, "Can you show me what you want, and I can help you tell Akisha?" It is important to give the child an opportunity to communicate his wishes by another means—for example, by gestures. If the child runs off, tell him he can show you later if he likes. Keep the door of communication open.

Goal: Child Will Talk with Peers during Play

At the beginning of this section, we discussed the ways children talk during play. They either talk from within the role, making comments that are appropriate to it, or interrupt the play momentarily to organize it. With this goal, either of these ways of communicating can be addressed. It is ideal if the child achieves a balance between these two types of communication.

Suggestions during Play

- Suggest that the child make requests and direct comments to other children. The adult can say, "Tell Jeremy that he can come to dinner."
- Direct other children's attention to the child's comments if they do not respond.
- Give the child the words to use when he is talking to other children. This is particularly necessary if he has been hesitant to use language. For example, he is setting the table and another child is cooking at the stove. You can suggest, "Jake, tell Darnell, 'You can serve the supper now.'"
- Pair the child with a partner and plan a special play theme for just the two of them. A child who has been shy about using words can begin more easily with only one child as a playmate.
- Give the pair of children puppets to use. Sometimes children talk through puppets when they won't talk on their own.
- Suggest that the child play a role that requires only a little verbal interaction, like a dog or cat, a bus driver, or a carpenter. Many of these roles use more physical action and mouth noises than words.
- Encourage the child to call another child on the play phone and talk, even if briefly.

Suggestions during Adult-Led Activities

- Ask the child to talk to puppets manipulated by other children. You may need to give words to him at first.
- Play Simon Says, and after you have played the leadership role, ask the child to lead the group with your help.
- Play a movement game in which each child has to copy the leader. Share the leader position so that each child gets a turn.
- Play a game similar to the one above using noises. You make a noise like "Shsh," and ask the children to copy it. Give each child a turn to lead.
- Play lotto games in which the children get to be leader. The leader announces the pictures.
- Create small-group murals in which each child paints part of the picture. Talk about each child's part.
- Highlight a Star of the Week. Have the child bring his favorite toys, pictures, and clothes from home. During group time, the Star of the Week can explain his special possessions.
- Dismiss children from the group one by one, asking each child a question, such as "How many brothers/sisters do you have?" or "What's your favorite thing to eat?" Be sure to match the question with the child's language ability. For some, ask a question that can be answered with one word, or ask a question and give a choice of one-word responses. Call on the nonverbal child last or second to last so that most of the group is already engaged in the next activity.

SHANITA SOUGHT OUT THE dramatic play area during free play. She was always running to operate the cash register, set the table, or ride on the bus. Darius, her teacher, saw that she never talked, even though she performed all the appropriate actions. The other children would leave her out when they moved to a new play theme. Although Shanita would move along with the group, she seemed to be outside of their play. Darius decided to sit near the area and give Shanita words that would connect her to the play of the other children. The first day, Darius and the children set up a bus with blocks and a steering wheel. Shanita was waiting in line to get on the bus. When it was her turn, Darius said to Shanita, "Shanita, ask the bus driver how much you need to pay." Shanita repeated, "How much?" The bus driver said, "Five cents." She pretended to give the bus driver the money and got on the bus. After a few minutes she got up. Darius said, "Shanita, tell the bus driver you want to get off." Shanita said, "I want off now." The bus driver said, "Okay, you can get off." She stepped out of the bus and smiled broadly. Darius continued to give her words to say throughout the play period. Although she wasn't speaking on her own yet, she was learning that using words in play can bring more response and involvement from other children.

Persistence in Play

Being able to play for an extended period helps a child develop many of the skills needed for play. When children can play only for a few minutes, the group barely has a chance to set up the play, much less develop a theme. The age of the child often determines how long he can sustain play in a group. A child of four should be able to persist from five to nine minutes, and a child of five or six should be able to persist for ten minutes or longer. Eventually, a child who engages in mature play can sustain a play theme until the next day or over several days. As children extend their play beyond one day, they learn to plan and enrich their original play theme (Bodrova and Leong 2007).

Getting Ready to Persist in Play

This section's goal is to increase the child's time in sociodramatic play, but you'll find that many children who cannot stay with play also have short attention spans for other activities. If this is the case, you need to help them lengthen their attention spans outside of group play as well.

Intensive play sessions with you or another adult are a good starting point to build longer attention spans. Playing next to or with an adult often keeps children at an activity longer. Once the child's ability to stay with a task has increased, you can begin addressing the goal within sociodramatic play. Following are activities and suggestions that help a child increase his attention span:

- Stand or sit next to the child and play with the same materials. For example, he is at the water table splashing water and starts to leave. The teacher brings funnels to use in the water table and sits by him. They both pour water through the funnels. This parallel play brings value to the activity and helps the child sustain it longer (see chapter 7).
- Plan a play sequence for you and the child that combines sensorimotor activity and dramatic play. For example, you could
  - wash babies
  - feed dolls with beans, playdough, and other objects
  - build roads in sand and drive to the store
  - cook with playdough
  - make pizza with playdough
  - wash cars (trikes) outside

- When the child is doing an activity and begins to leave, ask him to do one more thing. For instance, if he is doing a puzzle and begins to leave before he finishes, ask him to put one more piece in the puzzle.
- Hold back props to introduce when the child begins to lose interest. For example, have towels available to dry wet dolls, or add small plastic animals to the block or sand play.
- Minimize the number of distractions to the child throughout the day. Look at your environment. Use a limited number of props in the play areas. Do not use too many colors or pictures on the walls. Minimize the number of mobiles or art projects hanging from the ceiling; motion from these can be a source of overstimulation. Keep the noise level down in the room. When you limit distractions in such ways, you are helping the child who has difficulty concentrating.
- Comment positively when the child displays a long attention span.
- Provide adult support as often as possible. This tends to keep the child involved in any activity a little longer.
- Encourage the child to choose an area to play in "for a long, long time." Notice when he does.

Goal: Child Will Engage in Sociodramatic Play for XX Minutes

Occasionally a child can play for a long time when alone with his favorite activity but cannot play for long in a group of children. If this describes a child in your care, you can use the following suggestions to help him play longer in a group. These suggestions also help a child who has a short attention span throughout the day.

Suggestions during Play
- Choose one or two other children whom the child enjoys. Organize a new play theme for them. This is especially effective in a separate room, where there are fewer distractions. Start with the themes of playing doctor, riding a bus, or playing restaurant.
- Play with the group to establish a theme and roles. If the child starts to leave the group, encourage him to do something new. For example, the group is playing doctor, and you are pretending you are the patient and the child is the doctor. He is just starting to examine you, and he begins to wander off. You say, "Oh doctor, I think I have a temperature. Will you take my temperature?" When he starts to wander off again, bring in another patient who has a stomachache.
- Hold back a few props to introduce as interest flags. For example, as you play doctor, bring out a doll and bandages when children become restless.

- Choose play themes for groups of children that combine sensorimotor play and dramatic play. (See earlier discussion in this section.)
- Reduce your direct involvement if the child is remaining in the group for play, but stay close by. Continue making suggestions, commenting, and asking questions to maintain the children's interest in the play theme.

Suggestion during Adult-Led Activities
- Play Simon Says. Ask the child to be the leader. He may persist longer if you combine movement and a chance for him to lead an activity.

> MARCUS PLAYED ALONE WITH blocks, puzzles, or art projects for long periods of time. He would occasionally join an adult on the playground if he was playing car wash with the trikes, but if other children joined in, he would wander away. Margaret, his family child care provider, was concerned about this. She decided that she wanted to increase the time Marcus would play in a group of children. She had observed that Marcus enjoyed any play with water.
>
> One morning she took the trikes out to the playground, put up a car wash sign, and invited Marcus and two other children to wash cars with her. She asked Marcus to set up the scrubbing brushes and put soap in the water. She provided only one bucket of water, so the children would be playing together when they washed the trikes. The three children scrubbed the trikes using the water and soap. Marcus started to leave after a few minutes. Margaret asked him to help her set up the rinse bucket. Marcus enjoyed rinsing a few trikes, then started to leave again. Margaret showed him how to dry the trikes with cloths. By this time, Marcus had played with the group for at least ten minutes. Throughout the next several weeks, she offered additional activities for Marcus and two or three other children, all involving water. Marcus began to wander off less and needed fewer suggestions to stay in the play.

Interactions

To be part of a group engaged in sociodramatic play, children must be able to participate in joint activities and communicate with one another. Children who are skilled in getting to know and interacting with others usually have had successful relationships with adults, have played in pairs, and have learned to coordinate their actions with other children. They have learned to join others' play, maintain relationships, and solve problems. Interacting with others gives children an opportunity to take risks with peers and try different roles, such as leader, follower, or clown, and provides them with a sense of belonging. Children spend the most time interacting with those they consider their friends.

In the preschool years, children tend to think a friend is someone you play with most often or someone you are playing with at a certain time. Children can be drawn to one another because of a possession, physical appearance, or a physical skill ("I like him because he runs really fast"). When first choosing a friend, preschoolers tend to focus on outward similarities such as gender, race, and age (Kostelnik, Stein, Whiren, and Soderman 1998).

TUCKER, A PRECOCIOUS AND highly verbal five-year-old, came in from the playground looking rather dejected. His teacher asked what was wrong. Tucker said, "I just found out that Will doesn't like me that much." His teacher was shocked and exclaimed, "You two live next door and play together all the time at school. What do you mean?" Tucker replied, "Yeah, but I gave him a little test." Again his teacher dropped her jaw and said, "You gave him a test?" "Yeah, I asked him if he liked me or my stuff," Tucker explained. Confused but curious, his teacher asked, "What did he say?" "He said he liked my stuff, my superheroes, and my four-wheeler."

Tucker was stating the truth about some preschool friendships. Sometimes an interest in an object or activity is what brings children together. A more satisfying relationship may result from what they learn about each other as they play.

Help children who are monolingual English speakers learn about English-language learners:

- Have books in various languages in the classroom.
- Place books on tape in different languages in the listening center.
- Listen to music with lyrics in a variety of languages.
- Label common objects throughout the room in a variety of languages.
- Talk about the languages spoken in different families. Say, "Your family speaks English. Alexis's family speaks Spanish. They are learning to speak English too."
- Help an English-speaking child simplify what he is trying to tell a child who is learning English.

TWO GIRLS WERE PUTTING a puzzle together. When they completed it, each one wanted to do it by herself. The teacher explained to the child who spoke English, "You know that Tran is learning to use English. I'm not sure she understands what you want. What if Tran does the puzzle by herself first? Then you can say, 'My turn,' and she will understand."

A desire to interact is a highly motivating reason for some children to learn to speak English. English-language learners who want to learn to communicate with others during play may be particularly willing to risk trying some of their newly acquired English words. Their peers also provide models of words to use.

While interacting can be important, sometimes a child chooses to play alone. Playing alone may be developmentally appropriate for infants, toddlers, and even very young preschoolers. Playing alone at any age can be appropriate when it is rich in imagination. It becomes a concern, however, if an older child seems unable to make connections with others. A child who consistently plays alone or isolates himself may lack the interaction skills that would make it possible for him to play successfully with others.

When it appears that a child enjoys playing alone, you may hesitate to encourage him to interact. We suggest observing the child often enough to determine if he is alone because he lacks the requisite skills or because solitude is his preference. Watch to see if he can interact with others at times. Remember, it is the quality of his interactions that are important, not the quantity. Also observe if he seems to be anxious about his inability to interact. If he appears to be upset or looks as if he wants to join the others but does not know how, use the information that follows to teach him the skills he needs. When you know he has the skills yet chooses to play alone, you can feel assured he has truly made a choice.

Getting Ready to Play with Others

You may be able to help a child who is not yet interacting with others during play by fostering informal interactions and a sense of community in your setting. Create a setting in which every child feels accepted and vital to the community.

- Allow uninterrupted time for children to interact with their peers.
- Take photographs of the group that show each child fully engaged in the life of the classroom. Post them in your environment.
- Read and discuss books about friends. Karen Stephens (2002) suggests asking: Why are they friends? What do the friends do together? What made them decide to be friends? How did friends help each other? Try books like Pat Hutchins's *My Best Friend.*
- Help children learn the names of others in the group. If you don't make this effort, children don't know how to address each other or learn only the names of those you call out often.
- Play Who's Missing? Have the children close their eyes. Ask one child to go behind a divider. Ask the rest of the group to guess who is missing.
- Play a guessing game about the children. Say, "I'm thinking of someone who has long black hair and brown eyes and is a girl, and her name starts with the letter B. Guess who it is."
- While children are waiting in line or for a group time to start, you can give them a chance to move by using the tune to "The Farmer in the Dell" and singing, "Justin stand up, Meera stand up, hi-ho, the derry-o, now sit down." Then move on to two other children.

- Chant and clap, "Claire is here today, Claire is here today, Claire is here today, Yeaaaa! Claire."
- Write each child's name on a large card. Hold up one card at a time and ask the children to read whose name it is.

Goal: Child Will Play with an Adult

Very young children need positive, successful interactions with adults to learn some of the skills they need to interact with their peers. Older children who are having difficulty with interactions may also need to return to this first playmate.

Suggestions during Play
- Build your relationship with this child.
- Share a joke, silly action, or funny activity.
- Follow the child's lead in play situations. Do what he suggests, or copy some of his behaviors. Use parallel play to build trust and to demonstrate that you value what he does as well as the ideas he has.
- Recognize the child's play strengths and comment on them.
- Arrange a time each day when you are available to interact with the child under low-stress conditions.

Suggestions during Adult-Led Activities
- Build your relationship with the child by finding out his likes and dislikes. Ask him or ask his parents about his favorite toys, games, and activities. Place some of these in your environment. This helps provide a link between home and the early childhood setting.
- Visit the child at home. This can be difficult to arrange with busy schedules, but in many situations it is worthwhile. When you visit a child in his home, he is sometimes more comfortable and outgoing. You may get an indication of what he is capable of more quickly than in the early childhood setting.
- Establish a positive relationship with the child's family. The child will sense how you feel about his parent(s) and absorb it.

- Tell the child about your movements and touch so he knows what you are about to do. For example, say, "I'm going to push your chair in."
- Build a history of respectful experiences with the child so he knows he is firmly connected to you.

Goal: Child Will Play with One Other Child, Always the Same Person

As children grow older, they begin to move their attention from the adults they know to the children they are around frequently. After a child has had many opportunities to interact with an adult, arrange activities in which he spends more time in child-to-child contacts than in child-to-adult interactions.

Interactions with caregivers don't automatically transfer to peers. Recognize that peer interactions are qualitatively different from interactions with an adult, because children try out roles, behaviors, and actions with peers that they might not try out with an adult. For some children, beginning to interact with other children is a slow process.

When you first start to encourage child-to-child interactions, it may appear to the child that you are pushing him away. If he perceives it this way, he is more likely to cling to you. Be sure to balance your support of his developing peer relationships without pushing him into an uncomfortable position. He may begin playing with others by playing only with one other child. Children can sometimes have difficulty maintaining more than one friendship at a time (Kostelnik, Stein, Whiren, and Soderman 1998). It is through these important relationships with each other that children learn a great deal about coordinating behaviors and ideas for maintaining play.

This goal and the next involve encouraging the child to play with only one child at a time. Use this goal if the child plays primarily with adults and you want him to play with one other preferred peer. There are no activity ideas listed for this goal; those are listed under the following goal since they are so closely related.

Goal: Child Will Play with Different Play Partners

Use this goal when the child plays with only one peer and you want to encourage him to change play partners sometimes. He may still play with just one child at a time, but one day you encourage him to play with Sam and the next with Wayne.

Suggestions during Play
- Arrange times when the child can be involved in pretend play with one other child. Find out what he likes to pretend when he plays alone. Look for ways to include another child. If he likes to build roads in the sand, ask

the other child to dig a lake next to the road. Then they can both drive their cars around the lake.

- Watch for times when the child is playing next to another child and comment on their actions. Say something like, "I see you and Christa are playing in the grocery store. And you both have your grocery lists written too."
- Talk on behalf of the child who is learning to speak English when children are sharing an object or a glance to facilitate further interaction.
- Take on a role and guide the scenario. You can invite other children to join the play by assigning roles that are compatible. For example, if you are playing race car, you can ask another child to pump gas into your car.
- Phase out your involvement when the children begin to interact with one another.

Suggestions during Adult-Led Activities
- Point out ways in which the child is similar to others in the group. Call attention to very simple things, such as similarities in shoe color or two children sharing the same first letter in their name. Pay particular attention to times when the child is playing like the other children and comment on it.
- Describe friendly behaviors, like offering a toy or being careful not to knock down another child's block structure. Have the children help make a list of other things that are friendly. Help them be specific by asking, "What does that look like?" or "What do they do?" Friendly actions may include saying hello, playing together, sharing toys, smiling, and not fighting. Identifying friendly actions helps a child define what friends do and helps him believe he can make friends.
- Pair the children for certain activities. Assign the child who has difficulty interacting to a partner who is likely to accept him. He is more likely to get along easily with someone who is like him in activity level, temperament, and level of impulsivity (Gower, Hohmann, Gleason, and Gleason 2001). Paired activities can include
  - fingerpainting
  - running errands within the room
  - doing puppet plays
  - cleaning an area of the room
  - telling stories to each other
- Try an art activity pairing children with paint, paint brushes, and textured rollers. Allow them to decide how they will work together to make one painting.
- Be aware of informal contacts children make on their own. Do not interrupt or draw their attention away from each other. For example, if two children are counting crackers at snacktime, don't interrupt their interaction to ask them how many girls are sitting at the table.

- Use graphs to draw attention to children with similar interests—for example, children can indicate their favorite flavor of ice cream, toy to play with, book to read, or time of day at school.

Goal: Child Will Play with Two or Three Children All Together

To interact with two or three children at one time, a child must learn to engage in a joint activity, coordinate his behaviors with others, and see how his ideas fit.

Suggestions during Play

- Help children see that what they are playing fits with what others are doing. Weave story lines that include a number of children. In one family child care home, Gabriel, Tyler, and Sophie, all four-year-olds, were playing in the building area. Gabriel had the school, Tyler the barn, and Sophie the house. Although they were all near each other, they were playing without much interaction. Darren got out the school bus and wanted to join them. When the provider asked how they might all play together, Darren thought they might have some people ride his bus. The other children were not too excited about the idea until the adult helped to tie the play themes together with a story. She told them that the children woke up in their beds one morning excited about going to school that day because they were going on a field trip to the farm. The children were able to play out the story for about ten minutes before Sophie decided to play elsewhere. The next day, the children set up the same play and told the story again.
- Teach the child to respond each time another child talks to him. It is not important that he agree with the statement or comply with the request but important that he respond. Popular children acknowledge the comments made by other children whether they agree with the statements or not (Kemple 2000).
- Help the child focus on each player in the group for short periods of time. Children who are successful in groups tend to divide their time among the players. This seems to reduce their chances of being rejected by the rest of the group (Kostelnik, Stein, Whiren, and Soderman 1998).
- Be aware that even children who can play with others quite well sometimes get stuck and need the help of an adult. For example, they may become stuck when the children have reached the end of a story they've been enacting or when they have played out a story for quite some time. When play begins to fall apart, materials may be used inappropriately, scenes become repetitive, children wander out of the area, or noise level increases. Before play reaches one of these points, offer a unique way to expand the play, or help the children draw it to a close by saying something like "I think the animals look tired. It's time for the zookeeper to put them to bed and go home." Then suggest two or three new play themes they can act out (see chapter 3).

Suggestions during Adult-Led Activities

- Designate certain times of the day for small groups. Working in small groups can help children get to know each other. Make sure each child has opportunities to form relationships with others before changing group members.
- Read a book to a small group of three to four children and then act out the story. Have them perform it for the whole group.
- Give a small group of children a task to complete together, such as making a mural, building something, or doing a classroom chore. After they complete the task, take a picture and ask them to dictate a story about it.

TYRELL AND SHAWN WERE friends at home as well as at child care. They preferred one another as playmates and even received comfort from each other when they were upset. On days when one of them was absent, the other tended to play alone rather than join the play of another child.

Tyrell was at a loss when Shawn's family moved out of the city. For weeks he had difficulty playing with any other child at the center. His caregivers felt it was important to bring him together with others. To work on this, they invited Tyrell to join them as they played with the other children. They also paired him with children during art and table time. After a few weeks of helping him make connections with others, his caregivers observed that Tyrell was able to play with a few of the other children. He still preferred to play with only one child at a time, but now he had more children as play partners.

Entrance into a Play Group

When a child attempts to interact with other children or join their play, he needs a number of strategies to help him be accepted by the group. Two strategies are most effective. In the first, a child makes comments about the established play, but the comments aren't directed toward anyone in particular. In the second, the child makes comments about the play directly to an individual. As a child enters the group, he must learn not to disrupt the play or to draw undue attention to himself by being aggressive, barging in, criticizing, or being bossy (Kostelnik, Stein, Whiren, and Soderman 1998). Some children learn successful strategies for acceptance into group play by watching others. Others need more direct instruction as they learn to join a group.

Getting Ready to Enter a Group

There are a number of reasons a child might not be ready to enter group play; we list three here:

1. If the child is not comfortable interacting with others in structured activities, he may also be uncomfortable attempting to join group play. Before asking him to join, make sure he is competent in paired activities and in small-group activities (see the section on Interactions in this chapter). Help him become more comfortable with group play by trying some of the suggestions below.

- Tell stories about the benefits of being a group member (for example, playing kickball or having a tea party is more fun with a group than alone).
- Do a group puzzle. Use a large floor puzzle, or create one by pasting a poster on cardboard and cutting it into as many pieces as you have children. Give each child a piece, and then help them put the puzzle together. Emphasize how the group needs every person's contribution to make the puzzle whole.
- Do a puppet play for the group in which two puppets pretend to run a drive-through restaurant. One puppet is the cashier and the other the customer. Have the puppets say that they need more people to help with the restaurant. Ask the group to list the roles others can play, such as a second customer, someone to wipe the table, or someone at the drive-up window. Emphasize that there's room for lots of people/puppets to play in the group.

2. If the child plays with toys that isolate him, he may not be noticing items that interest him in theme centers. His favorite toys may be those typically used in solitary play, such as puzzles, books, or painting. Move these materials into another area of the room that encourages group play.

- Set up a pretend toy store. Move the puzzles into the toy store and have the children pretend to buy them before they play.
- Set up a pretend library where the children need to check out their books before reading them.
- Arrange an art gallery. Have the children create art and display it for others to come and view. Have the children write a brochure or invitation to the event and pretend to sell tickets.
- Place a book and the props for its story in the reading center. Have one child read or retell the story as the other children act it out with the props.

3. Occasionally a child uses physical contact as an entrance strategy. This child may use force as a way to get attention from group members. Some children

rely on physical contact with others to initiate or enter play because they do not understand the more complex verbal strategies used successfully by others.

- Reinterpret the child's physical contacts for the other children. When Jonathan arrived at the center, he called to the children from the car. He ran out to the playground at full speed and pushed Sam as he said, "You're it!" Sam turned and yelled, "Don't push me, Jon! You're not playing." A caregiver had been watching. She felt Jonathan had been trying to make contact with the rest of the children. She said to Sam, "I think Jonathan would like to play with you. Should he be 'it' or one of the runners?"

- Let the child know what the effect of his actions is on the other children, and suggest alternatives. In a confidential conversation with Jonathan, his caregiver let him know that other children didn't want to play with him if he hurt them. She didn't shame or embarrass him. Instead, she told him what to do rather than pushing: "Sam doesn't like it when you push him. He didn't know you wanted to play. You could tell Sam, 'Hi, Sam! I like to play tag too.'"

- Model the words the child can use to join the play. Suggest that he say, "I'm playing. I bet you can't catch me."

- Help this child watch the play of others and imitate some of their actions. This is often a successful strategy for a child because it does not depend on words. Stand with him on the sidelines of play and draw his attention to what others are doing. Find another toy like the one others are using and give it to this child. Suggest that he do what they are doing. For example, if the children are making a long chain with plastic links, hand this child some links and show him how to hook them together as the other children are doing. When he has a few on his chain, suggest that he add them to the chain the other children are making so it can be even bigger.

- Use a developmental checklist to pinpoint the child's language skills. Perhaps he resorts to physical contact because he has a hard time making himself understood by others. Are his skills age-appropriate or lagging behind age expectations? Does this child need to have his language skills assessed in more detail? (See children's language development in the section on Verbalizations about the Play Scenario, beginning on page 141.)

Imagine that you arrive late to a party. Pairs and small groups of people are already gathered and engrossed in conversation. You hang up your coat and look around the room. How would you join one of these already existing groups? What entrance strategy would you use? Here are some strategies that other adults have suggested:

- Find someone I know and stand by her.
- Stand next to a group and listen to their conversation.
- Hang around others and wait until I have something relevant to say.
- Go say hello and start a conversation.
- Look for someone else who is alone and join him.

Look for similarities in the entrance strategies adults and children use.

Goal: Child Will Stand Near the Group and Watch

One thing children do when they begin to show an interest in joining group play is to watch others at play. Sometimes standing nearby is enough to envelop them in play.

Suggestions during Play

- Help a child plan what to do during a play activity, or walk with him to a few areas where groups of children are playing and see what they are doing. Talk about their activities and what he would do if he were to join them.
- When you notice that the child is observing the play of others from where he sits or stands, invite him to walk closer to the group with you and watch for a while.
- Call attention to a child's good play ideas so others will notice.
- Help the child identify which play group is appropriate for him to join. If a child wants to play spaceship, help him find the ongoing activity that is most related to his idea. Point out that it may be more appropriate for him to be an astronaut with a group of children playing with the blocks or in the housekeeping corner than with children who are playing library. In simple terms, explain to him that if he attempts to join play too unrelated to his idea, his attempt may be considered so disruptive that he will be rejected. You can say something like, "The children in the library are reading quietly. If you blast off in your spaceship, it may make a lot of noise, and they won't like it. The children in the block area are making noise when their buildings crash. It may be better to play near them."

Suggestion during Adult-Led Activities

- Help the child get used to watching others play by having him watch while you demonstrate how to play at a theme center. Emphasize that he should watch what you are doing. Ask him to describe your actions. Then expand the activity by asking him to suggest other things he can play at the theme center.

Goal: Child Will Imitate the Behavior of the Group

Many children enjoy being imitated. Imitating another child can be a good way to gain entry into group play (Kostelnik, Stein, Whiren, and Soderman 1998). By doing what the others are doing, a child will sometimes be included.

Suggestions during Play

- Adopt the role of a parallel player and begin to imitate some of the actions of the others while remaining on the fringes of the play. Encourage the child to do the same. Playing on the outskirts may give him some practice performing the play actions and build his confidence before he joins the group.
- Coach the child by suggesting that he do what others are doing.
- Discuss in confidence with the child what he would like to do in play. Name another child who likes to play the same thing and suggest that he play next to that child. Suggest partners who are similar in development,

temperament, and level of impulsivity because they are the most likely to accept him (Gower, Hohmann, Gleason, and Gleason 2001).

- Facilitate opportunities for the child to join play by becoming a member of the group play. Once you are an active member of the play, invite this child to take on a role and join you. If he does not respond to your invitations right away, place positive expectations that the child will join you later. Say, "If you don't want to get on the bus right now, we'll stop for you next time around."
- Join the child and discuss the activity of the group when he is watching other children play. Talk about the roles he can take and how they fit into the ongoing play. For example, if there is a group of three playing in the housekeeping area and one is the mom, one the dad, and one the child, perhaps the newcomer can be the grandpa or the babysitter. See if he can list some of the things that a grandpa would do in the setting.
- Make sure the roles you suggest are ones the child can enact. This helps to ensure success and increases his willingness to participate in the future. For example, do not give a child with poor language skills a role that may require him to be highly verbal. He can set the tables at a restaurant rather than place the orders.
- Help the child who is an English-language learner and is unable to communicate in play so he is not ignored. If ignored, he may not be able to participate in play situations that can help him learn more communication skills. Help him learn to copy the play of others and to offer related props.

Suggestions during Adult-Led Activities
- Play Copy-Cat. Ask the children to do what you do. Twirl in a circle, stand on one foot, or clap your hands.
- Play Copy-Cat with a set of toys. Give each child in a small group the same materials you have and then ask them to copy what you do. For instance, drive a toy truck in a circle, bounce a ball, or rock a doll. Remind children that when friends play together, they often do the same things and use the same toys.

Goal: Child Will Make Comments Related to Play

A child who says something related to what is taking place in the play has learned to add to the play rather than enter it in ways that call undue attention to himself or suggest a big change in the play theme. Help a child learn this strategy by trying these ideas.

Suggestions during Play
- Spend time playing with the child in paired activities. Set up your play near the play of other children. Watch for opportunities to join the play of the

others and to bring this child with you. Perhaps you and he can play house near another group of children who are also playing house. Send him to their house to borrow some sugar for the cookies you are making. Help a child who has limited English proficiency join group play by demonstrating how he can knock at the door of the housekeeping area (rather than make a comment) or gather food in a bag and then pay for it at the pretend farmers' market.

- Teach English-speaking children that a child who is learning English may not respond to their invitation to play. Help them interpret this as not understanding their words rather than as a rejection. Encourage English-speaking children to gesture to the other child to follow or come closer. The English-speaking children can offer a toy for the other child to use so he can join the fun.
- Talk with the child about how he can fit in with what the other children are doing. Model the words for him to use in joining the others. He could say, "We could build a garage for the cars with the blocks I have."
- Help the child make comments that correspond to the ongoing play. Question him about what he is doing and how his play idea fits with what the other children are already doing. If he is unable to see how the ideas go together, you may need to provide some help. For example, he may want others to come to the store he has set up, while they are playing pretend camping trip. Help him to think about what someone who is camping may need to buy. Suggest that he sell batteries for flashlights and firewood for campfires.

Suggestions during Adult-Led Activities
- Do a puppet play that shows a puppet trying to play with others. Demonstrate the strategies he tries and the responses he gets. End with the children brainstorming some things that the puppet can do to gain entry. Act out the ideas with the puppets.

- Ask open-ended questions about entering a group: What can you do to let someone know you want to play? What can you say? What if someone wants to play with you? Why would someone want to play with you? What if you want to play alone for a little while?

Goal: Child Will Get the Attention of Another Child before Making Comments Related to Play

Comments that are not directed to anyone can go unnoticed and the child's attempt to gain entry may be ignored. Help a child learn to increase his chances of being heard by getting the attention of another child before saying something about the play.

Suggestions during Play

- When a child tries to enter a group by making a comment but his remarks are ignored, remind him to use the name of the other child. Model how to do this by repeating what was said but prefacing it with one of the children's names. For example, if the child says, "Hey, I've got the tomato soup for supper," you can model using the name of one of the other children before entering the group. Suggest to Grady that he say, "Henry, I've got the tomato soup for supper."

> **When Teaching through Puppets**
> - Introduce a short puppet story.
> - Act out the story up to the point of the conflict or problem to be solved.
> - Ask the children how the puppets could solve the problem.
> - Review the solutions.
> - Demonstrate the solution(s).
> - Let the children use the puppets to act out the story.

- Ask the child, "Who are you talking to?" Point out that the other child might not know he was being spoken to. Say, "I'm not sure Nathan knew you were talking to him. Say his name, and when he looks at you, tell him your idea again."

Suggestions during Adult-Led Activities

- Teach all children to gain each other's attention or call another child's name before beginning conversations.
- Encourage children to call your name rather than tap your shoulder or tug your sleeve when they want your attention. Model the way—say, "Erika, can you help me?"

CHAD ENTERED THE BLOCK area, saying, "We could play skateboarders!" There was no response from any of the boys who were building a tall tower of blocks. Chad tried again, saying, "Anybody want to play skateboarders?" but still got no response from the others. Chad stood watching but was not invited to play.

A few weeks later, Chad came into the housekeeping area, where two children were pretending to set the table for breakfast. He carried a cup and said, "Here's your coffee." Chad continued to help with the imaginary breakfast preparations by cooking some bacon at the stove. This time Chad's attempt to enter was much more successful.

Asking "Can I play?" is considered to be the least effective of all entrance strategies, yet it is one that adults often suggest. Children who ask, "Can I play?" too often hear the answer "NO!" (Hazen, Black, and Fleming-Johnson 1984).

Children reject others for many different reasons. One may be to protect play materials. Another might be that they do not want to open their play to another child because they realize they will have to share materials with the newcomer. Some children are rejected because they have used aggression or have been destructive in the past. Children remember these upsetting behaviors and don't want them to happen again. Unfortunately, the reputation for being disruptive can live beyond the actual behavior. Work with the child who has been disruptive or aggressive to teach him new behaviors. Offer your support during play so the others can be assured that play will go smoothly. Highlight the strengths of this child so others will begin to change their impression of him.

Children may reject others because they are so engrossed in their play script that they don't expand their thinking to include another child. For example, if two children are playing service station and one is the mechanic and the other the owner of a broken car, they may not see a role for another child. In this case, you can point out that the newcomer can be the next customer or the cashier.

Children may also have difficulty seeing how to spatially fit in one more player. In one such situation, Lisa was setting the table for lunch. She had four chairs and four place settings for her guests. She set dolls at two of the place settings and invited Shelley to sit in one of the other chairs. Martin was watching, and the adult tried to draw him into the play.

Adult: Where is Martin going to sit?
Lisa: He can't come. There isn't any room. Two babies are in these chairs, one chair for Shelley and one chair for me.
Adult: Maybe one of the babies could sit on Martin's lap during lunch.
Lisa: Oh yeah! Martin, do you want to come for lunch?

Lisa had rejected Martin simply because she saw no room for him! The adult was able to find a simple way to make space for one more.

Even highly skilled children are rejected at times. When one child rejects another, help him recognize the rebuff as temporary. Tell the child who has been rejected, "He must want to play by himself for a while. Maybe later he will be ready to play together again." Teach all children to respond to invitations to play politely, even if they don't want to play. Help them learn to say, "I'll play with you later, but right now I want to build by myself."

He had learned to match his comments and actions to the ongoing play. In addition, his entrance did not take anything away from the existing play. Chad's comments would have had an even greater chance of drawing a favorable response if he had said, "Simone, here's your coffee," or if he made sure that he had the attention of one of the other children before presenting his idea.

Problem Solving

Conflict is inevitable when young children come together. Children can learn to resolve conflict by using problem-solving skills. When they learn these skills, they can resolve their disagreements in mutually acceptable ways. Negotiating conflicts requires the ability to listen and compromise. In order to problem solve, children must learn to regulate strong emotions, find ways to express their feelings, and make appropriate choices.

Unfortunately, some children try to resolve conflicts in inappropriate ways. Doing so makes them less likely to be accepted by others in the group when they attempt to join in sociodramatic play (Asher, Renshaw, and Hymel 1982). Other children remain passive in problem solving: they don't stick up for themselves or make clear what they want.

Getting Ready to Problem Solve

Two inappropriate ways children respond to conflict include passivity and aggression. Before being able to problem solve independently, the passive child must learn to stand up for himself, and the aggressive child must learn to stop his actions before he hurts someone.

Teach Children to Be Assertive

Toddlers sometimes don't know how to respond to others who take their toys or hurt them. They allow another child to take their toy without any type of response. Some older preschoolers also lack assertiveness. If a child remains consistently passive when faced with conflict, he will not learn the skills of compromise and negotiation. Help a passive child learn to be assertive by trying some of the following suggestions.

- Model words for the child to use in conflict situations, such as "Mine!" "Stop!" or "I'm not done." Very young children or children for whom English is their second language can learn to use simple words such as these.
- Ask the child how he feels when another takes his toy. Ask him if that is okay with him. Help him identify his feelings about the situation.
- Teach him to get an adult if he needs help in a conflict.
- Do a puppet play in which one puppet is playing with a toy. The other puppet walks up and grabs it away. Stop and ask the children if it was okay to grab it. Ask them what the first puppet should say. Act out some of their ideas. Provide the words if they can't think of any.

> ### Signs a Child Needs Support
> Problem solving may be called for in challenging situations in which children experience heightened emotion and anxiety. When a child experiences anxiety, he often needs support. Signs of anxiety are different for each child. Your observations of a child will help you learn his signs. Catch his anxiety in its earliest stage so you can head it off. By responding with support, you can help him avoid aggression and challenging behaviors. Below are some of the signs that a child may be feeling anxious.
>
> - tearing up or crying
> - having a toileting accident
> - clenching teeth
> - getting pale
> - becoming rigid
> - breathing rapidly
> - sweating
> - fidgeting
> - becoming red in the face
> - getting louder
> - withdrawing
> - twirling hair
> - sucking thumb
> - sucking on clothes
> - hoarding toys
> - clinging
> - biting nails
> - whining
> - screaming

Help Children Get Ready to Problem Solve Peacefully

If a child uses force to solve problems, help him learn to stop aggressive behavior by using the following suggestions. At the same time, teach him new behaviors to replace the inappropriate one by using the goals and suggestions throughout this section.

- Teach the child to cross his arms over his chest and to rehearse words that will remind him not to hit. Say, "Don't hit. Do something different." This can be a reminder to help the child self-regulate when an adult isn't present.
- Stop the action in a conflict, and have the children think of ways they can solve the problem. In one family child care setting, the caregiver used this technique very effectively. She had the children who were arguing come and sit by her. She asked each child what he thought the problem was. After they

all had their turn to describe the situation, she asked, "How could you work it out so that everyone is happy?" The caregiver claimed that although it sometimes took a while, the children usually came up with their own solutions. The caregiver attributed the success of this technique to the opportunity it gave the children to calm down as well as to do the problem solving.

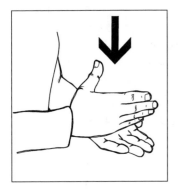

- Use the American Sign Language gesture for stop as you say the word *Stop*. This gives the child a visual cue as well as a verbal direction. To sign stop, extend your fingers on both hands. Extend one hand out horizontally, palm up. Place your other hand so that it faces outward and "chops" down on the palm of the first hand. The little finger of the second hand should rest on the palm of the first.

- Arrange associative play experiences for a time when sociodramatic play fails repeatedly. Set the children down side by side and have them play with similar materials, such as building blocks. This gives both the players and you a break. You can try cooperative play again later, perhaps with more success. Even children with complex play skills occasionally find it difficult to play together.

- Teach ways for the child to control his impulses. Play lots of stop-and-freeze games with the children. In these games, the child can learn to stop in response to auditory cues, such as a whistle, a drum, a bell, or the silence when music stops.

- Teach the child to stop and freeze when you call his name. When he can do this successfully in game-like situations, have him practice stopping when you call his name in the middle of playtime. Practice enough that he can transfer this skill to a conflict situation.

- When you recognize that the child is becoming upset, but before he becomes aggressive, call his name and ask him to freeze. When he does, you have a few seconds to get to him and guide him through the situation.

- Give the child opportunities to be powerful in other ways, like helping to make decisions, helping to set rules, planning an activity or a celebration, providing directions for you to follow, following his lead in play, or even moving furniture.

- Teach the child to relax at various times throughout the day. Then when he is upset, you can help him relax using these techniques. Reaching a more relaxed state before trying to resolve the conflict can help everyone involved respond more calmly. For more ideas, see *The Power of Relaxation* (Thomas 2003).

- Build the child's vocabulary of words about feelings. Include words like *frustrated, angry, scared,* and others.

- Identify the feelings of people pictured in a book or a magazine.

- Play Feelings Lotto, in which children match pictures of faces that exhibit the same feelings.

- Read books and have the child identify how the characters are feeling.
- Ask the child to show you how he looks when he feels angry, happy, or surprised.
- Remember that children from different cultures may express their feelings in different ways. For example, some Asian families do not encourage their children to express their feelings to adults.
- Ask the child to show you how he would feel in different circumstances, such as "Show me how you would feel if you were at a park and couldn't see your mom" and "Show me how you would feel if someone gave you a present."
- Teach the child that there are different levels of intensity in emotion. For example, you can explain that the words *frustrated, angry, upset, really angry,* and *mad* all describe anger. When the child can use many words rather than just one, he has more options for expressing his feelings.

Many caregivers find it challenging to deal with children who use force or aggression. There are many good resource materials available (see appendix B for book titles) to help an aggressive child learn more appropriate skills. Consult these resources and attend classes to learn more about these behaviors and to enhance your skills.

> Teach children to use the steps in problem solving when they experience difficulties:
>
> 1. Identify the problem.
> 2. Gather information.
> 3. Brainstorm solutions.
> 4. Pick the best idea.
> 5. Try it.
> 6. Decide if it's working.
> 7. Revise if needed.

Goal: Child Will Ask Adult for Help

Asking for help when problems arise is a growth step for some children. If a child who has been aggressive in the past is left to solve a problem on his own, he may rely on the aggressive behaviors he already knows. For example, if Jenise wanted a turn on the swing a few months ago, she might have attempted to knock another child off. Now she has learned to ask an adult to help her with turns. By turning to an adult, Jenise gets help in learning more appropriate ways to ask for what she wants.

You may become concerned because you feel that teaching a child to involve an adult fosters tattling. Children tell adults about other's behavior for a variety of reasons:

- They are concerned that a child may cause injury to himself or others.
- They are scared by another child's actions.
- They feel powerless.
- They need help working out a situation.
- They are trying to define the rules.

- They need affirmation and approval for staying within the rules themselves.
- They are trying to get another child in trouble.

The last of these reasons for telling is what is considered by many as tattling. Our experience has been that preschool children rarely tell to get another child in trouble. Determine when a child needs help with a situation, when suggesting that he solve the problem on his own may work, and when to let him know you are watching and that he doesn't need to worry. We believe that children who are just learning to solve conflicts need help from an adult. Later in this section, we discuss ways to teach the child to be more responsible for solving the problem on his own.

Suggestions during Play
- Encourage the child to ask for help when he begins to get frustrated.
- Help de-escalate the emotions before beginning to problem solve.
- Go with the child to the area in which the problem is taking place and help him settle the problem.
- Speak for the children in a conflict situation. You could say to Jonathan, "Michael would like a turn with that." If Jonathan isn't ready to give it up, say, "It doesn't look like Jonathan is done yet." Say to Michael, "Let's watch to see when Jonathan leaves the dump truck, and then it can be your turn. In the meantime, here is a car you can play with." Talk for the child who is learning English if he is not being understood by others or if his vocabulary is too limited to support his efforts.
- Ask "What" questions to help children resolve the problem. What is the problem? What could you do to work it out so you are both happy? What's another idea? What will work best?

Suggestions during Adult-Led Activities
- Make sure the children understand that asking for help is acceptable in many situations. You can do this by acknowledging that we all need help with certain things. Point out that you ask for help in getting the room cleaned up, Tineja asks for help when cutting things that have lots of corners, and Jeremy likes help carrying the snack tray.
- Use dolls or puppets to act out various solutions to common upsets so English-language learners have a chance to see the solutions as well as hear about them. The strategies you use to teach problem solving to English-language learners benefit all learners. For example, pretend two children want the same toy truck at the same time. Have the puppets argue over it while they pull the truck back and forth. Stop the puppet play and ask the children, "What can the puppets do to solve their problem?" Act out a few of their ideas.

- Draw simple pictures of things children can do when they have a problem. They can walk away, share, take turns, ignore, or tell a grown up. Post the pictures so children, including those who are learning to use English and may need pictures to support their words, can go to the pictures and show other children their idea for solving the problem (Hewitt and Heidemann 1998).

Learning to use words is the primary skill a child needs in order to solve his conflicts appropriately. There appears to be a sequence in the way in which an adult helps a child learn to use words. Adults need to scaffold the level of support for the child; depending on the child's ability, the adult needs to accompany the child and provide words before gradually shifting the responsibility to the child for solving the problem on his own. The chart below helps to visualize what the adult does, the child's likely response, and the adult's reaction.

Adult	Child	Adult
Provides words or a strategy	No response	Provides words or a strategy during the next conflict
Provides words or a strategy	Imitates	Acknowledges the child's attempt
Prompts the child to use words or try a strategy	Recalls words or a strategy used in the past	Recognizes the child's efforts
	Initiates the use of words or a strategy without adult prompt	Acknowledges the child's use of words and problem-solving strategy every time at first, then on occasion

Goal: Child Will Imitate Verbal Solutions or Strategies Provided by the Adult

A child may not know all of the phrases he can use in trying to resolve a conflict or ask for a toy. He needs many opportunities to hear words that may help him get what he wants without resorting to force. With this goal, you are encouraging the child to use words or strategies that you give him. Provide varied learning opportunities during teachable moments and during adult-led activities, such as role plays, puppet plays, and using real props to tell stories about successful problem solving.

Suggestions during Play
- Model the words for the child to use frequently. Tell him to say, "That's mine," "I want that back," or "I've been waiting for a turn for a long time." Eventually the child begins to imitate the words that have been provided. Be sure to recognize the child's efforts each time he repeats the words you have given him.
- Provide the child occasionally with a play partner who is more skilled and can act as a mentor or who can model problem-solving strategies.
- Remember that if you remove the toy or materials whenever there is a conflict, you remove the child's opportunity to learn more effective problem-solving skills. (You may need to put things away for a short time for your own sake.)

Suggestions during Adult-Led Activities
- Teach the child to imitate by playing echo games. Learning to imitate in game-like situations helps him learn to imitate the words to use in solving problems. Clap a simple rhythm for the children to repeat. Play the game with many different rhythms and different leaders. You can also have the children play this game with simple phrases like "your nose is blue." Or use a chant to teach children to echo. Gather plastic farm animals and say, "We went for a walk, and this is what we saw. We saw a cow, and the cow said, 'Mooo.'" Ask the children to repeat the animal sounds as you repeat the chant, using different animals.
- Model problem solving by talking out loud when you have a problem. Say, "I have a problem. I can't reach the paper we need for art. I could stand on a chair. No, that's not safe. I could stand on my tiptoes. No, I still can't reach it. I could get a step stool. I think that's the best idea. I'll try it."

Goal: Child Will Recall Words or Strategies to Use When Reminded

At this stage, the child should be ready to say the words he has been taught when you remind him. You can say, "What could you say? Go try your idea. Come back if it doesn't work and I'll help."

We often expect children to come up with effective words on their own before they have heard appropriate words modeled often enough by adults. If a child is given the responsibility to use words before he is ready, the words he comes up with may be inappropriate. When Benjamin was told to use words, he went back to the other child and said, "Get off my Big Wheel bike, or I'll push you off."

Suggestions during Play
- Prompt the child who has a problem with other children in play by asking him, "What could you say to him?" The child should go back to the situation and use words he recalls having been taught in the past.
- Make sure that the child's words work. This does not mean that he should always get his way but that the other children should listen to him and respond. If Keisha had a toy first and she says to Sara, "Give it back; I had it first," it is important that Sara respond to the words Keisha uses either by giving the toy back or by saying, "But you left it."

Suggestions during Adult-Led Activities
- Make a large poster of a stoplight and post it in your room. Teach the children that in your classroom, red means stop. Yellow means think about what you can do. Green means try your best idea. You can make your stoplight on a whiteboard and add a space for children to place a check mark next to the steps as they complete them. When the child experiences a conflict, he goes to the whiteboard and makes a check mark as he works through the steps. Make and carry a pocket-sized stoplight to use as a visual reminder during children's conflicts.
- Teach problem solving in all sorts of situations, not just in conflict situations. You can problem solve how to get a box open while wearing mittens, how to decide which movie to watch on a special movie day, or how to go through an obstacle course in a new way.

Goal: Child Will Initiate Use of Words or Strategies

Eventually, all of your teaching of appropriate words and strategies pays off. You overhear a child using words on his own! Now he no longer needs to be told the exact words to use or reminders to use words. Be sure that you notice this growth and his abilities to solve problems and comment on them periodically. Help the child cope if he uses words but the problem is not immediately solved to his satisfaction.

Suggestions during Play
- Recognize the child's appropriate behavior and comment to him about his growth in this area. You can whisper to Emma, "I heard you use your words to ask Ty for a turn. That used to be hard for you. You are learning to use words when you want a turn. Good for you."
- Help the child learn to wait for a turn or to cope with disappointment when he uses words to ask for a turn and the answer is "NO!" Redirect him to another activity while he is waiting (Katz 1984).

Suggestion during Adult-Led Activities
- Enact a puppet play in which you and the puppet have trouble. Maybe you have trouble deciding what to play or whose turn it is with a toy. Ask the children to think of things they can do when they have trouble. Make a list of their ideas. Strategies may include ideas like walk away, get help, ignore, or make a trade. If you can, find or draw pictures to show the children's ideas, or use the pictures in *The Optimistic Classroom* (Hewitt and Heidemann 1998).

Goal: Child Will Accept Reasonable Compromises

This child has learned to regulate his own emotions and behaviors so he can make suggestions for problem solving. Now he must listen to others and agree to their solutions at times.

Suggestions during Play
- Ask the children to think of a number of solutions as conflicts arise in play. Do not evaluate the solutions at this time. When a list of solutions has been developed, decide which idea would work the best. Have the children try it.
- Make sure that children listen to the suggestions of others when they try problem solving on their own.
- Guide a problem-solving discussion when you see that play is falling apart or the children need help settling on a play scene. Ask them what they will play, who will do what, and what props they will need. Ask clarifying questions to get them started, such as "What will you do first?"

Suggestion during Adult-Led Activities
- Tell a story about Helene and Simone. Helene tries to take the toy Simone is using. Helene hits Simone when she doesn't give it to her. Soon Helene and Simone are both crying. Ask the children how Helene might have solved the problem without hitting. Have them dictate their own ending to the story. They may also enjoy illustrating it.

> SHAWN, A FOUR-YEAR-OLD, puffed out his chest, clenched his fist, and yelled in order to scare younger children into giving him a turn riding the tricycle. Unfortunately, Shawn's intimidation strategies worked and he was almost always successful at getting what he wanted.
>
> The adults working with this group of children decided there were three parts to solving this problem. First, they agreed to teach the younger children to say no to Shawn when he demanded a toy that they were using. Second, they would help Shawn learn to use words when he wanted a turn. Finally, they would teach Shawn to find other things to do when he needed to wait for a turn.

Turn Taking

If there were a toy of each kind for every child, turn taking would not be a skill children need. However, this is not the case and children must learn to share materials to play successfully together. Successful turn taking requires that children learn to give up toys when they have finished with them, participate in give-and-take situations, and learn to propose turn taking. Successful turn taking is essential to sharing props in sociodramatic play.

Getting Ready to Take Turns

When a child is not able to take turns, set the stage for him to learn about turn taking and giving to others by practicing these skills in everyday situations.

- Set a good example by sharing with others. You might say, "We have lots of scarves to wave while we dance. We can share them. Let's find out who wants one," or "It's not my turn for a drink yet. I'll have to wait for my turn until Sadie is done."
- Don't demand that children share. Doing so can cause additional stress for those children who may not be sharing because they already feel anxious. Instead, place positive expectations for the future: "I'm sure you will share it after you have had a chance to play with it for a while."
- Recognize times throughout the day when children must wait for turns—for example, when it's time to use the bathroom or the drinking fountain. Comment on how well they are doing while waiting for a turn. Waiting in routine situations like these may be easier for some children than waiting for a toy. When they hear that they can be good at waiting for these turns, they may also be encouraged to wait for turns in other types of situations.
- Give children concrete information about when it will be their turn. For instance, when a child is waiting for a turn on the slide, say, "Your turn is after Shiann. When Shiann is down the slide and out of the way, it will be your turn."
- Practice giving to others by making simple pictures, collages, or notes at the writing center for children to exchange among your group. One preschool periodically asks each child to bring in a gently used book from home to give in a book exchange.

Goal: Child Will Leave a Toy and Not Demand to Have It Back

Use this goal to help a child who leaves a toy but protests if someone else picks it up.

Suggestions during Play

- Make sure children have enough time with an object to feel as if they are done before someone asks them to give it up. Children are more likely to give up something they have had adequate time to explore and play with or something they have lost interest in than an object they just received and with which they are still actively engaged (Beaty 1986).

- Let a child feel in control when he passes on a toy. If you are unable to allow him to finish with it on his own, ask, "Are you going to give it to Tenisha in two minutes or in five minutes?"

- When a child is getting ready to leave a toy, remind him that if he leaves it, other children will think he is done. Check to make sure that the child is really done. Say, "Are you all done with Mr. Potato Head? Then is it okay for Jessie to use it next?" Reinforce this idea at other times of the day too. For example, if the child leaves the snack table, it means that he is done with snack. A problem can come up if a child won't risk leaving a toy long enough to use the bathroom. To avoid this, you may need to make it clear that you will hold or protect a toy for him.

- Offer to save a child's block building by making a picture of it, having the child draw it, or taking a photograph of it. This way, he can leave the blocks and take his building with him.

Suggestions during Adult-Led Activities

- Practice taking turns with the child. It may be easier for him to learn to take turns with an adult at first. Play a game that has a back-and-forth rhythm. Try bouncing or rolling a ball or a car back and forth to each other. As you pass it back and forth, emphasize, "Your turn, my turn. Your turn, my turn." Return the toy right away, so the child knows he will get it back if he really wants it.

- Don't expect children to share all materials. Identify those objects that belong to the child, such as his special blanket or cuddly toy. Identify those things that belong to other individuals. You may have a water glass or apron that belongs only to you. Be sure that children have special places to put those things that do not need to be shared. Then, if a child is not willing to share his private toy, he can put it in this spot. This suggestion is meant for those children who truly need private spaces and materials. Keep in mind that some cultures encourage children to share everything; this value should be respected.

- Work with the child to take an inventory of all the toys in your setting. Decide which objects belong to the group. Refer to these objects as the group's toys or the school's toys. You can say, "Let's take good care of the school's toys and get them all put away."

Goal: Child Will Take Turns that Are Arranged by an Adult

A child at this level can take turns if an adult structures turn taking for him.

Suggestions during Play

- Help divide up materials so that each child has some. Have the children practice dividing things too. Practice giving one to everyone in the circle.
- Draw the attention of children playing together to the arrival of a new child. Say, "Jamie wants to play, but she doesn't have any playdough. Let's each give her a little of ours so she has some." Some children may give only a pinch of dough, while others give a little bigger chunk. Accept and thank each child for whatever portion he is willing to share.
- Coach the child through turn taking. If needed, provide words for him to ask for a turn. Make sure that he gets a response, even if the answer is "Not right now." Help the child find out when it will be his turn. He can ask, "When will you be done?" or "Will you give it to me when you are done?" Be sure to watch so that the child playing with the toy doesn't forget who is next.
- Some caregivers use a timer to structure the time each child has with popular pieces of equipment. Other providers object to this practice because it forces a child to give up an item even if he isn't done. We have found that many children begin to think about finishing their turn when given a warning that their time will be over soon. Then when the timer does go off, they are ready to give another child a turn.
- Teach the children a few turn-taking strategies. For example, teach the children to flip a quarter or draw the long straw to determine who will have the first turn. Place the quarter and the straws on a shelf where the children can reach them.
- When you must limit the number of children who can play in an area, make badges for them to wear. A child must have a badge on if he is going to play. If all of the badges are in use, other children can check back later to see if it is their turn. To help children know what area the badge is for, use a symbol that goes with the play theme (like a picture of an ice-cream cone for the ice cream parlor theme center). Be sure some areas are open to all children.
- Have the children sign up to play in a popular area like the listening center. They can do something else until their name is next on the list. When one child is done, he tells the next on the list that it is his turn.
- Place a chair in an area that has a limit on the number of children who can play there. Tell the children that this is the waiting chair. A child who wants to be next can sit in the waiting chair. If the wait gets too long, the child can say, "I've been waiting a long time." This sometimes prompts someone to play elsewhere so the child who is waiting can have a turn.

Suggestions during Adult-Led Activities
- Demonstrate ways to share toys. Do a role play in which one child has a car and another one wants to play with it. Ask the children what they can do. If someone suggests that they share or take turns, ask what that would look like. Act out their suggestions.
- Play turn-taking board and circle games. Let the child know how much longer he must wait by saying, "Sam is next, then Jake. Your turn will be right after Jake's."

Goal: Child Will Ask for a Turn and Wait for a Response

To accomplish this goal, a child needs to use words to ask for a turn and pause before expecting the turn or the item.

Suggestions during Play
- Check the rhythm of the children's turn taking. Remember that there must be a pause between asking for a toy and taking it. The pause allows the other child the opportunity to respond.
- Remind the child asking for a turn to wait for the other child to give the toy to him. One time Jamilla was leaning her doll on a stack of towels as she dressed it. Kelly came by and asked to use a towel and at the same time tried to take one off the pile. It happened so fast that Jamilla and her doll were nearly knocked over. The adult tried to steady Jamilla and said, "Give her a chance, Kelly. I'm sure she'll give you a towel."

Suggestions during Adult-Led Activities
- Check the child's ability to wait in other situations, like at snacktime. Make sure you consistently respond to his needs. This teaches him that you are trustworthy, even if he has to wait briefly for a reply.
- Teach patience, how to wait, and how to be calm so the child can tolerate the pause in having his needs met (Croft and Hewitt 2004).

Goal: Child Gives Up a Toy Easily If Done with It

A child who is capable of this gives the toy to another child when he is no longer using it.

Suggestions during Play
- Teach the child to say more than no. Help him explain why the other child must wait a bit longer. The child can say, "No, I only have one, and I'm using it right now" (Greene 1998).
- Children need many experiences in which they lend something and it comes back so they learn that others are trustworthy. Some children may need to

start lending a toy to others just to be looked at. Then the borrower needs to give it right back.

- Teach the child to say, "I'll give it to you when I am done." Then help the child who is waiting for a turn watch to see when the child using it sets the toy down. Remind the child using it to give the toy to the next child when he is done.

Suggestion during Adult-Led Activities
- Play a What-If game. Make up little stories like "What if Blake is on the swing. Jason is waiting, and Blake gets off. Whose turn is it?"

Goal: Child Willingly Gives Up a Toy If Another Child Asks for It

This goal differs from the one above because in this one, the child is still using a toy when another child approaches him and asks for a turn. Many times a child says, "Sure. I'm done anyway."

Suggestion during Play
- Propose trades. Have the child who wants the toy think about something that the other child may want and suggest a trade.

Suggestions during Adult-Led Activities
- Introduce the concept of trading by using puppets. Give each child in the group a toy to hold. Have the puppet play with a toy for a short time, then start looking at one of the toys being held by a child. Have the puppet ask to trade his toy for the one he is looking at (Committee for Children 1991).
- Have the children role-play making trades. Collect a number of popular toys. Have one child play with a toy. Ask another child to choose a different toy from the collection that he thinks the first child will like. Help him make a trade.
- Make a list of all the children. Next to each name, draw a simple picture of a toy the child likes. A child who is trying to make a trade can refer to the list to find a toy that will be attractive.

Goal: Child Suggests a Sequence of Turns

When a child initiates a sequence of turns with a toy or material, a back-and-forth rhythm of play or an agreement, such as "first me, then you," may follow.

Suggestions during Play

- Teach a child to use words to ask for a turn as described in the Problem Solving section of this chapter.
- Reinforce the child who is proposing turn taking. Point out his growth in this area. Natalie's ability to arrange turns was recognized when her teacher said, "I'm glad you think about ways that you and Claire both get a turn to use the steering wheel. You are really learning to take turns."

Suggestions during Adult-Led Activities

- Have pairs of children do a fingerpainting together. Ask them how they will share their painting. Some may suggest cutting it in half; others may suggest taking turns bringing it home.
- Read Pat Hutchins's *The Doorbell Rang.* In this story, two children start with a plate full of cookies. Each time the doorbell rings, more children come and they must divide their cookies further. Stop reading just before the last time the doorbell rings and Grandma comes with cookies. Ask the children what happens each time the doorbell rings and what the children do. Ask them to predict what will happen next. Use playdough or construction paper cookies to act out the story. Have cookies for snack.

MOLLIE HAD BEEN SETTING the table with the toy dishes. A few minutes later, she left to dress her doll. LaToya entered the housekeeping area and began to collect the dishes. All of a sudden, Mollie came running from across the room. She took the dishes out of LaToya's hands and said, "You can't have these. I'm playing with them." Mollie had not used the dishes for some time. But from her outburst, it was apparent that she was not done with them. LaToya had no way of knowing this and was quite surprised when Mollie appeared.

To help Mollie learn that when she left a toy others would think she was done, Mollie's caregiver started watching more carefully to see when Mollie left a toy. She checked with Mollie to see if she really was done. She reminded Mollie that if she played somewhere else, she couldn't expect things to stay exactly where she left them. Sometimes with this type of reminder, Mollie decided to stay and play with the toys a while longer. Other times, Mollie didn't seem to mind. Mollie's caregiver also reminded all of the children at snacktime that when they left the table, that meant that they were finished. Soon, Mollie learned she couldn't control materials she was not using.

Support of Peers

The relationships that children build with one another in early childhood settings can be very positive. Children who are in full-time child care can develop friendships that sometimes resemble or improve upon the relationships of siblings. In all types of early childhood settings, children's friendships provide companionship, support for emotional growth, and a context in which they learn how to join groups and problem solve (Asher and Williams 1993). To be successful in developing and maintaining relationships with others, children must learn to be supportive of their peers.

The goals in this section represent a group of skills that are essential for developing positive, accepting friendships. Attending to others, offering comfort or help when someone is distressed, sharing power and leadership in play, and showing approval are ways in which children demonstrate friendship skills (Kostelnik, Stein, Whiren, and Soderman 1998). Without these skills, a child may not be allowed to be a member of the group during sociodramatic play.

Getting Ready to Support Peers

In order for children to support one another, they must be aware of the feelings of others. Children sometimes miss the subtle clues that can help them know how another person feels. This is especially true for children with PDD/Autism Spectrum Disorder (see chapter 4). These children need adults to help make their own clues explicit and to learn to accurately identify another person's feelings. Once they know how another person is feeling, they can begin to learn how to respond.

- Help children learn to read the body language and facial expressions of others. Call attention to the eyes, eyebrows, mouth, forehead, etc. You can say, "See how his eyes are down and the corners of his mouth are down. He may be sad. Let's ask him."
- Ask the child to look at the faces of the people in the books you read. Ask the child what he thinks each person may be feeling. How can he tell?
- Be sure the child knows feeling words. Teach a variety of words to describe a variety of emotions.
- Play a guessing game. Act out some common situations and ask the child to guess "How am I feeling?" For example, try twirling in a circle, bumping

into a chair, or pretending to tie your shoe and not being able to do it. After each action, ask the children to guess how you are feeling (Hewitt and Heidemann 1998).

- Find pictures from magazines that show people expressing various emotions. Ask the child to act out some of the feelings the people in the pictures are showing. Talk about what is taking place, how the person is feeling, and what might happen next.
- Match and sort pictures of people showing similar facial expressions. Have the child guess what the feeling is. Ask how he can tell.
- Include books about feelings in your book area. Talk with children about the feelings that are depicted and why people feel those emotions at times.

Goal: Child Will Watch Peers

Some children do not look at or show interest in others in the group. Consequently, they don't notice facial expressions and body posture that give clues about how others are feeling. Help these children learn to tune in to the sights and sounds around them that suggest someone is sad, angry, or happy.

Suggestions during Play

- Draw the child's attention to sounds that express emotion. You can say, "I hear someone laughing. How do you think he is feeling?"
- Set up a mirror so you and the child can look in it. Make a facial expression and ask the child to imitate it, or ask the child to guess how you are feeling.

Suggestions during Adult-Led Activities

- Label other people's feelings as you notice them. If you are out on a walk and you notice people laughing or singing, talk about what they may be feeling and what clues lead you to believe they are happy.
- Play sound identification games to draw attention to auditory cues, especially those that indicate someone needs help. Record common sounds, like running water, a siren, a baby crying, or someone laughing. Play the recording and have the children guess what the sounds are.

Goal: Child Will Show Empathy or Offer Help

Part of supporting others is recognizing when someone is sad, frustrated, or can't manage on his own and then responding with care, concern, or an offer of help. This type of empathic response can be challenging for children who are at an egocentric stage of development. Help children learn this important skill with the following suggestions.

Suggestions during Play

- When a child watches another child who is crying, suggest that he take the crying child a toy or a tissue. He may be able to sympathize with the child who is crying but be unaware of how to help. One day, Vincent watched intently as Grace cried. As he watched, his bottom lip began to quiver. The caregiver suggested that Vincent take Grace a doll she enjoyed holding. Vincent's sympathetic crying suggests that he was beginning to understand how others feel.

- Encourage children to seek help from one another. For example, if a child asks you to find a game on the computer, you can say, "Tyler is good at finding games. See if he will help you. If he's too busy, come back and I will help."

- Model empathy and genuine caring for others. Use body language, tone of voice, choice of words, and behaviors that demonstrate your positive regard for others.

Suggestions during Adult-Led Activities

- Talk about a time when someone was sick or hurt. Ask the children to brainstorm a list of things they could have done to help. Make a picture list of all of the things the children suggest, like get the sick child a drink of water, get him something to eat, take a tissue to him, or get him a book to read.

- Teach children that sounds give clues to what is happening around them. Ask them what they can do to help when they hear a baby crying, their mom calling for their dog, or the teacher calling Joe's name and Joe doesn't hear him.

- Find magazine pictures of people who look sad. Help the children look to see if there are clues in the picture that explain why the person is sad. Ask the children to think of ways to make the sad person feel better—for example, bring him a toy, fix something that is broken, or clean up a mess.

- Play a What-If game. Ask the children what they could do to help if someone
  - spilled
  - fell down
  - couldn't get their jacket on
  - couldn't find their backpack

- Act out "Jack and Jill." Stop when Jack gets hurt. Ask the children what they could do to help him (Hewitt and Heidemann 1998).

- Hide a toy dog somewhere in the room. Sing the song "Where Has My Little Dog Gone?" and pretend to look for it. Ask the children how you are feeling. Ask them how they could help you. Then have them help find the dog.

- Set up dramatic play areas that encourage the children to act out caring for others. You could set up a veterinarian's office and use toy stuffed animals as the animals that visit the veterinarian. Ask a veterinarian to talk with your group to provide context for play.

- Take photographs of children as they help one another. Post them in your room. Talk about them to highlight how important helping one another is (Quann and Wien 2006).

> NIRAN HAD JUST RETURNED from a family trip to Thailand. In one corner of the room, the teacher had set out a big piece of butcher paper, markers, crayons, books about Thailand, plastic toy animals, and a variety of plastic foods. A group of children spontaneously formed around the butcher paper and the teacher said, "Let's draw what you see if you go to Thailand." Niran didn't speak much English, so the teacher said, "Niran, when you were in Thailand, did you eat an orange?" Niran said, "No, banana." The teacher said, "Who can draw a banana?" Darren grabbed a yellow marker and started right in. The teacher asked, "When you were in Thailand, did you see any dogs?" Niran said, "No, elephant." Isabel thought she could draw an elephant, but when she got frustrated, she ran for a plastic elephant from the block area and decided to draw the trees and the grass instead and placed the toy in the middle of it. The teacher asked Niran, "Did you see any cars or trucks?" Niran said, "Big trucks."
>
> With Niran's help, the children created a wonderful mural. They labeled it "What you see in Thailand" and posted it in the hallway for all to enjoy. It may not have been an accurate depiction in every sense, but for the couple of days the activity held the interest of the children, Niran was an expert.

Goal: Child Offers Suggestions to Ensure the Continuation of Play

This goal and the next one refer to turn taking with ideas and leadership rather than materials. Use this goal if a child does not offer suggestions. If he is not offering play ideas, he may be allowed to play and may even be sought out as a playmate. But by remaining passive, he may never learn what his creative potential can be.

Suggestions during Play
- Praise all the children for having good ideas. Emphasize that many children in the group have good ideas. Elicit lots of different thoughts about the ways that play can go. Ask the children, "Whose idea should we play first?"
- After play has been directed by one child for some time or if the play gets stuck and a new idea is needed, talk with him about expanding his play idea. If he is reluctant to offer a suggestion, ask questions that allow him to

choose, like "Do you think we should take the babies shopping or to the ice cream store?"

- Comment whenever this child takes turns with ideas.
- If this is a problem between two children, work with them at the beginning of playtime to develop a list of ideas. Try first one and then the other.
- Help children agree to "first your idea and then mine."
- Help children find ways to weave their ideas together so they can both play their ideas.

Suggestions during Adult-Led Activities

- Encourage the children to build on one another's story lines by drawing group pictures and telling group stories. To make a group picture, one child starts the picture by drawing a part and then passes the picture on to another child, who adds another part.
- Do a puppet play that shows two puppets trying to decide what to do together. One puppet suggests, "Let's say we're swimming in the ocean and the sharks are after us." The other puppet can say, "No, no. Let's pretend we're going to find the pirate's treasure." The first puppet says, "I don't want to play that." Stop the play and ask the children how they can take turns so both puppets get a chance to play their idea.

Goal: Child Accepts Play Suggestions from Others

This goal is similar to the one above. Both refer to sharing play ideas, but this one is about accepting *someone else's* play ideas. If the child does not learn to let others play their ideas on occasion, he may be considered bossy or controlling. In many cases, this leads to a clash among players. A child who cannot accept the suggestions of others may begin to be excluded.

Suggestions during Play

- Praise all the children for having good ideas. Emphasize that many children in the group have good ideas. Elicit lots of different thoughts about the ways that play can go. Ask the children, "Whose idea should we play first?"
- After he has been directing the play for a while, talk with the child about trying someone else's idea.

- Talk with the child confidentially about how his unwillingness to play other people's ideas may discourage them from playing with him. Tell him, "Your friends may not want to play if they don't get a chance to play their ideas." Emphasize what he can do differently so the others will play with him. Say, "But if you try Kia's idea about the spaceship, she may play with you a while longer."
- Emphasize the importance of all the roles assigned to children in a play scenario. Make less prominent roles more exciting by adding costumes or giving actors a special task. For instance, the role of the family dog can be enhanced by adding ears on a headband or suggesting that the player get the slippers and perform tricks.
- Praise this child when he takes turns with ideas.
- If taking turns with ideas is a problem between two children, work with them to develop a list of ideas at the beginning of playtime. Try first one and then the other.
- Help children agree to "first your idea and then mine."
- Help children find ways to weave their ideas together so they can all play their ideas.

Suggestions during Adult-Led Activities
- Encourage the children to build on one another's story lines by drawing group pictures and telling group stories. To make a group picture, one child starts the picture by drawing one part, then passes the picture on to another child, who adds another part.
- Do a puppet play that shows two puppets trying to decide what to do together. One puppet suggests, "Let's pretend we're walking on a tight rope." The other puppet says, "No, no. Let's say we are riding our horses, and we'll use the rope to tie our horses when we stop." Stop the play and ask the children how they can take turns so that they both get a chance to play their idea.

Goal: Child Will Encourage and Praise Others during Play

Children who do well socially are able to praise their peers. They say things like "That's a nice tower," "Good job," and "You're a fast runner" (Kostelnik, Stein, Whiren, and Soderman 1998). Help children learn to notice and say things that are supportive of others.

Suggestions during Play
- Recognize the child's efforts often. Comment on things he does well and things that he has learned. Offer him, in other words, a model of how to praise others.
- Encourage the child to say positive things about himself. Start by saying, "I really like the way you built your tower so high. What do you like about it?"

It is important for a child to feel good about himself before expecting him to be able to feel good about others and support them.

- Ask the child to tell another child when he notices something special. Sometimes when a child notices something nice about his friend, he tells an adult about it. Selma may say, "Did you see Mehdi's pretty picture?" Help Selma praise Mehdi directly by encouraging her to tell Mehdi she likes his picture.
- Turn negative conversations about another child into positive ones. If a child comments about Marcus's scribbling, help the child think of all of the things Marcus does really well. For instance, Marcus may be using a nice combination of colors, staying on the paper with his crayons, or working hard at getting the whole figure covered up with color. By turning the conversation around, you set the tone for a more positive discussion and demonstrate to the child that you will not talk negatively about a child's abilities.
- Coach the child to say something friendly when a peer does well. Help him learn to describe what he has seen by saying something like "I saw you climbing really high."

Suggestions during Adult-Led Activities
- Do a puppet play that models how to say something friendly. Have one puppet play with a toy while the second puppet says something friendly about it. Then ask the children, "What did he say that was friendly?" For example, the first puppet may be making a pattern out of red and blue counters. The second puppet can say, "I like the way you lined them up" (Hewitt and Heidemann 1998).
- Ask two children to role-play saying friendly things. One child plays with toys while the other practices saying something friendly. Prompt the second child by encouraging him to start his sentence with "I like . . ." or "I like the way you . . ." The child can say something like, "I like the way you stacked the blocks" (Hewitt and Heidemann 1998).
- Schedule a time each day when children compliment each other. One caregiver scheduled this as part of her lunchtime conversation. Each child at the table offered at least one compliment about the child sitting next to him. At first the comments were about the "pretty blue dress" or the "cool superhero" on a shirt. After some practice, the children were able to talk about things they saw another child do that morning. One child said, "I really liked the garage you were building today. I wish I could have played with you."
- Do a puppet play to teach children words they can use to encourage someone. Have the puppet stack blocks that keep falling down. Have the puppet say things that indicate she is getting discouraged, like "Oh, no! They're falling down again." Stop the puppet play and ask the children what they can say to the puppet so she will try again. Have the puppet try again and ask the children to say the encouraging words (Hewitt and Heidemann 1998).

AIDAN HIT LEXI. BOTH Aidan and Lexi were upset about the situation and started crying. Aidan was asked to sit down for a short time while the caregiver focused on comforting Lexi. Soon Lexi felt better but was concerned because Aidan was still crying. She asked the caregiver, "Is he just going to keep on crying all day?" The caregiver asked Lexi what she could do to help Aidan feel better. Lexi thought that Aidan might stop crying if he had his blanket. Lexi offered the blanket to Aidan and he took it gratefully. When things calmed down, the caregiver talked with the children about how they could resolve the situation that had caused them both to become so upset.

We've presented many teaching strategies here. Although we've described the activities in separate sections, there is a great deal of crossover; one strategy or a variation of it can fit many skills. Choosing an activity or making up one of your own can help children practice a desired skill. Doing this is one part of the planning process, which should also include the following:

- Design lessons that will appeal to the child and you.
- Create a variety of activities.
- Offer activities a number of times.
- Observe the child's performance during the activity.
- Gather data and observe to determine if the goal has been reached.
- If the goal has not been reached, plan and offer additional activities.
- If the goal has been reached, plan a new goal and start the process again.

This process helps a child learn play skills that will enrich and expand his play experience.

In the next chapter, we provide case studies that demonstrate how these techniques and strategies have been implemented in early childhood settings. You will see real situations in which the process and suggestions have made an impact.

Reflection Questions

1. Describe an activity you have used to teach one of the goals in this chapter.

2. Describe a child you thought of as you read this chapter.

3. What entrance strategy do you use at social gatherings? What have you seen children try?

4. Which of these skills do you find most challenging to teach? What can you do to improve your skills?

Case Studies: Putting It All Together

CHAPTER NINE

JESSICA LOOKS OVER AT the new dramatic play area, Dinosaur Land. Travis is pushing Letisha while he grabs a dinosaur out of her hands. Jessica hurries over to stop the fight. She is frustrated because, once again, Travis is in the middle of a conflict. At a planning meeting later that day, she talks with coworkers and they decide to complete a Play Checklist to develop a plan for Travis.

Jessica and her team recognize the play challenges Travis is experiencing. They know they can help him learn to problem solve through some careful planning. They begin the process of observing, evaluating his play skills, writing a goal, and implementing play activities.

In this chapter, we see what it looks like when we put it all together. We look more closely at how teachers used the continuous cycle of improvement to help two children, Asheley and Lori, become more successful in sociodramatic play. It is time to see how each step put into practice helps a child make progress on her play skills. In this chapter, we discuss the following topics:

Asheley: A case study
Lori: A case study
The value of reflection
The continuous cycle of improvement

Asheley: A Case Study

Observations

We first described some of Asheley's skills and behaviors in chapter 6. As you recall, Asheley was a four-year-old who was having trouble engaging in pretend play. The teacher observed Asheley during free play, as she prepared to complete the Play Checklist. During these observations, Asheley tended to play with the same materials each day, spending a great deal of time at the water or sand table. She did not speak to others very often, and when she did, they had difficulty understanding her. Her teachers often repeated her words to other children, especially when the children had a problem sharing toys. If Asheley used materials to pretend, she did one thing with them. For example, she would pat the baby on the back or rock it but then move on to another activity. These observations were used to complete the Play Checklist that follows.

Evaluating Play Skills

When her teacher evaluated her current level of performance, she found that Asheley was not using language to communicate during play, her role-playing skills were not well developed, and she rarely interacted with the other children. Her teacher wanted to help Asheley learn to play with others but was unsure where to begin.

It was obvious that Asheley's language skills needed further assessment by someone skilled in this area. Her teacher talked with Asheley's parents and suggested that they have her language skills assessed by a language specialist. Her parents were becoming concerned about her speech as she got older because although they could understand her, other people were having difficulty. Now that the teacher also expressed concern, they planned to set an appointment with a specialist.

In this initial evaluation of Asheley's play skills, her teacher decided to focus on role-playing. She felt that Asheley's poor pretend skills might be part of the reason Asheley did not comfortably join the play of others. The second area to be prioritized was interactions.

Play Checklist

Child's Name: __Asheley_____   Date: __September 20__

Date of Birth: __March 21 (four years and six months old)__

Check the highest level skills you consistently observe:

*1. Pretending with Objects
- ❏ Does not use objects to pretend
- ☒ Uses real objects
- ❏ Substitutes objects for other objects
- ❏ Uses imaginary objects

*2. Role-Playing
- ❏ No role play
- ☒ Uses one sequence of play
- ❏ Combines sequences
- ❏ Uses verbal declaration (for example, "I'm a doctor")
- ❏ Imitates actions of role, including dress

*3. Verbalizations about the Play Scenario
- ☒ Does not use pretend words during play
- ❏ Uses words to describe substitute objects
- ❏ Uses words to describe imaginary objects and actions (for example, "I'm painting a house")
- ❏ Uses words to create a play scenario (for example, "Let's say we're being taken by a monster")

*4. Verbal Communication during a Play Episode
- ☒ Does not verbally communicate during play
- ❏ Talks during play only to self
- ❏ Talks only to adults in play
- ❏ Talks with peers in play by stepping outside of role (for example, "That's not how mothers hold their babies")
- ❏ Talks with peers from within role (for example, "Eat your dinner before your dad comes home")

*5. Persistence in Play
- ☒ Less than five minutes
- ❏ Six to nine minutes
- ❏ Ten minutes or longer

*6. Interactions
☒ Plays alone
❑ Plays only with adults
❑ Plays with one child, always the same person
❑ Plays with one child, can be different partners
❑ Can play with two or three children together

**7. Entrance into a Play Group
☒ Does not attempt to enter play group
❑ Uses force to enter play group
❑ Stands near group and watches
❑ Imitates behavior of group
❑ Makes comments related to play theme
❑ Gets attention of another child before commenting

8. Problem Solving
❑ Gives in during conflict
❑ Uses force to solve problems
☒ Seeks adult assistance
❑ Imitates verbal solutions or strategies provided by adults
❑ Recalls words or strategies to use when reminded
❑ Initiates use of words or strategies
❑ Accepts reasonable compromises

9. Turn Taking
❑ Refuses to take turns
❑ Leaves toys, then protests when others pick them up
❑ Takes turns if arranged and directed by an adult
❑ Asks for turn, does not wait for a response
☒ Gives up toy easily if done with it
❑ Gives up toy if another child asks for it
❑ Proposes turn taking, will take and give turns

10. Support of Peers
❑ Shows no interest in peers
❑ Directs attention to distress of peers
☒ Shows empathy or offers help
❑ Offers and takes suggestions of peers at times
❑ Encourages or praises peers

Note: The developmental progression outlined in each segment of the Play Checklist can be used as a guideline when assessing most children's development. However, not all children will go through the same steps in development nor through the same developmental sequence.
*Smilansky, Sara. 1968. *The effects of sociodramatic play on disadvantaged preschool children.* New York: Wiley.
** Hazen, Nancy, Betty Black and Faye Fleming-Johnson. 1984. Social acceptance: Strategies children use and how teachers can help children learn them. *Young Children.* 39: 26–36.

Play by Sandra Heidemann and Deborah Hewitt, copyright © 2010. Redleaf Press grants permission to photocopy this page for classroom use.

Goals
Two SMART goals were developed for Asheley.

Goal Number 1

Who?	Asheley
Does what?	Will combine two sequences of play
Where?	In the housekeeping area
How well or how often?	During two out of three free play periods
By when?	December 15

Goal Number 2

Who?	Asheley
Does what?	Will play with an adult
Where?	On the playground
How well or how often?	Four out of five days a week
By when?	December 15

Planning Learning Activities and Strategies
Lesson Plan 1 for Goal 1

To work on the goal "Asheley will combine two sequences of play in the house-keeping area in two out of three play episodes by December 15," her teacher decided to expand Asheley's play when she was playing her favorite theme. She knew that when Asheley pretended, she chose to dress her favorite doll. Next, her teacher referred to chapter 8 and found the suggestions listed in the Role-Playing section for the goal "Child will combine sequences of play." One of the suggestions includes modeling sequences of play while pretending to care for babies. She knew that Asheley was familiar with what takes place when caring for a baby because she had a nine-month-old brother. The teacher used the Planning Form, shown on the next page, and her observations to further develop her lesson plan. She knew that Asheley needed real objects to use as she played, so she gathered real diapers, empty powder containers, bottles, and doll strollers. Asheley's teacher felt she needed to help Asheley by becoming a co-player. She planned to suggest that Asheley diaper the doll and then feed her.

Planning Form

Child's Name: __Asheley__   Date: __October 1__

GOAL: 1

Who? __Asheley__

Does what? __will combine two sequences of play__

Where? __in the housekeeping area__

How well or how often? __two out of three play episodes__

By when (target completion date for the goal)? __December 15__

ACTIVITY: Pretending to take care of a baby

Consider:

- the child's special interests __(dressing the doll)__
- ways to make the activity sensitive to the child's culture and home language __(Asheley has a younger brother at home; mom carries him in a back carrier.)__
- the appropriate level of difficulty __(Asheley needs life-sized, real items)__
- adaptive equipment __(none needed)__

When? (Circle one)

(Free play)   Group   Small Group   Transition   Meal/Snack

Outdoors   Home visit   Other: _____

Where? __Housekeeping area.__

What props/materials are needed? __Dolls, diapers, back carrier for the doll, empty cans of baby powder, bowls, plastic food, baby bottles, doll stroller, doll clothes and spoons.__

Who will be involved? __Children can come and go.__

What is the role of the adult? __Invite Asheley to come to the housekeeping area; co-player; provide suggestions and modeling—for example, diapers the doll, then feeds her; shift responsibility of combining sequences to Asheley after she successfully imitates two sequences a number of times.__

What data will be collected and how will it be recorded? __Record sequences of pretend play. Include whether the adult gave an instruction or Asheley initiated the sequence of play. For example, "rock the doll + pat its back. Teacher directed."__

REFLECTION (to be completed following the lesson):

How would you modify this activity if you were to repeat it? _____

_____

Implementing the Plan

This was an activity the teacher could work on periodically before the target completion date because the housekeeping area was always open during free play. She wrote a reminder in her calendar to work with Asheley a number of times over the next few weeks. In addition, she joined Asheley when she spotted her already playing with the dolls.

Reflecting on the Activity

The teacher found that Asheley was eager to play but continued to focus only on dressing the dolls. When the teacher suggested she try something new, like feed the doll, Asheley watched but went back to buttoning the doll's shirt without trying to imitate the teacher's actions. After reflecting on this, her teacher modified her plan and decided to make sure they would feed the doll and then pat its back the next time they worked on this goal. She also recognized that modeling and suggestions might not be enough. Instead, acting in the role of play leader, she needed to instruct Asheley to engage in a second action. For example, she could say, "First do this; then do that."

One day during free play, the teacher noticed that Asheley had successfully put on the doll's clothes, so she was no longer preoccupied by this task. The teacher used this opportunity to suggest a new play sequence: putting the doll in the stroller and pretending to take their two babies to the classroom grocery store. The teacher said, "Asheley, put your doll in the stroller. We'll take our babies to the grocery store." Asheley followed instructions, placing the doll in the stroller. She even drove the stroller around the room but did not stop at the grocery store, as the teacher had suggested.

Lesson Plan 1 for Goal 2

To work on the goal "Asheley will play with an adult on the playground four out of five days a week by December 15," the teaching team decided that during outdoor play or large muscle time, the assistant teacher would set up a special activity where she and Asheley could play together. Asheley really liked the song "Five Little Monkeys Sitting in a Tree," so the teachers decided they would use it as a way to interact with her. The song encouraged pretend skills when Asheley acted out the animals in the lyrics. The teacher planned the activity on the following page.

Planning Form

Child's Name: __Asheley__   Date: __October 10__

GOAL: 2
Who? __Asheley__

Does what? __will play with an adult__

Where? __on the playground or in the large-muscle room__

How well or how often? __four out of five days a week__

By when (target completion date for the goal)? __December 15__

ACTIVITY: Act out the action in "Five Little Monkeys Sitting in a Tree"
Consider:
- the child's special interests **(Asheley claps and sings with the song about the alligator and the monkeys during group time and has looked at the book before nap several times)**
- ways to make the activity sensitive to the child's culture and home language **(none needed)**
- the appropriate level of difficulty **(Asheley needs toy animals rather than imaginary ones)**
- adaptive equipment **(none needed)**

When? (Circle one)

Free play   Group   Small Group   Transition   Meal/Snack

(Outdoors)   Home visit   Other: _____

Where? __On the playground or in the large-muscle room.__

What props/materials are needed? __CD player, CD, monkey and alligator puppets.__

Who will be involved? __Assistant teacher and children, holding toy monkeys; additional children can play if they want to be monkeys without holding one; one person using the alligator puppet__

What is the role of the adult? __Stage Manager. Help with the CD player or help sing the song; help children share the props. Coach Asheley in her role.__

What data will be collected and how will it be recorded? __Check off on chart daily if Asheley plays with an adult.__

REFLECTION (to be completed following the lesson):
How would you modify this activity if you were to repeat it? _____

_____

Implementing the Plan

The first time they did the activity, the assistant teacher took the CD player, CD, props, and book outside with them. Asheley got to carry some of the props, so she was highly motivated to engage in the activity. Once outside, the assistant teacher let Asheley choose if she wanted to be the monkey or the alligator. The assistant teacher took the other role.

Reflecting on the Activity

When they first tried this activity, Asheley spent most of the time working to get the puppet on her hand so it felt just right. When the assistant teacher suggested she run away from the alligator, Asheley ran, but the assistant teacher was uncertain if Asheley was really pretending or engaging in a motor activity. The teacher decided that next time she tried the activity, she would encourage Asheley to perform some of the monkey's actions before they started playing the song. She thought she could prompt Asheley by saying, "Let's pretend to . . ." or by asking questions, such as, "What does the alligator do next?" She also thought that she could do the same basic lesson but offer variety by suggesting that they pretend they were mice being chased by a fox.

Evaluating Play Skills

When the target completion date of December 15 arrived, the teaching team looked at the data they had gathered on the daily chart they had created as part of the lesson plans. They evaluated the information and discovered they had reached the goal in which Asheley was to play with an adult. They also knew that although other children were often involved in the activity or situated close by, Asheley's focus remained on the adult. They had not yet made progress toward the next skill listed on the Play Checklist. This information led them to their next step—the goal of encouraging Asheley to play with another child.

When they evaluated the data on the goal to combine sequences, they found it was not convincing. There were many days when Asheley combined actions, but often she did so only at the suggestion or instruction of an adult. They felt that Asheley was not yet consistently performing this skill on her own. They decided to continue to work on this goal. They used the Planning Form to write another set of lesson plans to implement over the next few months.

Lori: A Case Study

Lori was a three-year-old with a very short attention span and limited play skills. She was old enough to move into the three-year-old class but because she couldn't sustain participation in group activities her teacher had not yet moved her up. She flitted from activity to activity without a look backward. Initial attempts to help Lori focus or extend her attention resulted in little improvement. She participated only minimally in pretend play sequences. Terry, her teacher, knew there were family circumstances that greatly influenced Lori's behavior. Lori's mom and boyfriend argued vehemently, resulting in calls to the police about their domestic disturbances. Although staff was sympathetic to the factors influencing her behavior, the fact remained that Lori couldn't move into the next class until her skills improved. Terry knew that she couldn't control what happened at home for Lori, but she could focus on Lori's behavior at school (adapted from Halfin, unpublished data).

Observations

Terry observed Lori several times during free play. During her observations, Terry noted that Lori rarely stayed with a play activity beyond one or two minutes. She saw that Lori might stay longer with an adult, but if the adult's attention was diverted for any reason, Lori ran off. She also saw that Lori would play a little longer if she was doing a sensorimotor activity. When playing with a group of children, Lori swore, called other children names, and had tantrums when she didn't get her way. Terry used her observations to complete the Play Checklist for Lori.

Play Checklist

Child's Name: __**Lori**_____   Date: __**March 12**_____

Date of Birth: **November 27 (three years and eight months old)**_____

Check the highest level skills you consistently observe:

*1. Pretending with Objects
☐ Does not use objects to pretend
☒ Uses real objects
☐ Substitutes objects for other objects
☐ Uses imaginary objects

*2. Role-Playing
☐ No role play
☒ Uses one sequence of play
☐ Combines sequences
☐ Uses verbal declaration (for example, "I'm a doctor")
☐ Imitates actions of role, including dress

*3. Verbalizations about the Play Scenario
☐ Does not use pretend words during play
☒ Uses words to describe substitute objects
☐ Uses words to describe imaginary objects and actions (for example, "I'm painting a house")
☐ Uses words to create a play scenario (for example, "Let's say we're being taken by a monster")

*4. Verbal Communication during a Play Episode
☐ Does not verbally communicate during play
☒ Talks during play only to self
☐ Talks only to adults in play
☐ Talks with peers in play by stepping outside of role (for example, "That's not how mothers hold their babies")
☐ Talks with peers from within role (for example, "Eat your dinner before your dad comes home")

*5. Persistence in Play
☒ Less than five minutes
☐ Six to nine minutes
☐ Ten minutes or longer

*6. Interactions
☒ Plays alone
❑ Plays only with adults
❑ Plays with one child, always the same person
❑ Plays with one child, can be different partners
❑ Can play with two or three children together

**7. Entrance into a Play Group
❑ Does not attempt to enter play group
☒ Uses force to enter play group
❑ Stands near group and watches
❑ Imitates behavior of group
❑ Makes comments related to play theme
❑ Gets attention of another child before commenting

8. Problem Solving
❑ Gives in during conflict
☒ Uses force to solve problems
❑ Seeks adult assistance
❑ Imitates verbal solutions or strategies provided by adults
❑ Recalls words or strategies to use when reminded
❑ Initiates use of words or strategies
❑ Accepts reasonable compromises

9. Turn Taking
☒ Refuses to take turns
❑ Leaves toys, then protests when others pick them up
❑ Takes turns if arranged and directed by an adult
❑ Asks for turn, does not wait for a response
❑ Gives up toy easily if done with it
❑ Gives up toy if another child asks for it
❑ Proposes turn taking, will take and give turns

10. Support of Peers
❑ Shows no interest in peers
☒ Directs attention to distress of peers
❑ Shows empathy or offers help
❑ Offers and takes suggestions of peers at times
❑ Encourages or praises peers

Note: The developmental progression outlined in each segment of the Play Checklist can be used as a guideline when assessing most children's development. However, not all children will go through the same steps in development nor through the same developmental sequence.
*Smilansky, Sara. 1968. *The effects of sociodramatic play on disadvantaged preschool children*. New York: Wiley.
** Hazen, Nancy, Betty Black and Faye Fleming-Johnson. 1984. Social acceptance: Strategies children use and how teachers can help children learn them. *Young Children*. 39: 26–36.

Play by Sandra Heidemann and Deborah Hewitt, copyright © 2010. Redleaf Press grants permission to photocopy this page for classroom use.

Evaluating Play Skills

Terry used the information from the Play Checklist to decide how to best help Lori improve her skills. Because of her age, Lori's skills were at the lower end of the Play Checklist in all areas. When Terry evaluated the information, she felt Lori had particular difficulty in the following areas:

Persistence in play
Interactions
Problem solving
Turn taking

Goals

Terry decided to write a goal on Persistence in Play. She felt that many of the other skills could be worked on when Lori was able to stick with a chosen activity. Terry used her knowledge of Lori and the Play Checklist to write a SMART goal. The goal she wrote was "Lori will persist in play with an adult in the preschool classroom for five minutes by the end of May."

Planning Learning Activities and Strategies
Lesson Plan 1

Once Terry had decided on a goal, she looked at the activity suggestions listed in the section on Persistence in Play in chapter 8 to help her frame plans for Lori. There she found suggestions that she thought would build on Lori's interests and strengthen her skills. Terry used playdough in a sensorimotor activity, coupled with pizza shop, a dramatic play theme. She predicted that Lori's interest in sensorimotor activities would help her stay involved. Because Lori would often run away when an adult's attention was divided, Terry included only herself and Lori in the activity. To do so, Terry had to plan with other staff how this activity would fit into class routines. This joint planning ensured that the plan would be supported by other staff members.

Planning Form

Child's Name: __Lori__   Date: __April 4__

GOAL: 1

Who? __Lori__

Does what? __will persist in play with an adult__

Where? __in the preschool classroom__

How well or how often? __for five minutes__

By when (target completion date for the goal)? __the end of May__

ACTIVITY: Making pizza with playdough

Consider:

• the child's special interests **(sensorimotor activities)**

• ways to make the activity sensitive to the child's culture and home language **(none needed)**

• the appropriate level of difficulty **(needs support of adult)**

• adaptive equipment **(none needed)**

When? (Circle one)

(Free play)   Group   Small Group   Transition   Meal/Snack

Outdoors   Home visit   Other: _____

Where? __Preschool classroom.__

What props/materials are needed? __Playdough, cardboard pizza rounds, plastic knives, garlic press, spatula__
__and other kitchen utensils, play oven, oven mitts, pot holders, pizza menu, pizza delivery boxes, play money.__

Who will be involved? __Lori and Terry__

What is the role of the adult? __Co-player__

What data will be collected and how will it be recorded? __Note the time the activity starts and when__
__Lori moves to a new activity.__

REFLECTION (to be completed following the lesson):

How would you modify this activity if you were to repeat it? _____

_____

Implementing the Plan

The staff arranged a corner of the room as a pizza shop. They allowed any children who were interested to play in the area for the first part of free play, and then they took all the children but Lori to the large-muscle room. They were able to arrange this schedule four days in a row.

Reflecting on the Activity

After Terry had done the activity the first time, she was able to proudly report that Lori had played for almost twenty minutes with the sensory activity and Terry's support. Lori had wandered off two times, but Terry was able to lure her back by reminding her she needed to pay for her pizza and showing her how to use the garlic press to make pretend cheese. In regular classroom play, Lori would rarely come back even when an adult called her.

Besides the obvious increase in Lori's attention span, Terry noted that Lori was able to demonstrate fine-motor control when she manipulated the play-dough in imitation of Terry's actions. (This was important data for Terry's overall classroom assessment system, and she noted it in Lori's portfolio.) Terry was surprised that Lori's attention lasted so long, especially the first time—it often takes longer to see such dramatic results. Terry felt the success of this lesson plan was due in part to her observation and her use of Lori's play preferences. Terry knew she was on the right track. She decided to plan two more play themes that combined sensorimotor activities and dramatic play.

Lesson Plan 2

Terry planned to have Lori play with cars and trucks in the sand when they went out to the playground. If the weather was bad, she thought she could use miniature cars and trucks in the sensory table filled with sand. She thought her role would be to take a truck and play with Lori, demonstrate how the grader worked, and offer suggestions about what they might do next.

Planning Form

Child's Name: __Lori__   Date: __April 8__

GOAL: 1

Who? __Lori__

Does what? __will persist in play with an adult__

Where? __in the preschool classroom__

How well or how often? __for five minutes__

By when (target completion date for the goal)? __the end of May__

ACTIVITY: Building roads in the sand

Consider:

- the child's special interests **(sensorimotor activities)**
- ways to make the activity sensitive to the child's culture and home language **(Lori's mom takes Lori to a nearby park to play in the sand a few times a week)**
- the appropriate level of difficulty **(needs support of adult)**
- adaptive equipment **(none needed)**

When? (Circle one)

Free play   Group   Small Group   Transition   Meal/Snack

(Outdoors)   Home visit   Other: _____

Where? __On the playground or at sensory table.__

What props/materials are needed? __Sand, cars and trucks, a small grader to build roads, shovels, miniature road signs.__

Who will be involved? __Lori and Terry (other children may play nearby)__

What is the role of the adult? __Co-player, moving to play leader if Lori needs more direction__

What data will be collected and how will it be recorded? __Note the time the activity starts and when Lori moves to a new activity.__

REFLECTION (to be completed following the lesson):

How would you modify this activity if you were to repeat it? _____

_____

Implementing the Plan

Terry arranged for Lori to look at some books that showed construction equipment building roads. She also asked Lori to carry one of the graders out to the playground. After Lori had a chance to do some climbing, Terry noticed her attention waning, so she approached Lori with the grader. Terry invited Lori to join her in the sand. They played together, moving the sand with the grader and driving the trucks on the roads they had built.

Reflecting on the Activity

Although Lori played for ten minutes building roads, she didn't play as long as she had in the first lesson. After some reflection, Terry believed this was because Lori knew more about going for pizza than about building roads. She also may have been more interested in other outside activities than playing in the sand. Terry decided to try one more variation of combining sensorimotor with pretend play, so she planned an activity in which they would pretend to cook and take care of babies.

Lesson Plan 3

In this lesson, Terry chose to do an activity in which she and Lori would pretend to cook and feed babies. To bring in Lori's sensorimotor interest, Terry decided to have pots and pans, spoons for stirring, dried beans for scooping, and empty salt and pepper shakers for seasoning. Terry decided to model cooking and then feeding the baby.

Planning Form

Child's Name: __Lori__   Date: __April 22__

GOAL: 1

Who? __Lori__

Does what? __will persist in play with an adult__

Where? __in the preschool classroom__

How well or how often? __for five minutes__

By when (target completion date for the goal)? __the end of May__

ACTIVITY: Pretending to cook and feed babies

Consider:

- the child's special interests **(sensorimotor activities)**
- ways to make the activity sensitive to the child's culture and home language **(none needed)**
- the appropriate level of difficulty **(needs support of adult)**
- adaptive equipment **(none needed)**

When? (Circle one)

Free play   Group   Small Group   Transition   Meal/Snack

Outdoors   (Home visit)   Other: _____

Where? __On a home visit.__

What props/materials are needed? __Pans, dishes, spoons, salt and pepper shakers, doll, bottle, and dried beans.__

Who will be involved? __Lori, Terry, and Lori's mother, who will join after observing for a short time.__

What is the role of the adult? __Co-player, moving to Play Leader if needed__

What data will be collected and how will it be recorded? __Note the time the activity starts and when Lori moves to a new activity. Record on a chart in Lori's file.__

REFLECTION (to be completed following the lesson):

How would you modify this activity if you were to repeat it? _____

_____

Implementing the Plan

The goal was to help Lori persist in play in the preschool classroom, doing a home visit offered an opportunity to practice the skill in another setting and to demonstrate for Lori's mom some of the things Terry was working on at school. Terry pulled Lori's mother into the play in an easy and nonthreatening way. After the lesson, Terry and Lori's mother talked about how Lori was learning fine-motor skills while she stirred the beans, learning sharing when she offered the food to her mother, and learning to pretend when she brought the spoonful of beans to the doll's mouth. Terry was not only articulating what skills were learned through play but also helping Lori's mother see their value.

Reflecting on the Activity

Terry again saw a dramatic increase in Lori's attention span. Lori played for twenty minutes and left the activity only once, then came back readily. She performed many of the actions of cooking and feeding: stirring, seasoning, smelling, dishing out, and feeding the doll and her mother. At home, with fewer distractions, she was better able to concentrate. Toward the end of the activity, Lori pretended to cook less and did more pouring, a sensorimotor activity. An unexpected benefit to this activity was having Lori's mother involved.

Terry wondered if the success of the activities she had planned was due to the fact Lori had an adult's attention or if it was the combination of sensorimotor and dramatic play. To test this out, Terry planned a classroom activity for Lori and herself. If it were only an adult's presence that helped Lori concentrate, Lori should play a similar length of time with any activity that involved an adult's support. Terry brought out bristle blocks and sat with Lori to play with them. Lori only sat there for two minutes and ignored Terry's requests to come back. From this small experiment, Terry concluded that Lori not only needed an adult to expand her attention span but also activities that combined dramatic play and sensorimotor play. With this information, Terry could safely assume her lesson plans worked.

Evaluating Play Skills

Terry planned eight more lessons that addressed her goal. When the target completion date arrived, she sensed that she had reached her goal. To be sure, she observed Lori for a week, evaluated the data, and found that Lori could persist in play with an adult for five minutes.

Terry had found a formula that worked for Lori. When Lori stayed with the dramatic play, she was able to extend and expand on the theme. Her behavior became more positive: no tantrums, less name calling, and less swearing. All these were positive benefits.

Thanks to Terry's continued focus on play skills, Lori was able to persist in play with another child for ten minutes at a time by the time she was four years old. She still had difficulties resolving conflict, so her preschool teachers continued to work on goals to address this in Lori's play. But she was making real progress.

The Value of Reflection

Both Asheley's and Lori's teachers spent time reflecting after they began implementing their activities. They reflected on how the child responded to the activity and on how the child responded to their own roles and participation. They used their reflections to generate new goals and activities for Asheley and Lori. The Planning Form contains space for you to record your important thoughts so you can incorporate them in the future. Both Asheley's and Lori's teachers wrote their reactions to the lessons. Examples are below:

Asheley: "Five Little Monkeys"

Reflection (to be completed following the lesson): How would you modify this activity if you were to repeat it?	Asheley pretends to be monkey before alligator chases. Try monkey sounds and actions.

Lori: Pretend Pizza

Reflection (to be completed following the lesson): How would you modify this activity if you were to repeat it?	Lori loved combined sensorimotor activity and dramatic play. Try sand and dramatic play.

From the case studies, you can see that reflection is an important step in the process. Reflecting on a lesson plan helps you decide whether or not your plan has accomplished its purpose. Reflection also helps you determine if you need to modify the level of difficulty, the choice in activities, or the people you included. Reflection helps you become more intentional during teachable moments, play, and adult-led activities. Being intentional means you have the words in mind when a teachable moment presents itself, can integrate an individual child with a group of children during play, and keep your goals in mind while leading a group. When you reflect, ask yourself three key questions:

- What worked?
- What didn't?
- What would you change if you were to repeat the activity?

Other possible questions include:
- Did the activity match the child's interests?
- Did the activity match the child's skill level?
- Was the adult role you used appropriate?
- How did the other children respond to and affect your lesson?

Taking time during a busy day to reflect on an activity you have just completed and write your reflections isn't easy. Here are hints about how to find time to reflect:

- Write only a word or two to remind yourself.
- Write immediately following the activity.
- Discuss patterns, changes, and successes with team members periodically.

Not only are you reflecting on the child's reactions and progress, you are also reflecting on your own reactions, planning, and participation. Sometimes you may become discouraged when you reflect. Take a longer view. In writing things down, you may actually see the smaller steps the child is making as she progresses. Remember: sometimes your lesson may work right away, sometimes it takes more than one try, and sometimes you may have to wait to try the lesson again in a couple of months.

Through reflection, you can see a possibility or opportunity you haven't seen before. Maybe you will see how one small gesture, word, or toy caught the child's attention. You can build your lesson around that next time.

The Continuous Cycle of Improvement

As you can see through the case studies and the examples throughout the book, play is the ideal time to help children learn skills they will need in school and adulthood. During play, children learn the basics of relationships, problem solving, self-regulation, and supporting one another. They develop the cognitive skills and language upon which further understanding is built. Children learn that one object can represent another when they pretend and learn about abstraction. Children learn they can take on different roles, and this helps them determine who they are. They practice new skills and integrate new information. Adults who give children the opportunity to play are supporting their growth and development in many ways.

Many children learn such lessons through pretend play when you arrange the environment for them, plan a schedule, include some props, and offer your support. You can provide these experiences for children by following the continuous cycle:

1. Observe and assess skills and interests of the group.
2. Evaluate the play needs of the group and of individuals who may need further assessment.
3. Develop classroom goals based on standards and widely held expectations.
4. Plan an environment, schedule, and activities that are appropriate for the group; implement the plan.
5. Recycle through the process, beginning with observe and assess.

As you observe and assess the group, you may discover children who—because of temperament, lack of experience, or special needs—may need planned activities specifically designed to teach them play skills. Children who benefit from this level of instruction need many opportunities to practice their new skills. Sometimes caregivers only devise one lesson plan and then become busy with other important demands of their job. This means that particular children do not receive reinforcement for the progress they have made, nor do they get the chances they need to extend their learning. Think of your involvement in a child's play as more than a one-time plan. For most children who are having difficulty, you will need to continue your involvement.

The list below reviews the steps in an expanded version of the continuous cycle you can use with individuals who need additional help:

1. Observe and assess:
   • Gather data from multiple sources.
   • Complete the Play Checklist based on your observations.
2. Evaluate play skills:
   • Following your initial observations, evaluate the child's need for planned activities to support her play skills.
   • Once you have reached your target completion date, evaluate progress.
   • Decide if you have met your goal. Determine if you will create a new goal.
3. Write a SMART goal using the items on the Play Checklist as the core.

4. Plan and implement activities and strategies designed to teach the desired skills:
   • Offer a number of activities and opportunities to practice the new skill prior to the target completion date.
   • Observe and assess the success of each activity.
   • Reflect on the activity and modify if necessary.
5. Recycle through the process; begin by observing and assessing the child's play skills.

Expanded Continuous Cycle of Improvement

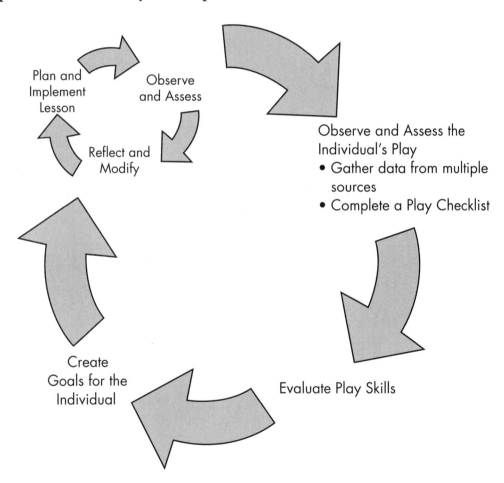

As you recycle through this process, you will help the child continue her learning throughout the year.

Afterword

While writing this book, we focused on each step in a rather orderly fashion. We are acutely aware that life rarely progresses in such a fashion, and children's growth probably never does. We know that as you try the ideas in this book, you are likely to experience discouragement. The decisions and plans you make as a caregiver may not work as quickly as you wish. You may intuitively do something that works for most of the group, yet your carefully laid plans for an individual may fizzle. You may see immediate progress when you work with a child, and then a plateau occurs in her growth. You may not see all the progress you hope for while the child is in your care. Some skills may not become natural to her until she matures. These are variables that we expect and even welcome. Each child's growth is individual and unique. Focus on the progress that *is* made, and be confident that you are making a difference when you help a child learn to become part of group play.

Despite the element of the unexpected in working with any group and individual children, we have outlined the steps of teaching play skills concretely and in a certain order. In our experience, the order has made our work with children more consistent and more helpful, especially with the children who are having trouble. After plans have been laid, actual play becomes spontaneous and alive.

When children learn to play more cooperatively, everyone gains. You will be able to observe and enjoy the unfolding of enriched and positive play instead of policing destructive play. You will be more aware of how an individual child is changing and growing because you have been an important part of that growth. Having learned more about play and its components, you will be able to help parents understand their children's progress with play skills and the importance of play.

While children are in your care, they will increase their positive self-esteem and confidence because they are more successful in play. They can elaborate the roles they play with greater accuracy. They can better fit into a play group. They can more easily solve problems, communicate their ideas with more fluency, and show more empathy toward their friends. They can even practice leadership skills when they put forth new play ideas. In enumerating the tremendous learning that can take place in play, we can see that the lessons of play extend far beyond childhood. Being able to think imaginatively, resolve conflict with grace, trade ideas with others, and be compassionate are the building blocks for human relationships. We hope that as you read this book, you may have wondered, like us, how different some adult lives would have been if they had learned these play skills as children.

Appendix A

Play Checklist

Child's Name: _____   Date: _____   Date of Birth: _____

Check the highest level skills you consistently observe:

*1. Pretending with Objects
- ❑ Does not use objects to pretend
- ❑ Uses real objects
- ❑ Substitutes objects for other objects
- ❑ Uses imaginary objects

*2. Role-Playing
- ❑ No role play
- ❑ Uses one sequence of play
- ❑ Combines sequences
- ❑ Uses verbal declaration (for example, "I'm a doctor")
- ❑ Imitates actions of role, including dress

*3. Verbalizations about the Play Scenario
- ❑ Does not use pretend words during play
- ❑ Uses words to describe substitute objects
- ❑ Uses words to describe imaginary objects and actions (for example, "I'm painting a house")
- ❑ Uses words to create a play scenario (for example, "Let's say we're being taken by a monster")

*4. Verbal Communication during a Play Episode
- ❑ Does not verbally communicate during play
- ❑ Talks during play only to self
- ❑ Talks only to adults in play
- ❑ Talks with peers in play by stepping outside of role (for example, "That's not how mothers hold their babies")
- ❑ Talks with peers from within role (for example, "Eat your dinner before your dad comes home")

*5. Persistence in Play
- ❑ Less than five minutes
- ❑ Six to nine minutes
- ❑ Ten minutes or longer

*6. Interactions
- ❑ Plays alone
- ❑ Plays only with adults
- ❑ Plays with one child, always the same person
- ❑ Plays with one child, can be different partners
- ❑ Can play with two or three children together

**7. Entrance into a Play Group
- ❑ Does not attempt to enter play group
- ❑ Uses force to enter play group
- ❑ Stands near group and watches
- ❑ Imitates behavior of group
- ❑ Makes comments related to play theme
- ❑ Gets attention of another child before commenting

8. Problem Solving
- ❑ Gives in during conflict
- ❑ Uses force to solve problems
- ❑ Seeks adult assistance
- ❑ Imitates verbal solutions or strategies provided by adults
- ❑ Recalls words or strategies to use when reminded
- ❑ Initiates use of words or strategies
- ❑ Accepts reasonable compromises

9. Turn Taking
- ❑ Refuses to take turns
- ❑ Leaves toys, then protests when others pick them up
- ❑ Takes turns if arranged and directed by an adult
- ❑ Asks for turn, does not wait for a response
- ❑ Gives up toy easily if done with it
- ❑ Gives up toy if another child asks for it
- ❑ Proposes turn taking, will take and give turns

10. Support of Peers
- ❑ Shows no interest in peers
- ❑ Directs attention to distress of peers
- ❑ Shows empathy or offers help
- ❑ Offers and takes suggestions of peers at times
- ❑ Encourages or praises peers

Note: The developmental progression outlined in each segment of the Play Checklist can be used as a guideline when assessing most children's development. However, not all children will go through the same steps in development nor through the same developmental sequence.

*Smilansky, Sara. 1968. *The effects of sociodramatic play on disadvantaged preschool children*. New York: Wiley.

** Hazen, Nancy, Betty Black and Faye Fleming-Johnson. 1984. Social acceptance: Strategies children use and how teachers can help children learn them. *Young Children*. 39: 26–36.

Planning Form

Child's Name: _____ Date: _____

GOAL:

Who?_____

Does what? _____

Where?_____

How well or how often?_____

By when (target completion date for the goal)?_____

ACTIVITY:

Consider:

• the child's special interests

• ways to make the activity sensitive to the child's culture and home language

• the appropriate level of difficulty

• adaptive equipment

When? (Circle one)

Free play   Group   Small Group   Transition   Meal/Snack

Outdoors   Home visit   Other: _____

Where?_____

What props/materials are needed? _____

Who will be involved?_____

What is the role of the adult?_____

What data will be collected and how will it be recorded? _____

_____

REFLECTION (to be completed following the lesson):

How would you modify this activity if you were to repeat it? _____

_____

_____

_____

_____

_____

Appendix B

Suggested Reading List

Berk, Laura, and Adam Winsler. 1995. *Scaffolding children's learning: Vygotsky and early childhood education.* Washington, DC: NAEYC.

Cherry, Clare. 1981. *Think of something quiet: A guide for achieving serenity in early childhood classrooms.* Belmont, CA: Pitman Learning.

Cohen, Dorothy, Virginia Stern, and Nancy Balaban. 1983. *Observing and recording the behavior of young children.* 3rd ed. New York: Teachers College Press.

Copple, Carol, and Sue Bredekamp, eds. 2009. *Developmentally appropriate practice in early childhood programs serving children from birth through age 8.* 3rd ed. Washington, DC: NAEYC.

Davidson, Jane Ilene. 1996. *Emergent literacy and dramatic play in early education.* Albany: Delmar Publishers.

Derman-Sparks, Louise, and the A.B.C. Task Force. 1989. *Anti-bias curriculum: Tools for young children.* Washington, DC: NAEYC.

Freyberg, J. T. 1973. Increasing the imaginative play of urban disadvantaged kindergarten children through systematic training. In *The child's world of make-believe: Experimental studies of imaginative play,* ed. J. L. Singer, 129–154. New York: Academic Press.

Gartrell, Dan. 2004. *The power of guidance: Teaching social-emotional skills in early childhood classrooms.* Washington, DC: NAEYC.

Glasser, Howard, and Jennifer Easley. 1998. *Transforming the difficult child: The nurtured heart approach.* Tucson: Nurtured Heart Publications.

Gronlund, Gaye. 2006. *Making early learning standards come alive: Connecting your practice and curriculum to state guidelines.* Saint Paul: Readleaf Press.

Henig, Robin Marantz. 2008. Taking play seriously. *New York Times Magazine,* February 17.

Hewitt, Deborah. 1995. *So this is normal too? Teachers and parents working out developmental issues in young children.* Saint Paul: Redleaf Press.

Jablon, Judy, Amy Laura Dombro, and Margo L. Dichtelmiller. 2007. *The power of observation.* Washington, DC: NAEYC.

Jacobs, Gera, and Kathy Crowley. 2007. *Play, projects, and preschool standards: Nurturing children's sense of wonder and joy in learning.* Thousand Oaks, CA: Corwin Press.

Jones, Elizabeth, and Renatta M. Cooper. 2006. *Playing to get smart.* New York: Teachers College Press.

Koralek, Derry, ed. 2004. *Spotlight on young children and play.* Washington, DC: NAEYC.

Leonard, Ann Marie. 1997. *I spy something! A practical guide to classroom observations of young children.* Little Rock: Southern Early Childhood Association.

MacDonald, James, and Yvonne Gillette. 1985. Taking turns: Teaching communication to your child. *Exceptional Parent* 15:49–52.

MacDonald, Sharon. 1997. *The portfolio and its use: A road map for assessment.* Little Rock: Southern Early Childhood Association.

Mooney, Carol Garhart. 2000. *Theories of childhood: An introduction to Dewey, Montessori, Erikson, Piaget, and Vygotsky.* Saint Paul: Redleaf Press.

Owocki, Gretchen. 1999. *Literacy through play.* Portsmouth, NH: Heinemann.

Roskos, Kathleen A., and James F. Christie. 2000. *Play and literacy in early childhood: Research from multiple perspectives.* Mahwah, NJ: Lawrence Erlbaum.

Turecki, Stanley, with Leslie Tonner. 2000. *The difficult child.* 2nd ed. New York: Bantam Books.

Wolfgang, Charles H. 2004. *Child guidance through play: Teaching positive social behaviors.* Boston: Pearson Education.

Appendix C

Children's Book List

Brett, Jan. 1989. *The mitten: A Ukrainian folktale*. New York: G. P. Putnam.

Browne, Eileen. 1999. *Handa's surprise*. London: Mantra.

Christelow, Eileen. 1991. *Five little monkeys sitting in a tree*. New York: Clarion.

Galdone, Paul. 1970. *The three little pigs*. New York: Houghton Mifflin/ Clarion Books.

———. 1992. *The three bears*. New York: Clarion.

Galdone, Paul, and Peter Christen Asbjørnsen. 1998. *The three billy goats gruff*. New York: Houghton Mifflin.

Hutchins, Pat. 1986. *The doorbell rang*. New York: Greenwillow.

———. 1993. *My best friend*. New York: Greenwillow.

Jama, Adam. 2001. *Walking through the jungle*. London: Mantra.

Kalan, Robert. 1981. *Jump, frog, jump!* New York: Greenwillow.

Krauss, Ruth. 1995. *The carrot seed*. New York: HarperCollins.

Martin, Bill, Jr. 1983. *Brown bear, brown bear, what do you see?* New York: Henry Holt.

McDonnell, Flora. 1999. *Splash*. London: Mantra.

Morgan, Pierr. 1990. *The turnip*. New York: Philomel Books.

Seeger, Pete, and Michael Hays. 2004. *Abiyoyo*. New York: Aladdin.

Slobodkina, Esphyr. 1996. *Caps for sale*. New York: Harper Trophy.

Williams, Sue. 1992. *I went walking*. Orlando: Harcourt Children's Books.

Glossary

Anecdote: a story or an account of an event.

Assessment: gathering data in order to make evaluative statements.

Associative Play: children play in the same area doing the same activity, watch each other, and imitate the actions of others, but verbal exchanges are limited.

Attention Deficit Disorder (ADD): a neurobiological disorder that affects a child's ability to attend and focus.

Attention Deficit Hyperactivity Disorder (ADHD): a neurobiological disorder that affects a child's ability to attend and focus; child may also have high activity levels, especially when overstimulated.

Auditory Cue: the signal a child hears that lets him know to stop or begin an action. A cue can be a verbal direction, a bell, a whistle, a clap, etc.

Authentic Assessment: a way to gather information about children while they are in a familiar setting and engaged in familiar activities.

Autism Spectrum Disorder: a disorder that affects a broad range of children whose symptoms can include detachment from people, poor social skills, delayed language skills, unusual play, repetitive body movements, difficulty with changes, and sensory sensitivities.

Bilingual: speaking two languages.

Coach: a teaching strategy involving one-on-one conversation with a child to give hints, suggestions, encouragement, and instruction. Conversation may focus on behavior, play, cooperation, and other skills.

Constructive Play: a child's use of materials to make or build things.

Continuous Cycle of Improvement: a guide or way to visualize the elements involved in teaching. The elements include observing and assessing, evaluating, writing goals, planning, and implementing activities.

Cooperative Play: an activity in which two or more children organize and participate in the play.

Co-playing: the adult joins play that is already started. Children remain in control of the play.

Depression: a neurological disorder that affects a child's mood, thinking, and sense of self-worth. Can be caused by a traumatic event and/or genetic tendency.

Developmental Assessment: a formal investigation of a child's skills to determine how his skills compare to those of other children the same age.

Developmental Checklist: a written tool that lists skills and behaviors. Those demonstrated by a child are checked off.

Dramatic Play: an advanced form of play in which a child pretends with objects and uses roles to act out scenes and make-believe.

Egocentric: self-centered; the way a child thinks about all things in terms of himself or how they affect him.

Empathy: the child's ability to put himself into another person's position and understand the other's feelings.

English-Language Learners (ELL): people learning English in addition to their home language.

Environmental Print: the print children see at home or in the community, including print on food containers and other kinds of product boxes, store signs, road signs, and advertisements.

Evaluation: judging how close something comes to a standard.

Expansion: adult adds words and/or phrases to child's words.

Free Play: periods throughout the day when the child is allowed to choose how he will spend his time in learning areas of the early childhood setting.

Frequency Tally: a count of the number of times a behavior or skill is demonstrated during a specific time frame.

Games with Rules: a group of children agree upon rules to structure their play so it can continue. Rules can be formal, as in board games, or informally agreed upon before play begins.

Goodness of Fit: the match between the child's needs and the adult's mannerisms and strategies.

Imitate: to copy an example or to repeat a word or behavior that has been modeled.

Impulsive: to act suddenly or spontaneously. Sometimes the child behaves as if he can't stop himself from responding in certain ways.

Inclusion: the act of building community; providing plans, activities, and materials; and adapting the environment to ensure all children feel welcomed and successful in their early childhood settings.

Initiate: to engage in or start a behavior on one's own.

Inside the Play: adult plays with children to model play skills.

Interactions: the ways in which people act with one another.

Language Sample: a record of what a child says during a given period of time.

Large-Motor: the use of the large muscles of the body.

Level of Assisted Performance: behaviors that a child can perform with assistance from adult or peers.

Level of Independent Performance: behaviors that a child can perform alone and without help.

Monolingual: speaking only one language.

Objective: observable, without interpretation or judgment.

Observation: gaining a better understanding of a child's skill level by noting a fact or occurrence.

Obsessive Compulsive Disorder (OCD): a neurobiological disorder that causes a child to repeat actions over and over to relieve overwhelming anxiety.

Onlooker: adult stays near play and observes, sometimes commenting and suggesting to assist children.

Outside the Play: adult makes comments and suggestions from outside of the play and is not a player in the play scenario.

Parallel Play: (1) children play side by side with different activities and very little exchange of materials or conversation; or (2) adult plays next to the child.

Parallel Talk: adult is near child and describes child's actions to model language.

Peers: people of approximately the same age.

Persistence: the ability to stick to a task for a certain amount of time.

Pervasive Developmental Disorder: a large category that covers other diagnoses such as autism, Asperger's Syndrome, and Rhet's Syndrome. All disorders affect social skills and language development and involve repetitive motions and sensory sensitivities.

Play Checklist: a written tool developed to assist caregivers in planning for individual children; used in teaching the skills that help a child to successfully engage in sociodramatic play.

Play Leader: adult plays with children, influencing roles, themes, use of props, and language from within her role.

Play Scenario: the play scene or story.

Play with Objects: the ways in which a child uses toys and materials to discover and create.

Prompt: to give a cue or direction to stimulate a behavior.

Props: materials available to use in dramatic play. Enhance a child's ability to act out a role. May be replicas of real objects or substitutes for real objects.

Recall: to remember what has been modeled or taught.

Representational Skills: a child begins to use objects to pretend; the cognitive ability to have one item represent another.

Role-Playing: when a child pretends to be someone other than himself. May be playing a role, such as firefighter, parent, or waitress.

Running Record: a recording technique in which all that a child does and says is written down during a specific time period to be analyzed later.

Scaffolding: the process of providing external support for learning. Gradually the support from adults and peers is removed as the learner gains more skill.

Self-Regulation: the ways a child regulates his own behavior.

Self-Talk: (1) a child talks to self; comments are not directed to another person; or (2) an adult talks about his actions, thoughts, or feelings to model language for the child; comments are not directed to the child.

Sensorimotor Play: the activities performed by a child to explore the physical properties of toys or other materials.

Sequence: an orderly succession of learning.

SMART Goal: a written goal with the following characteristics: specific, measurable, attainable, realistic, and timely.

Social Play: play with others.

Sociodramatic Play: two or more children acting out a play scenario. Children use roles, pretend with objects and actions, and communicate verbally from within the role for at least five minutes.

Solitary Play: playing alone rather than with peers.

Speech Therapist: a specialist who identifies and works with people who have communication disorders.

Stage Manager: adult as an observer and provider of props, comments, suggestions, and other assistance outside of the play.

Standards: achievement goals set by state or federal governments or professional organizations that define what children should know and be able to do by each age or grade level.

Strategies: plans for teaching that include activities and words to use.

Subjective: assessment based on personal opinion, included in a description of a child's behavior.

Substance: a material or element, such as water or sand.

Teachable Moments: spontaneously teaching when a child indicates interest in a topic or when a suitable situation occurs.

Temperament: mode of emotional response typical of a particular child.

Thematic Fantasy Play: a well-known story is enacted by a group of children. Usually the adult narrates and keeps the story moving.

Tourette's Syndrome: a neurobiological disorder that can produce tics (involuntary movements). Sometimes child also has accompanying disorders, such as ADD, learning issues, and emotional volatility.

Work Sample: an example or a sample of what the child is able to do. For example, you might collect a sample of something the child has cut.

Zone of Proximal Development (ZPD): behaviors that are emergent. ZPD is defined by the distance between what the child can do independently and what the child can do with assistance.

References

Asher, S., P. Renshaw, and S. Hymel. 1982. Peer relations and the development of social skills. In *The young child: Reviews of research*, eds. S. Moore and C. Cooper, 137–158. Washington, DC: NAEYC.

Asher, Steven R., and Gladys A. Williams. 1993. Children without friends; Part 1: Their problems. In *Day care center connections,* ed. C. M. Todd, 3–4. Urbana-Champaign: University of Illinois Cooperative Extension Service.

Beaty, Janice J. 1986. *Observing development of the young child.* Columbus: Charles E. Merrill.

Berk, Laura E. 1994. Vygotsky's theory: The importance of make-believe play. *Young Children* 50:30–39.

Bodrova, Elena, and Deborah J. Leong. 2007. *Tools of the mind: The Vygotskian approach to early childhood education.* Upper Saddle River, NJ: Pearson Education.

Christie, James F. 1982. Sociodramatic play training. *Young Children* 37:25–32.

Committee for Children. 1991. *Second step: Violence prevention curriculum.* Seattle, WA: Committee for Children.

Community Action Partnership Head Start of Washington and Ramsey Counties. 2007. *Educational philosophy.* Saint Paul: Community Action Partnership of Washington and Ramsey Counties.

Cothran, Henry, and Allen Wysocki. 2005. *Developing SMART goals for your organization.* Gainsville: University of Florida IFAS Extension.

Crary, Elizabeth. 1993. *Without spanking or spoiling: A practical approach to toddler and preschool guidance.* 2nd ed. Seattle: Parenting Press.

Croft, Cindy, and Deborah Hewitt, eds. 2004. *Children and challenging behavior: Making inclusion work.* Eden Prairie, MN: Sparrow Media.

Erikson, Erik. 1950. *Childhood and society.* New York: Norton.

Federlein, Anne Cairns. 1979. A study of play behaviors and interactions of preschool handicapped children in mainstreamed and segregated settings. Paper presented at the Annual International Convention of the Council for Exceptional Children, Texas.

Freud, Sigmund. 1961. *Beyond the pleasure principle.* New York: Norton.

Gartrell, Dan. 2006. Guidance matters: Boys and men teachers. *Young Children* 61:92–93.

Gillespie, Linda Groves, and Nancy L. Seibel. 2006. Self-regulation: A cornerstone of early childhood development. *Beyond the Journal* 61(4):34–39.

Golomb, Claire. 1979. Pretense play: A cognitive perspective. In *Symbolic functioning in childhood,* eds. N. R. Smith and M. B. Franklin, 101–116. Hillsdale, NJ: Lawrence Erlbaum.

Gower, Amy L., Lisa M. Hohmann, Terry C. Gleason, and Tracy R. Gleason. 2001. The relation among temperament, age, and friendship in preschool-aged children. Paper presented at the Biennial Meeting of the Society for Research in Child Development, Minnesota.

Greene, Alan. 1998. Learning to share. Drgreene.com. http://www.drgreene.org/blank.cfm?print=yes&id=21&action=detail&ref=196.

Hazen, Nancy, Betty Black, and Faye Fleming-Johnson. 1984. Social acceptance: Strategies children use and how teachers can help children learn them. *Young Children* 39(6):26–36.

Hewitt, Deborah, and Sandra Heidemann. 1998. *The optimistic classroom: Creative ways to give children hope.* Saint Paul: Redleaf Press.

Johnson, James, James Christie, and Francis Wardle. 2005. *Play, development, and early education.* Boston: Pearson Education.

Johnson, James E., James F. Christie, and Thomas D. Yawkey. 1987. *Play and early childhood development.* Glenview, IL: Scott, Foresman.

———. 1999. *Play and early childhood development.* 2nd ed. New York: Longman.

Katz, Lilian G. 1984. The professional early childhood teacher. *Young Children* 39:3–10.

Kemple, Kristen M. 2000. Understanding and facilitating preschool children's peer acceptance. *ERIC Digest.*

Koralek, Derry G., Amy Laura Dombro, and Diane Trister Dodge. 2005. *Caring for infants and toddlers.* 2nd ed. Washington, DC: Teaching Strategies.

Kostelnik, Marjorie, Laura Stein, Alice Whiren, and Anne Soderman. 1998. *Guiding children's social development.* 3rd ed. Albany, NY: Delmar Publishers.

Levin, Diane. 2003a. Beyond banning war and superhero play: Meeting children's needs in violent times. *Young Children* 58:60–64.

———. 2003b *Teaching young children in violent times: Building a peaceable classroom.* 2nd ed. Cambridge, MA: Educators for Social Responsibility; Washington, DC: NAEYC.

McAfee, Oralie, Deborah J. Leong, and Elena Bodrova. 2004. *The basics of assessment: A primer for early childhood educators.* Washington, DC: NAEYC.

Mednick, Barbara. 2005. Set S.M.A.R.T. goals: Reach the impossible dream by creating practical steps to concrete goals. *Star Tribune,* December 16, 2005. http://www.startribune.com/jobs/career/11397481.html.

Minnesota Department of Education. 2005. *Early childhood indicators of progress: Minnesota's early learning standards.* Saint Paul: Minnesota Department of Education.

National Association for the Education of Young Children. 1996. *Responding to linguistic and cultural diversity: Recommendations for effective early childhood education.* Washington, DC: NAEYC.

Oliver, Susan J., and Edgar Klugman, 2004. Speaking out for play-based learning: Becoming an effective advocate for play in the early childhood classroom. *Child Care Information Exchange* (January/February): 22–26.

Paley, Vivian Gussin. 1992. *You can't say you can't play.* Cambridge, MA: Harvard University Press.

Parten, Mildred B. 1932. Social participation among preschool children. *Journal of Abnormal and Social Psychology* 27:243–269.

Piaget, Jean. 1962. *Play, dreams, and imitation in childhood.* New York: Norton.

Program for Infant/Toddler Caregivers, The. 1998. *Early messages: Facilitating language development and communication.* Video. Sacramento: WestEd and California Department of Education.

Quann, Valerie, and Carol A. Wien. 2006. The visible empathy of infants and toddlers. *Beyond the Journal* 61(4):22–29.

Rebus Planning Associates. 1995. *Learning to use the work sampling system.* Ann Arbor: Rebus Planning Associates.

Reschke, Kathy. 2002. Power play: The good, the bad and the ugly. National Network for Child Care. http://www.nncc.org/Curriculum/power.html.

Smilansky, Sara. 1968. *The effects of sociodramatic play on disadvantaged preschool children.* New York: Wiley.

Smilansky, Sara, and Leah Shefatya. 2004. *Facilitating play: A medium for promoting cognitive, socioemotional and academic development in young children.* Silver Spring, MD: PS&E Publications.

South Dakota Department of Education. 2006. *South Dakota early learning guidelines.* Pierre: South Dakota Department of Education.

Stephens, Karen. 2002. Friendship skills: Children's books for preschool to age 8. Parenting Exchange. http://www.oh-pin.org/articles/pex-10-friendship-skills-childre.pdf.

Tabors, Patton O. 1997. *One child, two languages: A guide for preschool educators of children learning English as a second language.* Baltimore, MD: Brookes Publishing.

Thomas, Alexander, Stella Chess, and Herbert G. Birch. 1970. The origin of personality. *Scientific American* 223(2): 102–109.

Thomas, Patrice. 2003. *The power of relaxation: Using tai chi and visualization to reduce children's stress.* Saint Paul: Redleaf Press.

Tokarz, Barb. 2008. Block play: It's not just for boys anymore. *Child Care Exchange* (May/June).

Vygotsky, Lev S. 1976. Play and its role in the mental development of the child. In *Play: Its role in development and evolution,* eds. J. S. Bruner, A. Jolly, and K. Sylva, 537–554. New York: Basic Books.

Zigler, Edward F., Dorothy G. Singer, and Sandra J. Bishop-Josef, eds. 2004. *Children's play: The roots of reading.* Washington, DC: Zero to Three Press.

Index